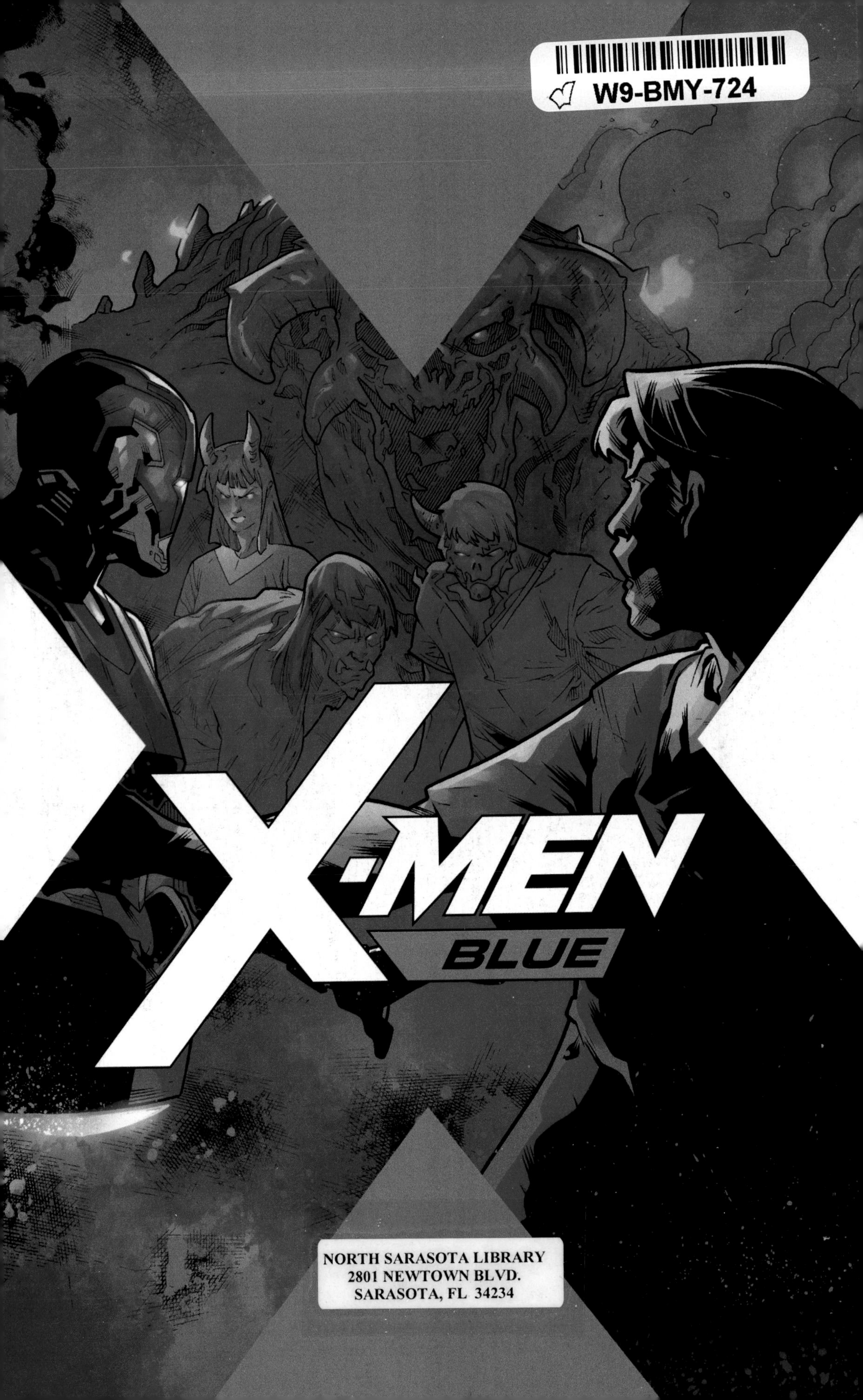
X-MEN
BLUE

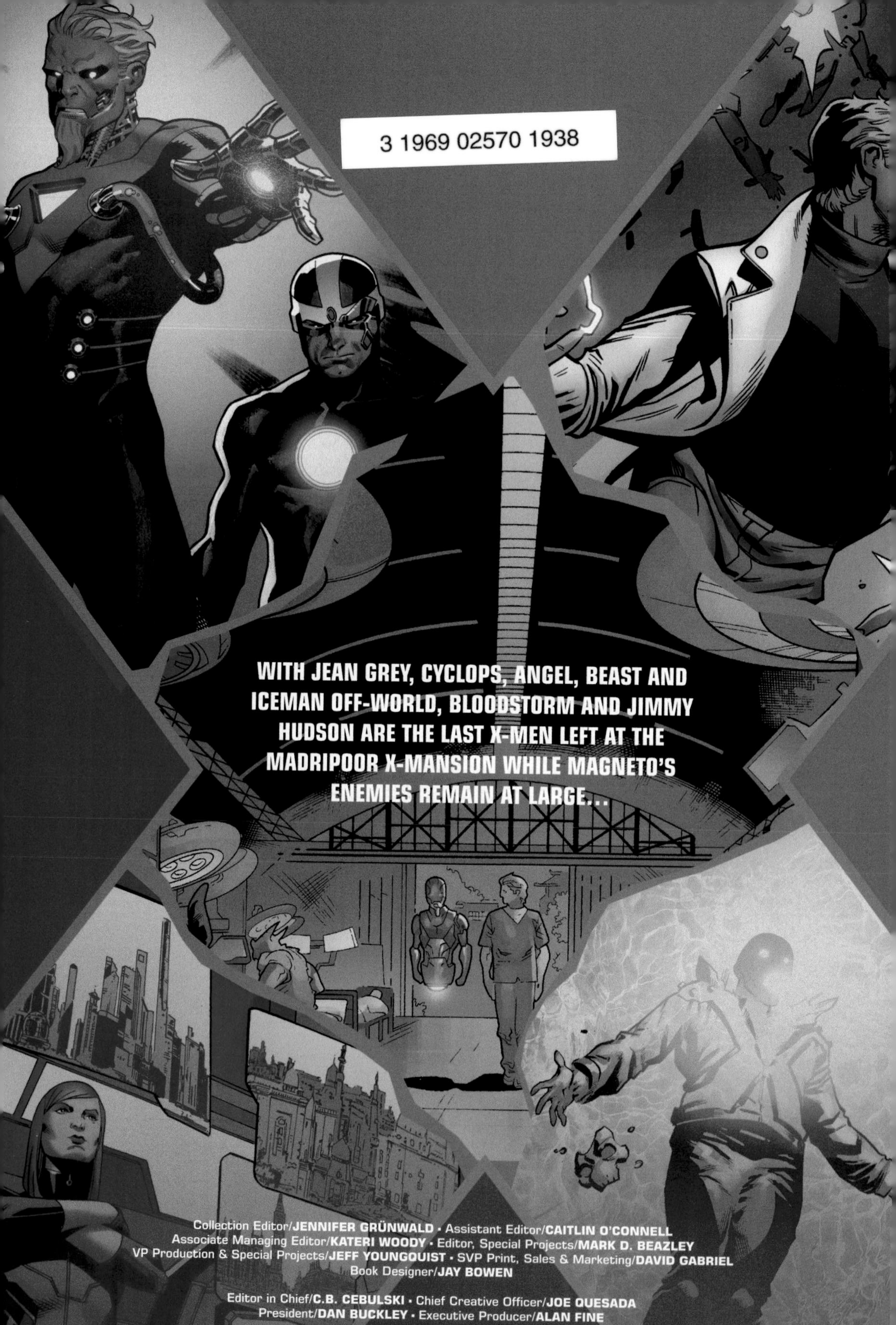

WITH JEAN GREY, CYCLOPS, ANGEL, BEAST AND ICEMAN OFF-WORLD, BLOODSTORM AND JIMMY HUDSON ARE THE LAST X-MEN LEFT AT THE MADRIPOOR X-MANSION WHILE MAGNETO'S ENEMIES REMAIN AT LARGE...

Collection Editor/**JENNIFER GRÜNWALD** • Assistant Editor/**CAITLIN O'CONNELL**
Associate Managing Editor/**KATERI WOODY** • Editor, Special Projects/**MARK D. BEAZLEY**
VP Production & Special Projects/**JEFF YOUNGQUIST** • SVP Print, Sales & Marketing/**DAVID GABRIEL**
Book Designer/**JAY BOWEN**

Editor in Chief/**C.B. CEBULSKI** • Chief Creative Officer/**JOE QUESADA**
President/**DAN BUCKLEY** • Executive Producer/**ALAN FINE**

X-MEN BLUE VOL. 4: CRY HAVOK. Contains material originally published in magazine form as X-MEN BLUE #23-28. First printing 2018. ISBN 978-1-302-90979-6. Published by MARVEL WORLDWIDE, INC., a subsidiary of MARVEL ENTERTAINMENT, LLC. OFFICE OF PUBLICATION: 135 West 50th Street, New York, NY 10020. **Printed in the U.S.A.** DAN BUCKLEY, President, Marvel Entertainment; JOHN NEE, Publisher; JOE QUESADA, Chief Creative Officer; TOM BREVOORT, SVP of Publishing; DAVID BOGART, SVP of Business Affairs & Operations, Publishing & Partnership; DAVID GABRIEL, SVP of Sales & Marketing, Publishing; JEFF YOUNGQUIST, VP of Production & Special Projects; DAN CARR, Executive Director of Publishing Technology; ALEX MORALES, Director of Publishing Operations; DAN EDINGTON, Managing Editor; SUSAN CRESPI, Production Manager; STAN LEE, Chairman Emeritus. For information regarding advertising in Marvel Comics or on Marvel.com, please contact Vit DeBellis, Custom Solutions & Integrated Advertising Manager, at vdebellis@marvel.com. For Marvel subscription inquiries, please call 888-511-5480. **Manufactured between 6/1/2018 and 7/3/2018 by QUAD GRAPHICS SARATOGA, SARATOGA SPRINGS, NY, USA.**

10 9 8 7 6 5 4 3 2 1

X-MEN BLUE

CRY HAVOK

Writer/**CULLEN BUNN**

ISSUES #23-25
Artist/**JORGE MOLINA**
Inker, #25/**CRAIG YEUNG**
Color Artists/**MATT MILLA**
with **JAY DAVID RAMOS** (#23-24)
Cover Art/**JORGE MOLINA**

"MEANWHILE..."
Artist/**MIKE PERKINS**
Color Artist/**ANDY TROY**

ISSUE #26
Penciler/**R.B. SILVA**
Inker/**ADRIANO DI BENEDETTO**
Color Artist/**RAIN BEREDO**
Cover Art/**MIKE CHOI** & **FEDERICO BLEE**

ISSUES #27-28
Artist/**MARCUS TO**
Color Artist/**RAIN BEREDO**
Cover Art/**R.B. SILVA** & **RAIN BEREDO**

Letterers/**VC's JOE CARAMAGNA**

Assistant Editor/**CHRIS ROBINSON**
Editor/**DARREN SHAN**
X-Men Group Editors/**MARK PANICCIA** & **JORDAN D. WHITE**

X-MEN CREATED BY **STAN LEE** & **JACK KIRBY**

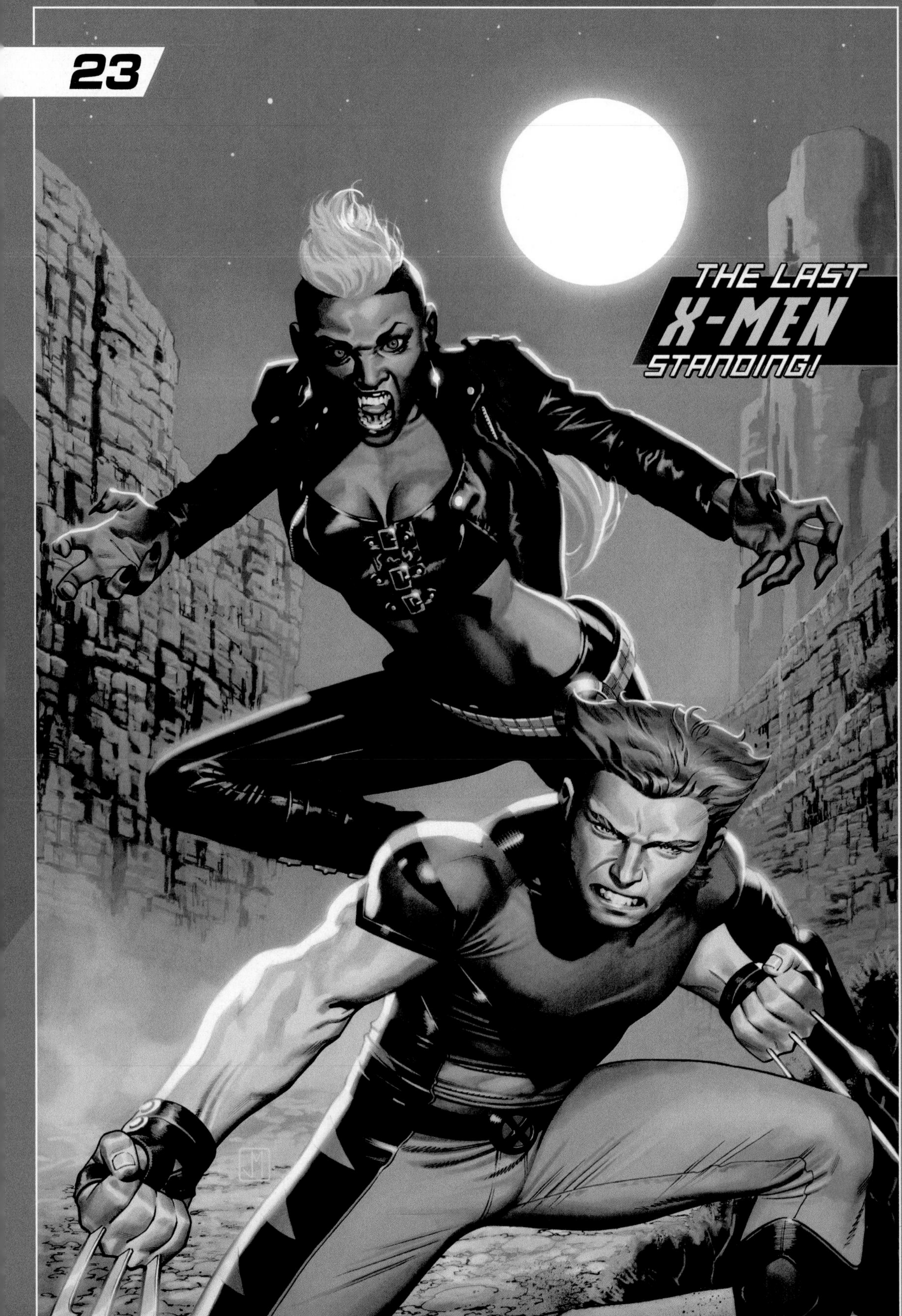
23
THE LAST
X-MEN
STANDING!

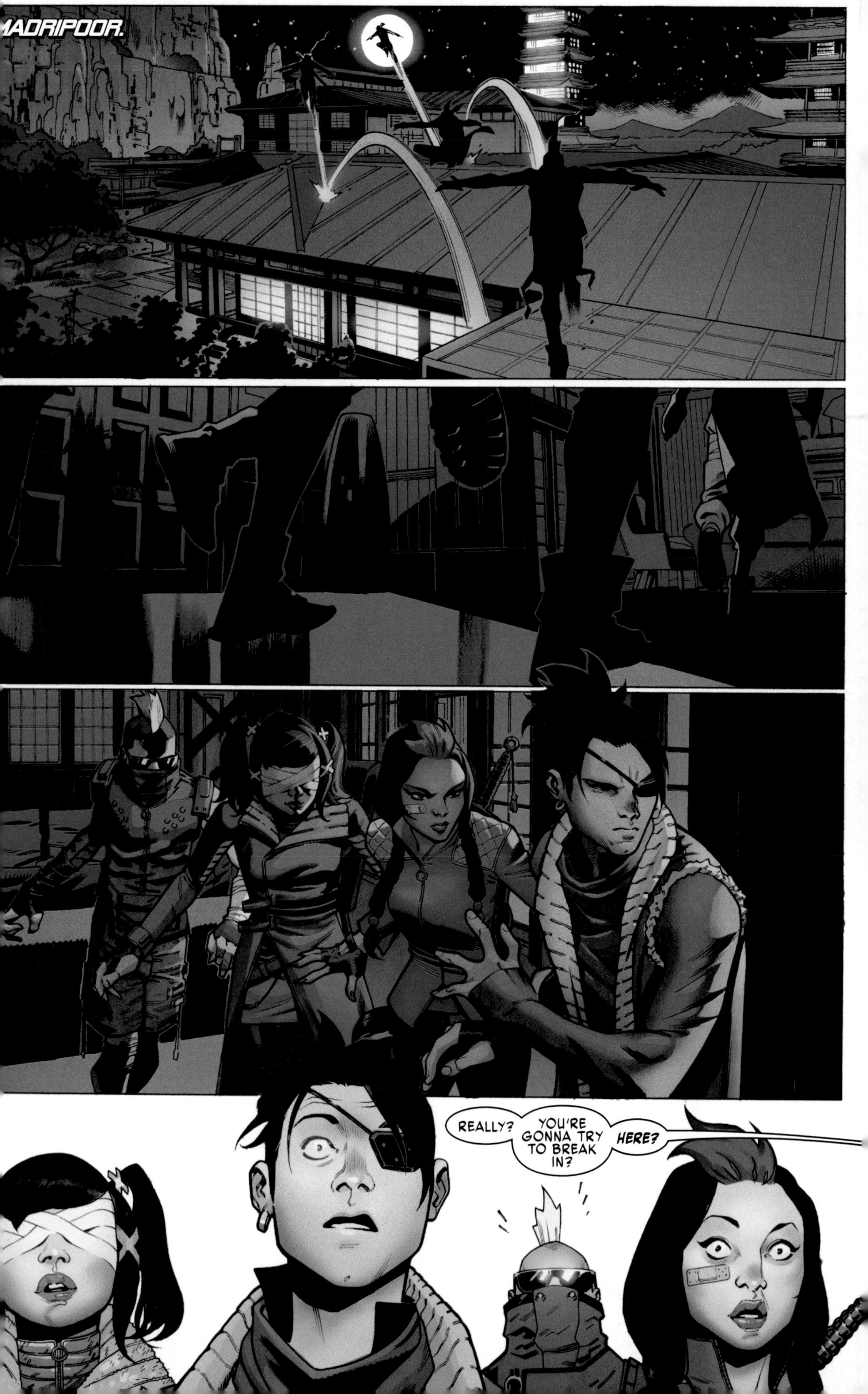
MADRIPOOR.
REALLY?
YOU'RE GONNA TRY TO BREAK IN?
HERE?

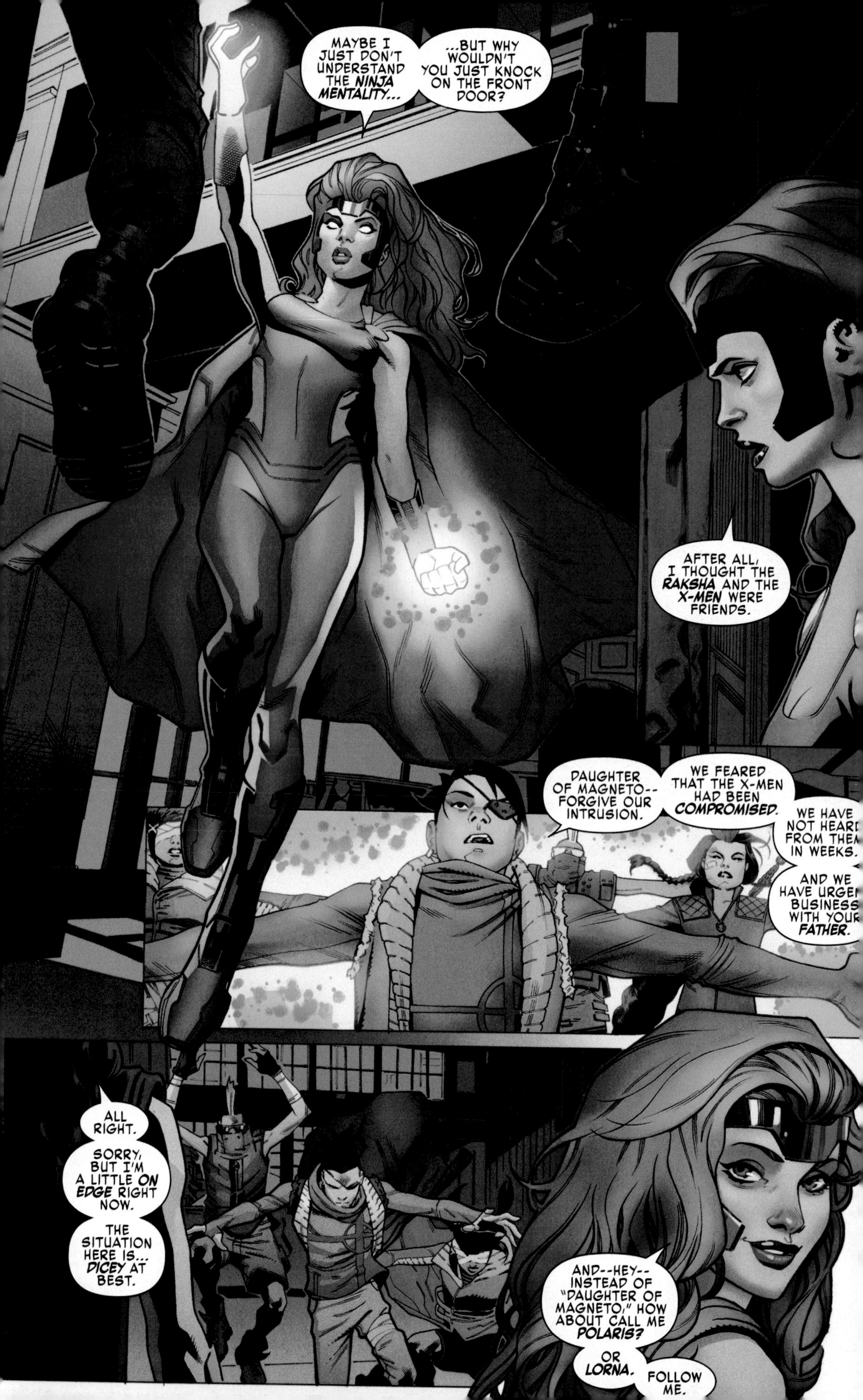
MAYBE I JUST DON'T UNDERSTAND THE NINJA MENTALITY...
...BUT WHY WOULDN'T YOU JUST KNOCK ON THE FRONT DOOR?
AFTER ALL, I THOUGHT THE RAKSHA AND THE X-MEN WERE FRIENDS.
DAUGHTER OF MAGNETO--FORGIVE OUR INTRUSION.
WE FEARED THAT THE X-MEN HAD BEEN COMPROMISED.
WE HAVE NOT HEARD FROM THEM IN WEEKS.
AND WE HAVE URGENT BUSINESS WITH YOUR FATHER.
ALL RIGHT.
SORRY, BUT I'M A LITTLE ON EDGE RIGHT NOW.
THE SITUATION HERE IS... DICEY AT BEST.
AND--HEY--INSTEAD OF "DAUGHTER OF MAGNETO," HOW ABOUT CALL ME POLARIS?
OR LORNA.
FOLLOW ME.

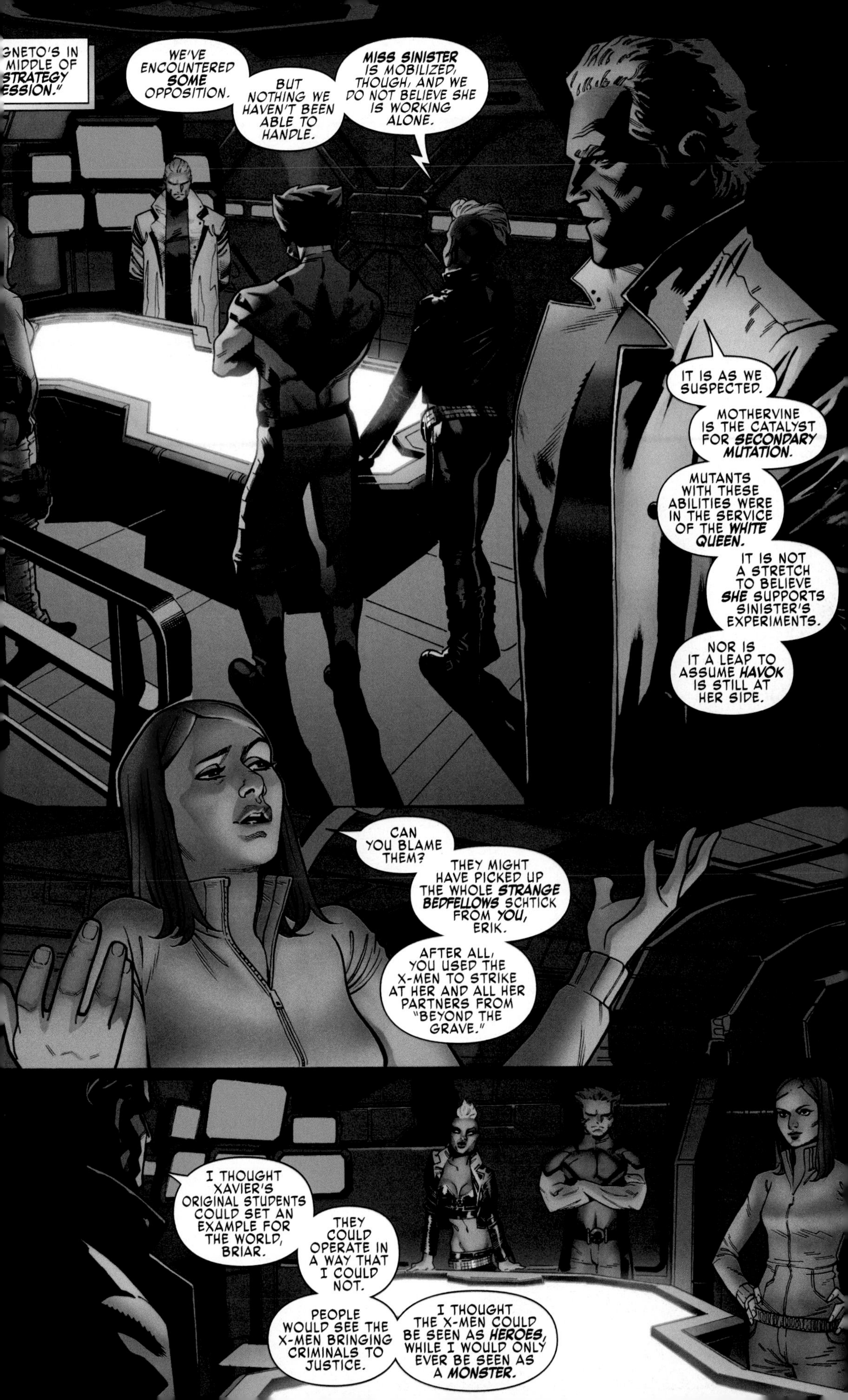
GNETO'S IN MIDDLE OF STRATEGY ESSION."
WE'VE ENCOUNTERED SOME OPPOSITION.
BUT NOTHING WE HAVEN'T BEEN ABLE TO HANDLE.
MISS SINISTER IS MOBILIZED, THOUGH, AND WE DO NOT BELIEVE SHE IS WORKING ALONE.
IT IS AS WE SUSPECTED.
MOTHERVINE IS THE CATALYST FOR SECONDARY MUTATION.
MUTANTS WITH THESE ABILITIES WERE IN THE SERVICE OF THE WHITE QUEEN.
IT IS NOT A STRETCH TO BELIEVE SHE SUPPORTS SINISTER'S EXPERIMENTS.
NOR IS IT A LEAP TO ASSUME HAVOK IS STILL AT HER SIDE.
CAN YOU BLAME THEM?
THEY MIGHT HAVE PICKED UP THE WHOLE STRANGE BEDFELLOWS SCHTICK FROM YOU, ERIK.
AFTER ALL, YOU USED THE X-MEN TO STRIKE AT HER AND ALL HER PARTNERS FROM "BEYOND THE GRAVE."
I THOUGHT XAVIER'S ORIGINAL STUDENTS COULD SET AN EXAMPLE FOR THE WORLD, BRIAR.
THEY COULD OPERATE IN A WAY THAT I COULD NOT.
PEOPLE WOULD SEE THE X-MEN BRINGING CRIMINALS TO JUSTICE.
I THOUGHT THE X-MEN COULD BE SEEN AS HEROES, WHILE I WOULD ONLY EVER BE SEEN AS A MONSTER.

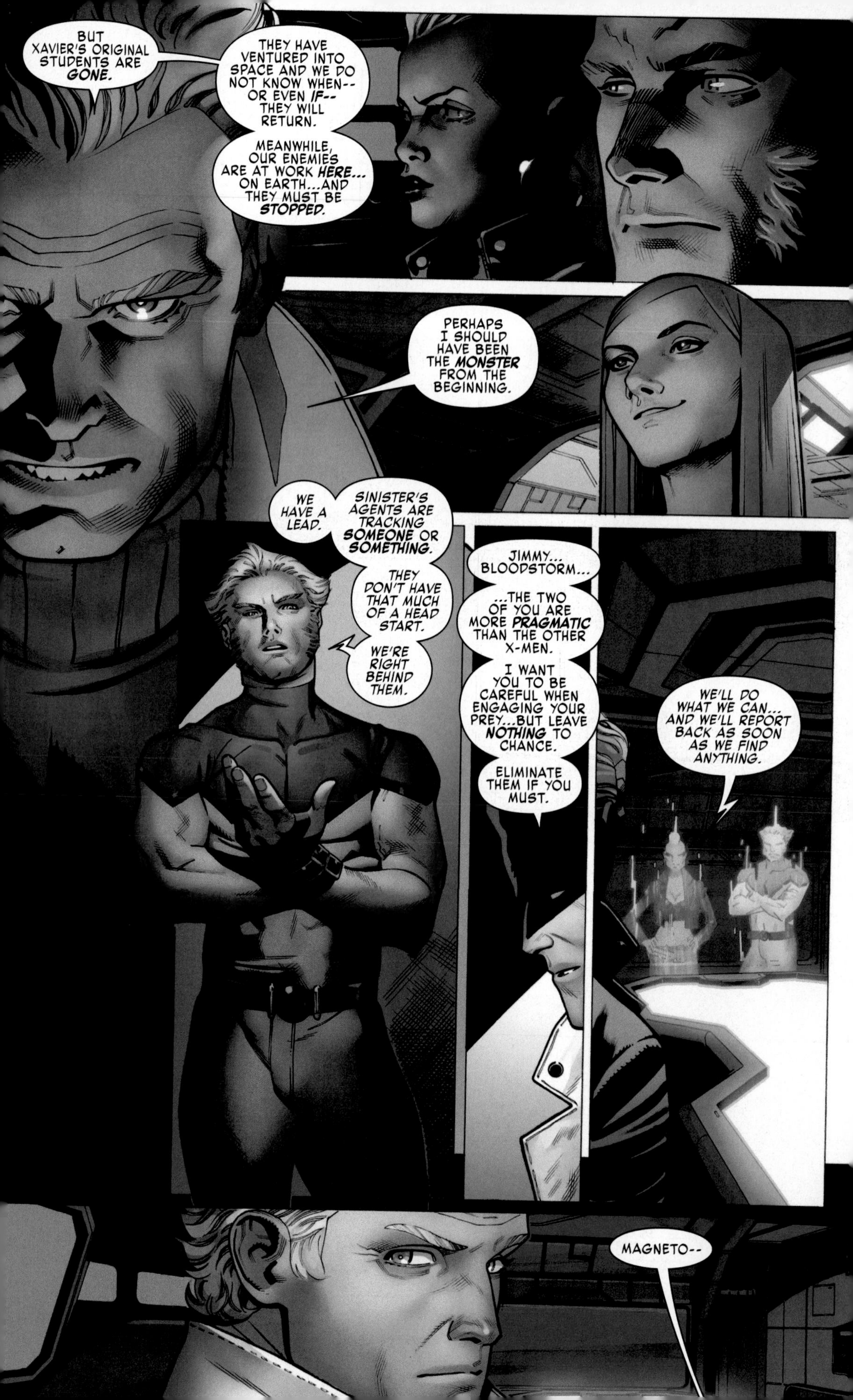
BUT XAVIER'S ORIGINAL STUDENTS ARE GONE.
THEY HAVE VENTURED INTO SPACE AND WE DO NOT KNOW WHEN-- OR EVEN IF-- THEY WILL RETURN.
MEANWHILE, OUR ENEMIES ARE AT WORK HERE... ON EARTH...AND THEY MUST BE STOPPED.
PERHAPS I SHOULD HAVE BEEN THE MONSTER FROM THE BEGINNING.
WE HAVE A LEAD.
SINISTER'S AGENTS ARE TRACKING SOMEONE OR SOMETHING.
THEY DON'T HAVE THAT MUCH OF A HEAD START.
WE'RE RIGHT BEHIND THEM.
JIMMY... BLOODSTORM...
...THE TWO OF YOU ARE MORE PRAGMATIC THAN THE OTHER X-MEN.
I WANT YOU TO BE CAREFUL WHEN ENGAGING YOUR PREY...BUT LEAVE NOTHING TO CHANCE.
ELIMINATE THEM IF YOU MUST.
WE'LL DO WHAT WE CAN... AND WE'LL REPORT BACK AS SOON AS WE FIND ANYTHING.
MAGNETO--

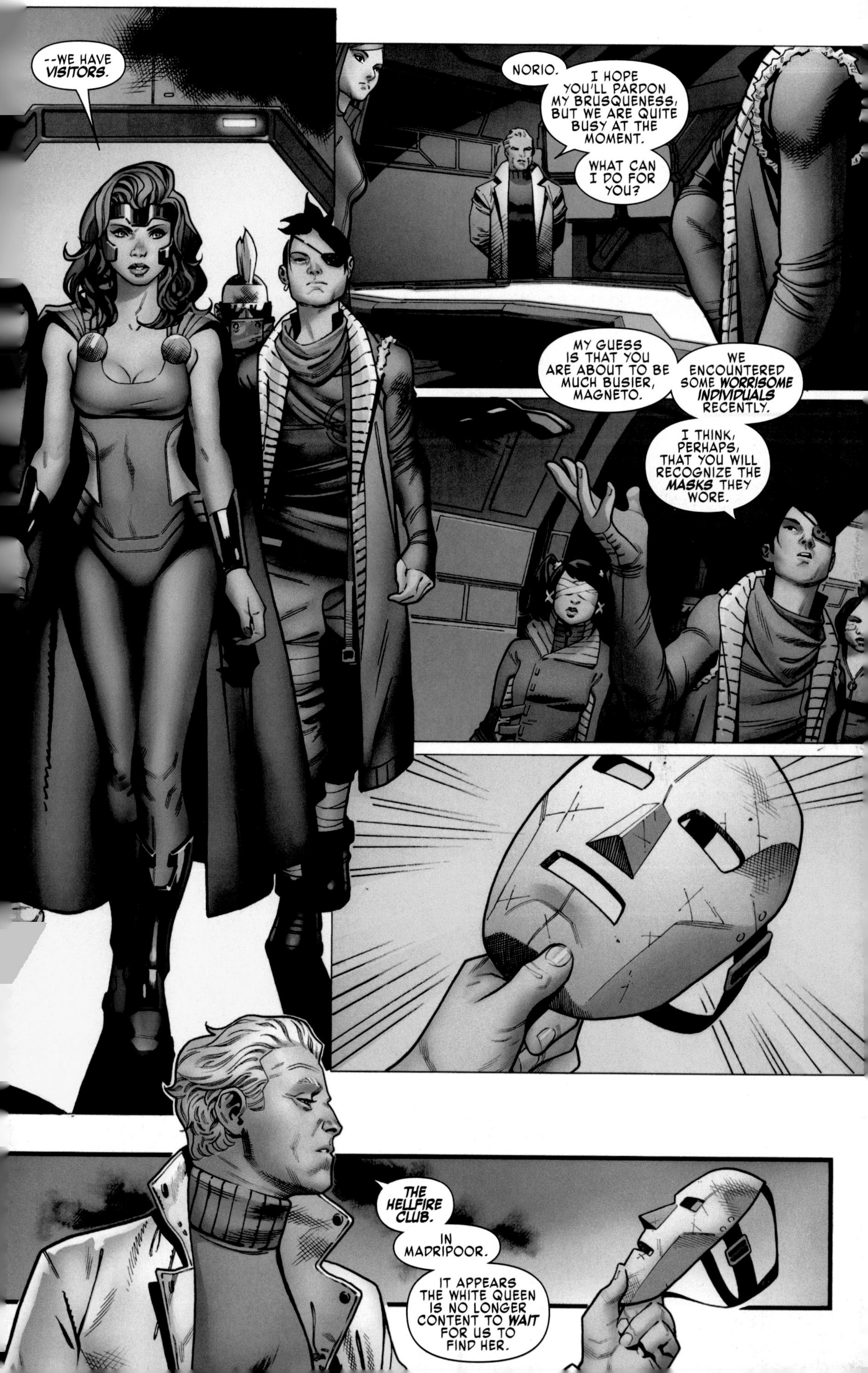
--WE HAVE VISITORS.
NORIO.
I HOPE YOU'LL PARDON MY BRUSQUENESS, BUT WE ARE QUITE BUSY AT THE MOMENT.
WHAT CAN I DO FOR YOU?
MY GUESS IS THAT YOU ARE ABOUT TO BE MUCH BUSIER, MAGNETO.
WE ENCOUNTERED SOME WORRISOME INDIVIDUALS RECENTLY.
I THINK, PERHAPS, THAT YOU WILL RECOGNIZE THE MASKS THEY WORE.
THE HELLFIRE CLUB.
IN MADRIPOOR.
IT APPEARS THE WHITE QUEEN IS NO LONGER CONTENT TO WAIT FOR US TO FIND HER.

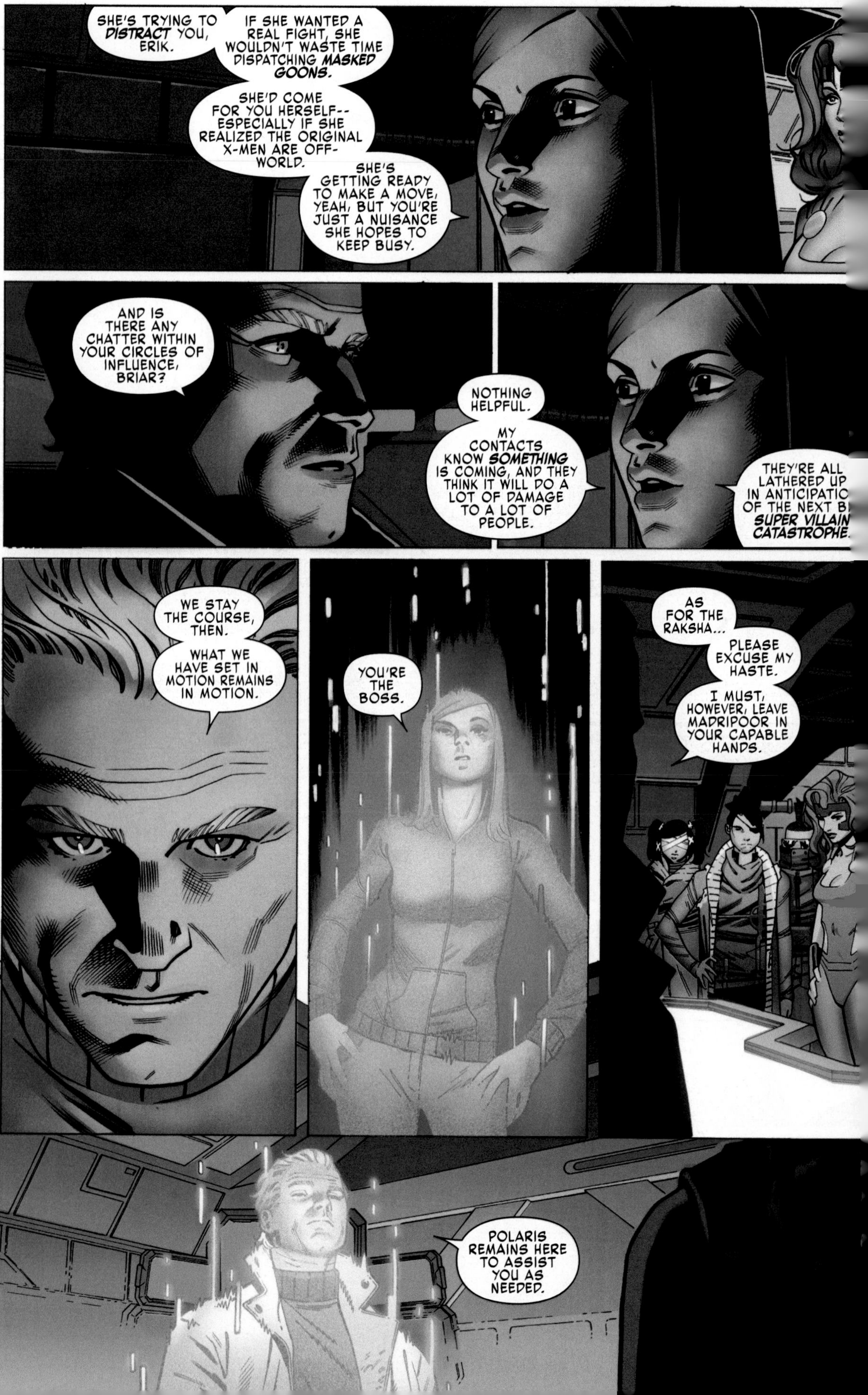
SHE'S TRYING TO DISTRACT YOU, ERIK.
IF SHE WANTED A REAL FIGHT, SHE WOULDN'T WASTE TIME DISPATCHING MASKED GOONS.
SHE'D COME FOR YOU HERSELF-- ESPECIALLY IF SHE REALIZED THE ORIGINAL X-MEN ARE OFF-WORLD.
SHE'S GETTING READY TO MAKE A MOVE, YEAH, BUT YOU'RE JUST A NUISANCE SHE HOPES TO KEEP BUSY.
AND IS THERE ANY CHATTER WITHIN YOUR CIRCLES OF INFLUENCE, BRIAR?
NOTHING HELPFUL.
MY CONTACTS KNOW SOMETHING IS COMING, AND THEY THINK IT WILL DO A LOT OF DAMAGE TO A LOT OF PEOPLE.
THEY'RE ALL LATHERED UP IN ANTICIPATIO OF THE NEXT BI SUPER VILLAIN CATASTROPHE.
WE STAY THE COURSE, THEN.
WHAT WE HAVE SET IN MOTION REMAINS IN MOTION.
YOU'RE THE BOSS.
AS FOR THE RAKSHA...
PLEASE EXCUSE MY HASTE.
I MUST, HOWEVER, LEAVE MADRIPOOR IN YOUR CAPABLE HANDS.
POLARIS REMAINS HERE TO ASSIST YOU AS NEEDED.

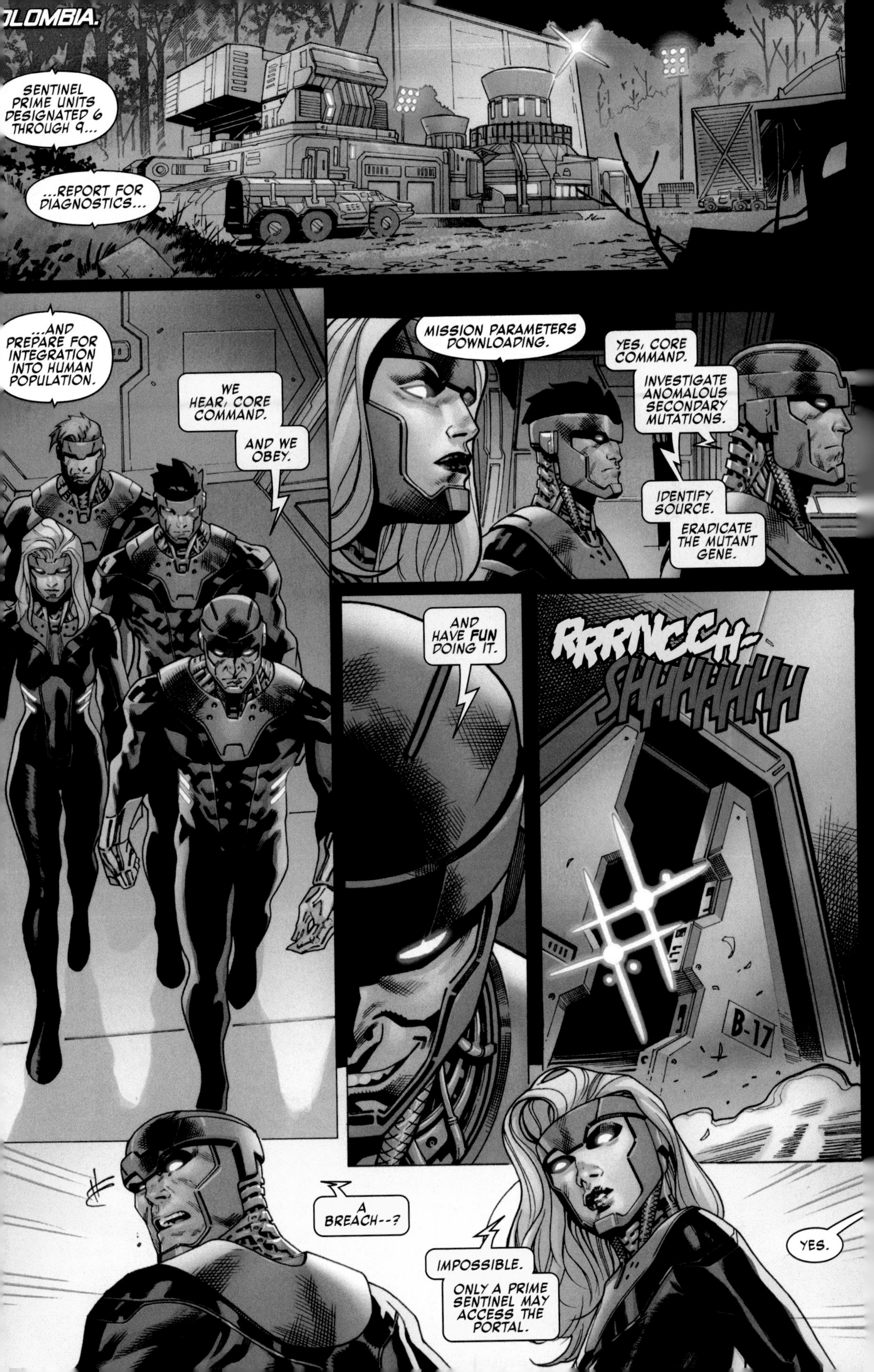
OLOMBIA.
SENTINEL PRIME UNITS DESIGNATED 6 THROUGH 9...
...REPORT FOR DIAGNOSTICS...
...AND PREPARE FOR INTEGRATION INTO HUMAN POPULATION.
WE HEAR, CORE COMMAND.
AND WE OBEY.
MISSION PARAMETERS DOWNLOADING.
YES, CORE COMMAND.
INVESTIGATE ANOMALOUS SECONDARY MUTATIONS.
IDENTIFY SOURCE.
ERADICATE THE MUTANT GENE.
AND HAVE FUN DOING IT.
RRRNCCH-SHHHHHHH
B-17
A BREACH--?
IMPOSSIBLE.
ONLY A PRIME SENTINEL MAY ACCESS THE PORTAL.
YES.

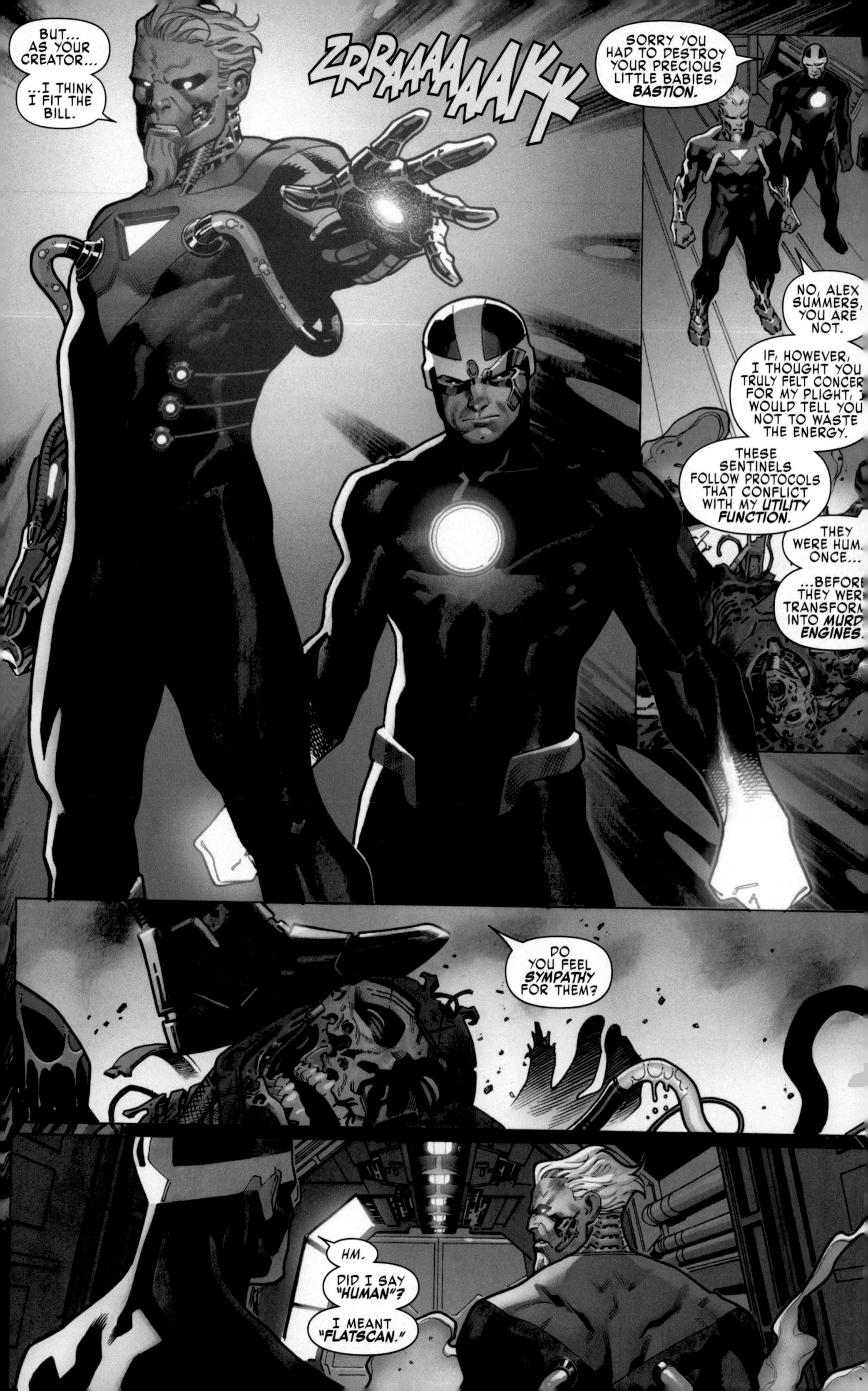
BUT... AS YOUR CREATOR...
...I THINK I FIT THE BILL.
ZRRAAAAAAKK
SORRY YOU HAD TO DESTROY YOUR PRECIOUS LITTLE BABIES, BASTION.
NO, ALEX SUMMERS, YOU ARE NOT.
IF, HOWEVER, I THOUGHT YOU TRULY FELT CONCER FOR MY PLIGHT, I WOULD TELL YOU NOT TO WASTE THE ENERGY.
THESE SENTINELS FOLLOW PROTOCOLS THAT CONFLICT WITH MY UTILITY FUNCTION.
THEY WERE HUM ONCE...
...BEFOR THEY WER TRANSFOR INTO MURD ENGINES.
DO YOU FEEL SYMPATHY FOR THEM?
HM.
DID I SAY "HUMAN"?
I MEANT "FLATSCAN."

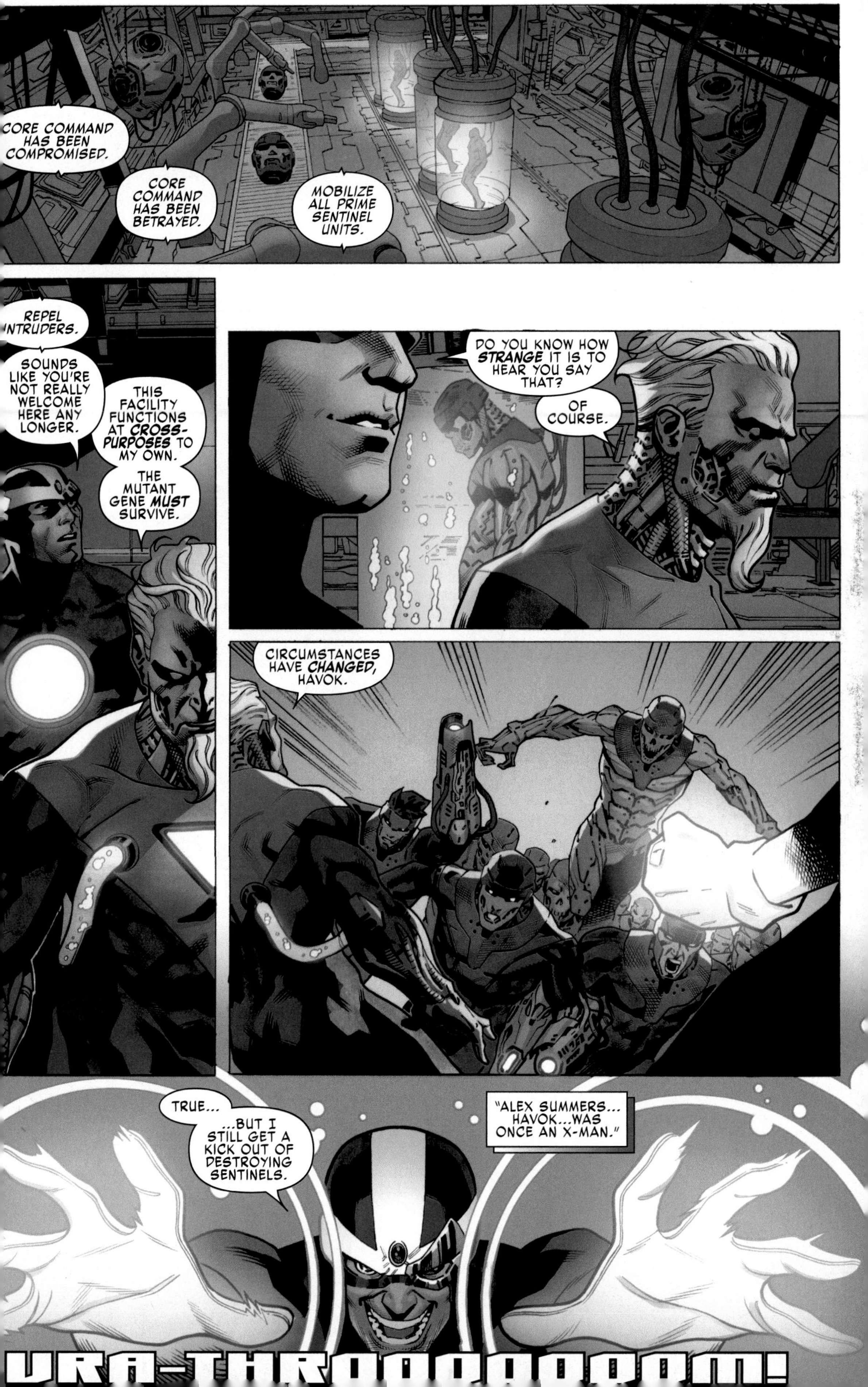
CORE COMMAND HAS BEEN COMPROMISED.
CORE COMMAND HAS BEEN BETRAYED.
MOBILIZE ALL PRIME SENTINEL UNITS.
REPEL INTRUDERS.
SOUNDS LIKE YOU'RE NOT REALLY WELCOME HERE ANY LONGER.
THIS FACILITY FUNCTIONS AT CROSS-PURPOSES TO MY OWN.
THE MUTANT GENE MUST SURVIVE.
DO YOU KNOW HOW STRANGE IT IS TO HEAR YOU SAY THAT?
OF COURSE.
CIRCUMSTANCES HAVE CHANGED, HAVOK.
TRUE...
...BUT I STILL GET A KICK OUT OF DESTROYING SENTINELS.
"ALEX SUMMERS... HAVOK...WAS ONCE AN X-MAN."
URA-THROOOOOOOOM!

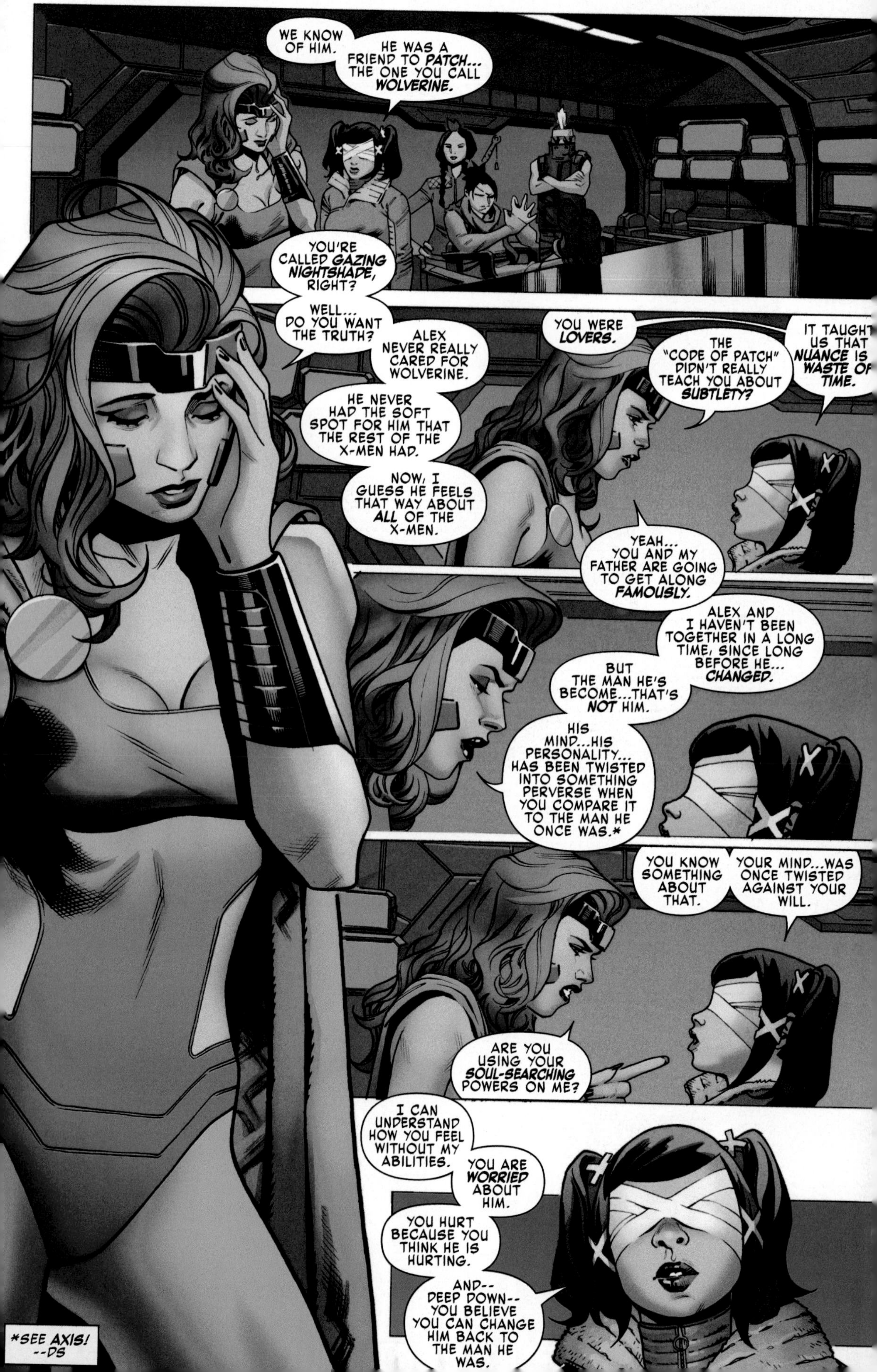
WE KNOW OF HIM.
HE WAS A FRIEND TO PATCH... THE ONE YOU CALL WOLVERINE.
YOU'RE CALLED GAZING NIGHTSHADE, RIGHT?
WELL... DO YOU WANT THE TRUTH?
ALEX NEVER REALLY CARED FOR WOLVERINE.
HE NEVER HAD THE SOFT SPOT FOR HIM THAT THE REST OF THE X-MEN HAD.
NOW, I GUESS HE FEELS THAT WAY ABOUT ALL OF THE X-MEN.
YOU WERE LOVERS.
THE "CODE OF PATCH" DIDN'T REALLY TEACH YOU ABOUT SUBTLETY?
IT TAUGHT US THAT NUANCE IS WASTE OF TIME.
YEAH... YOU AND MY FATHER ARE GOING TO GET ALONG FAMOUSLY.
ALEX AND I HAVEN'T BEEN TOGETHER IN A LONG TIME, SINCE LONG BEFORE HE... CHANGED.
BUT THE MAN HE'S BECOME...THAT'S NOT HIM.
HIS MIND...HIS PERSONALITY... HAS BEEN TWISTED INTO SOMETHING PERVERSE WHEN YOU COMPARE IT TO THE MAN HE ONCE WAS.*
YOU KNOW SOMETHING ABOUT THAT.
YOUR MIND...WAS ONCE TWISTED AGAINST YOUR WILL.
ARE YOU USING YOUR SOUL-SEARCHING POWERS ON ME?
I CAN UNDERSTAND HOW YOU FEEL WITHOUT MY ABILITIES.
YOU ARE WORRIED ABOUT HIM.
YOU HURT BECAUSE YOU THINK HE IS HURTING.
AND-- DEEP DOWN-- YOU BELIEVE YOU CAN CHANGE HIM BACK TO THE MAN HE WAS.
*SEE AXIS! --DS

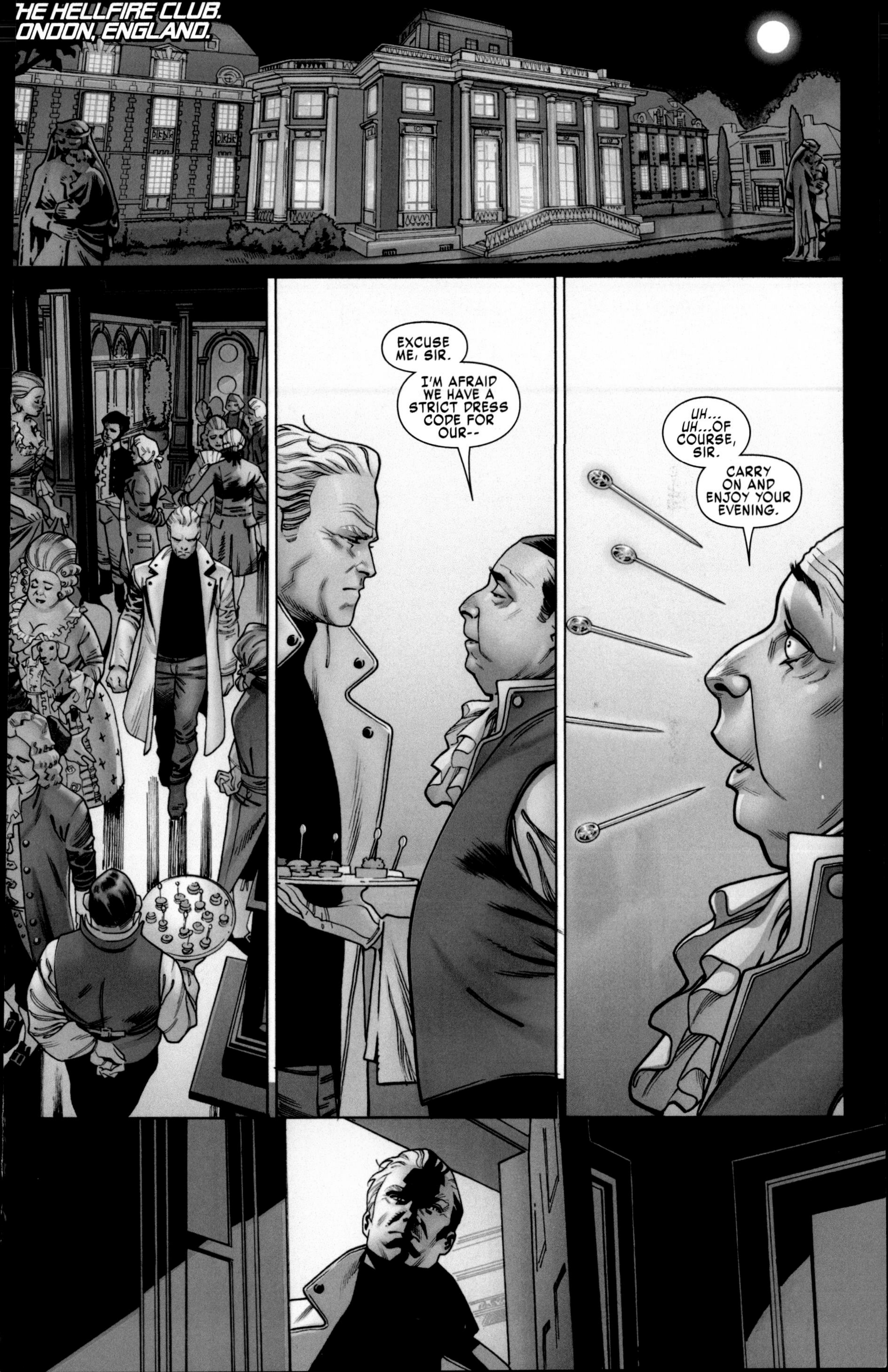
HE HELLFIRE CLUB.
ONDON, ENGLAND.
EXCUSE ME, SIR.
I'M AFRAID WE HAVE A STRICT DRESS CODE FOR OUR--
UH... UH...OF COURSE, SIR.
CARRY ON AND ENJOY YOUR EVENING.

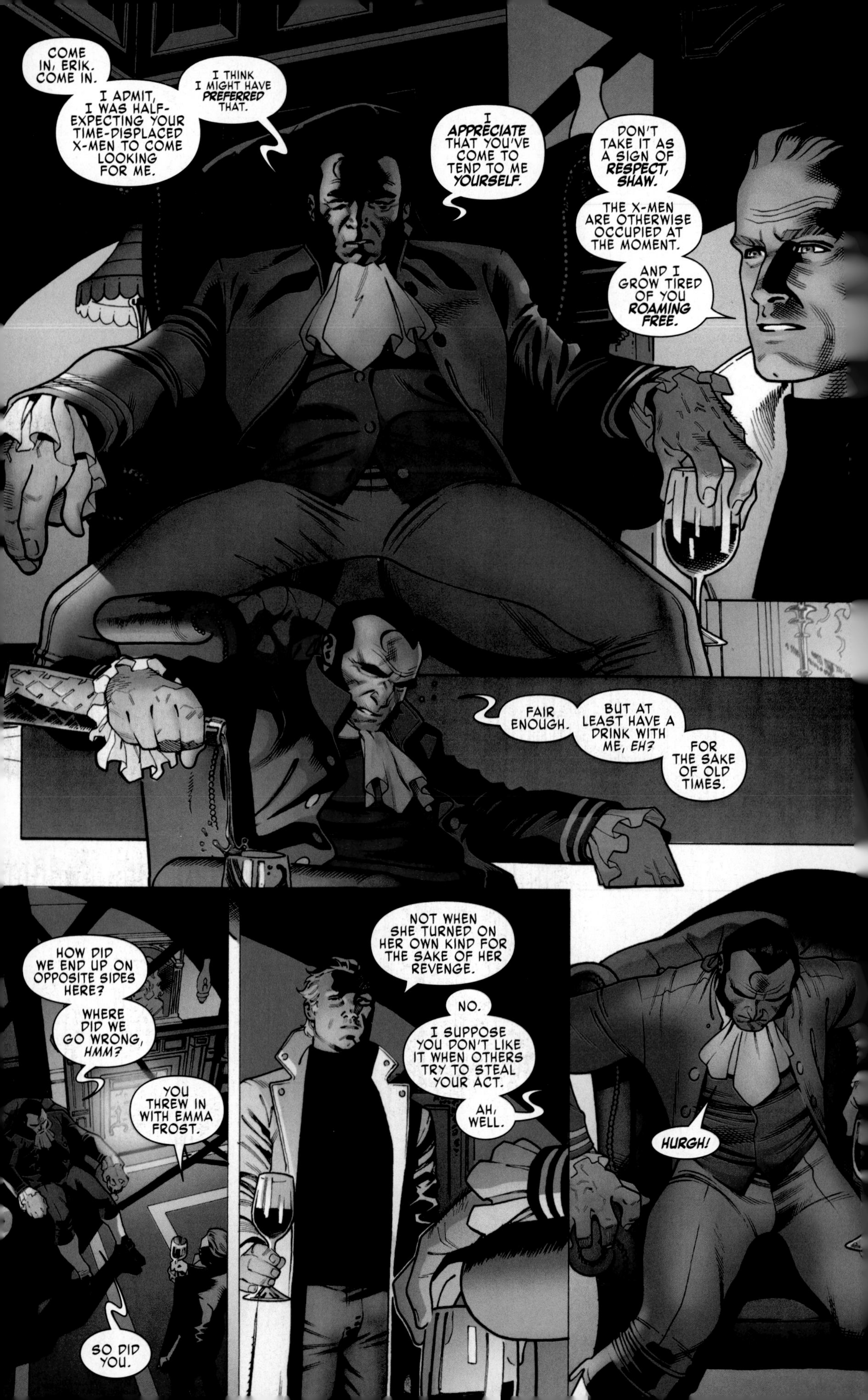
COME IN, ERIK. COME IN.
I ADMIT, I WAS HALF-EXPECTING YOUR TIME-DISPLACED X-MEN TO COME LOOKING FOR ME.
I THINK I MIGHT HAVE PREFERRED THAT.
I APPRECIATE THAT YOU'VE COME TO TEND TO ME YOURSELF.
DON'T TAKE IT AS A SIGN OF RESPECT, SHAW.
THE X-MEN ARE OTHERWISE OCCUPIED AT THE MOMENT.
AND I GROW TIRED OF YOU ROAMING FREE.
FAIR ENOUGH.
BUT AT LEAST HAVE A DRINK WITH ME, EH?
FOR THE SAKE OF OLD TIMES.
HOW DID WE END UP ON OPPOSITE SIDES HERE?
WHERE DID WE GO WRONG, HMM?
YOU THREW IN WITH EMMA FROST.
SO DID YOU.
NOT WHEN SHE TURNED ON HER OWN KIND FOR THE SAKE OF HER REVENGE.
NO.
I SUPPOSE YOU DON'T LIKE IT WHEN OTHERS TRY TO STEAL YOUR ACT.
AH, WELL.
HURGH!

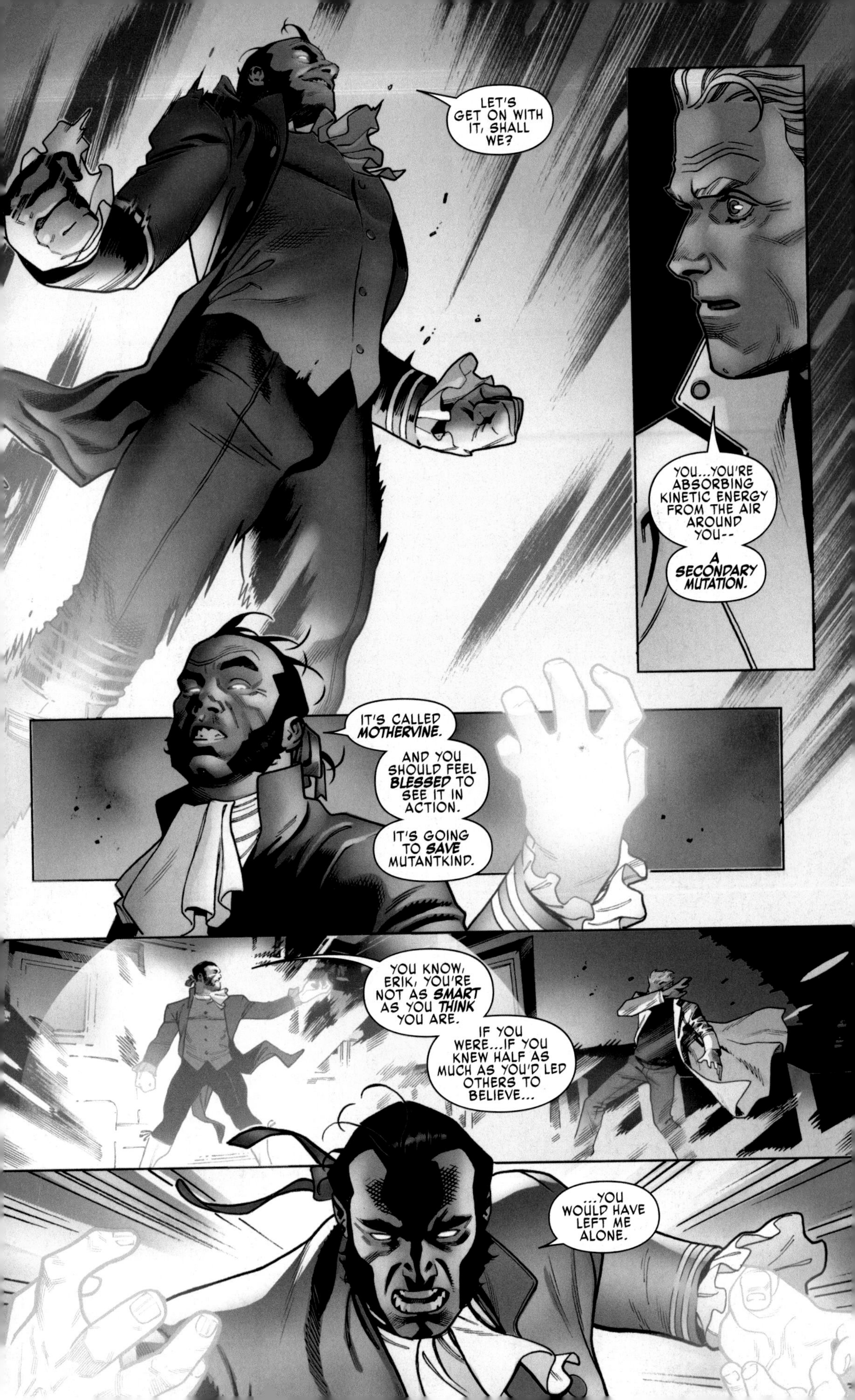
LET'S GET ON WITH IT, SHALL WE?
YOU...YOU'RE ABSORBING KINETIC ENERGY FROM THE AIR AROUND YOU--
A SECONDARY MUTATION.
IT'S CALLED MOTHERVINE.
AND YOU SHOULD FEEL BLESSED TO SEE IT IN ACTION.
IT'S GOING TO SAVE MUTANTKIND.
YOU KNOW, ERIK, YOU'RE NOT AS SMART AS YOU THINK YOU ARE.
IF YOU WERE...IF YOU KNEW HALF AS MUCH AS YOU'D LED OTHERS TO BELIEVE...
...YOU WOULD HAVE LEFT ME ALONE.

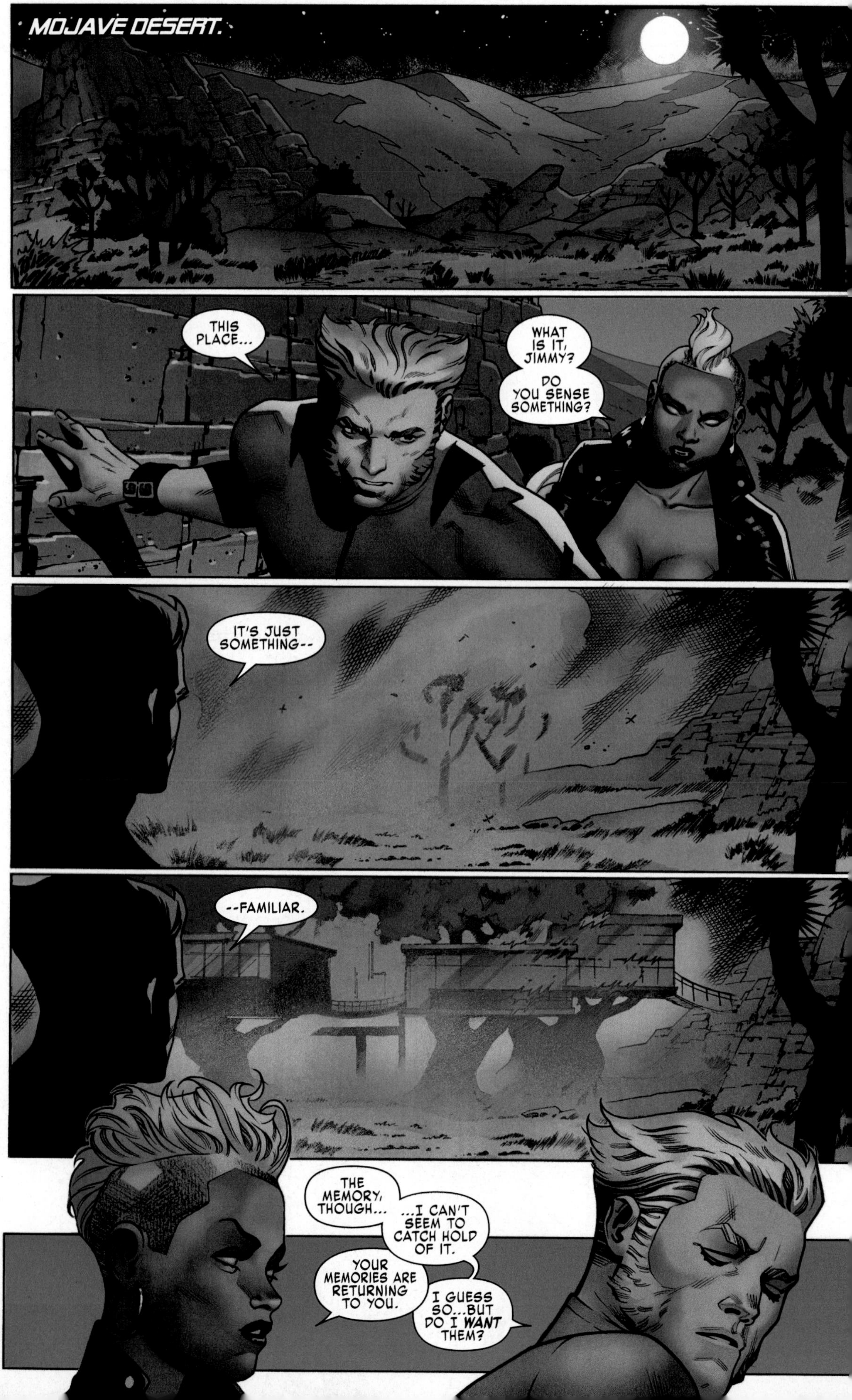
MOJAVE DESERT.
THIS PLACE...
WHAT IS IT, JIMMY?
DO YOU SENSE SOMETHING?
IT'S JUST SOMETHING--
--FAMILIAR.
THE MEMORY, THOUGH...
...I CAN'T SEEM TO CATCH HOLD OF IT.
YOUR MEMORIES ARE RETURNING TO YOU.
I GUESS SO...BUT DO I *WANT* THEM?

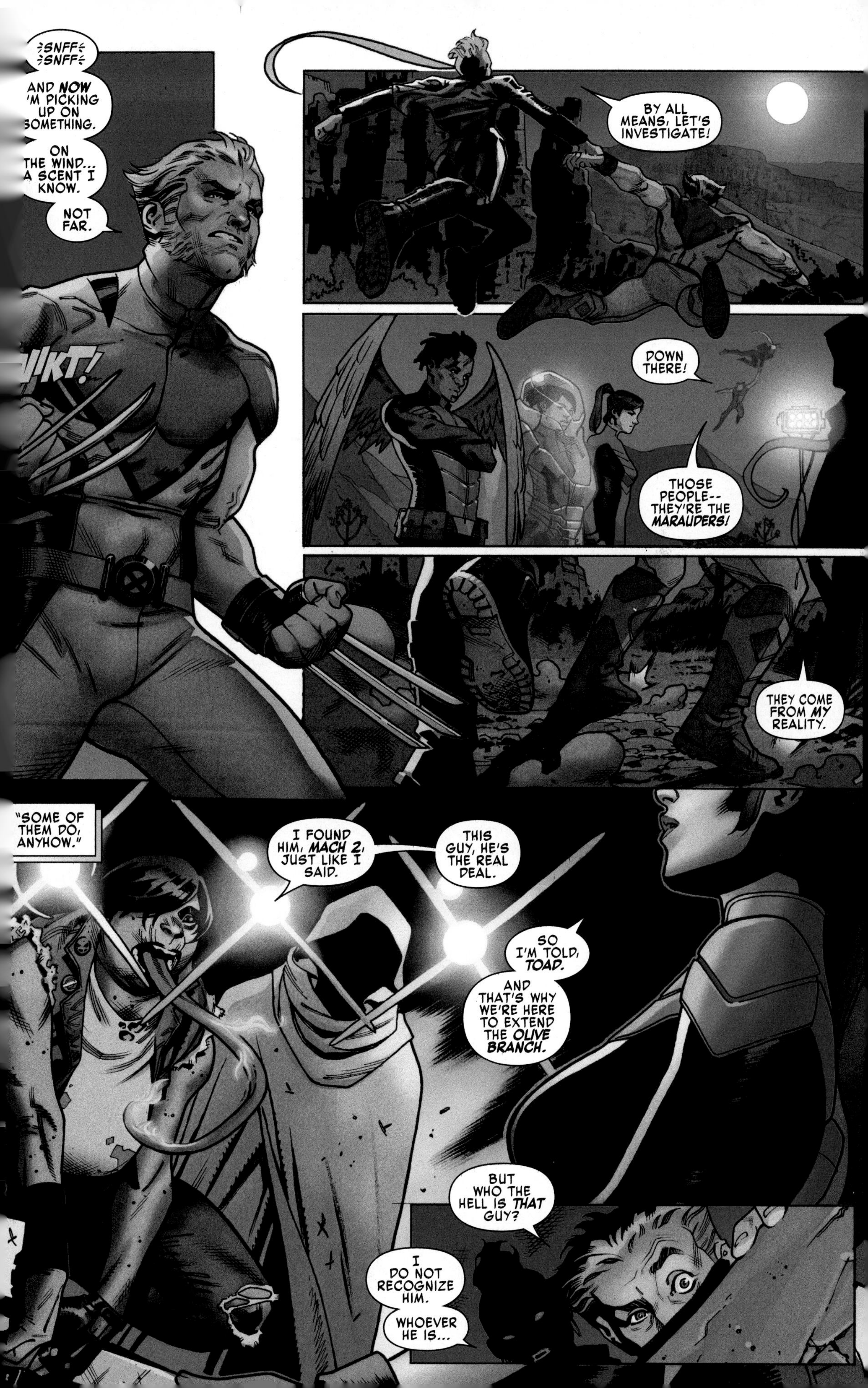

SNFF SNFF
AND NOW I'M PICKING UP ON SOMETHING.
ON THE WIND... A SCENT I KNOW.
NOT FAR.
BY ALL MEANS, LET'S INVESTIGATE!
DOWN THERE!
THOSE PEOPLE-- THEY'RE THE MARAUDERS!
THEY COME FROM MY REALITY.
"SOME OF THEM DO, ANYHOW."
I FOUND HIM, MACH 2, JUST LIKE I SAID.
THIS GUY, HE'S THE REAL DEAL.
SO I'M TOLD, TOAD.
AND THAT'S WHY WE'RE HERE TO EXTEND THE OLIVE BRANCH.
BUT WHO THE HELL IS THAT GUY?
I DO NOT RECOGNIZE HIM.
WHOEVER HE IS...

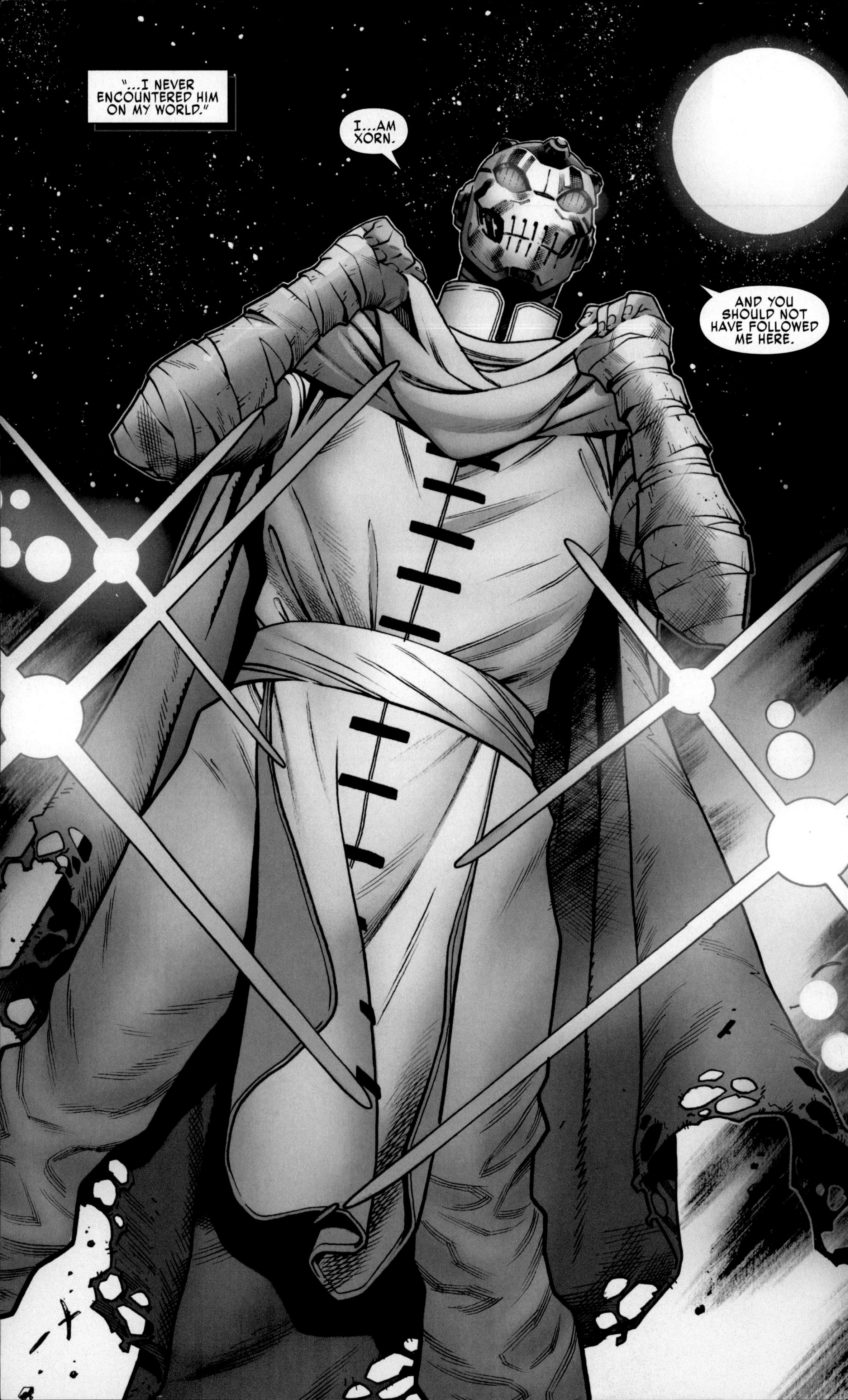
"...I NEVER ENCOUNTERED HIM ON MY WORLD."
I...AM XORN.
AND YOU SHOULD NOT HAVE FOLLOWED ME HERE.

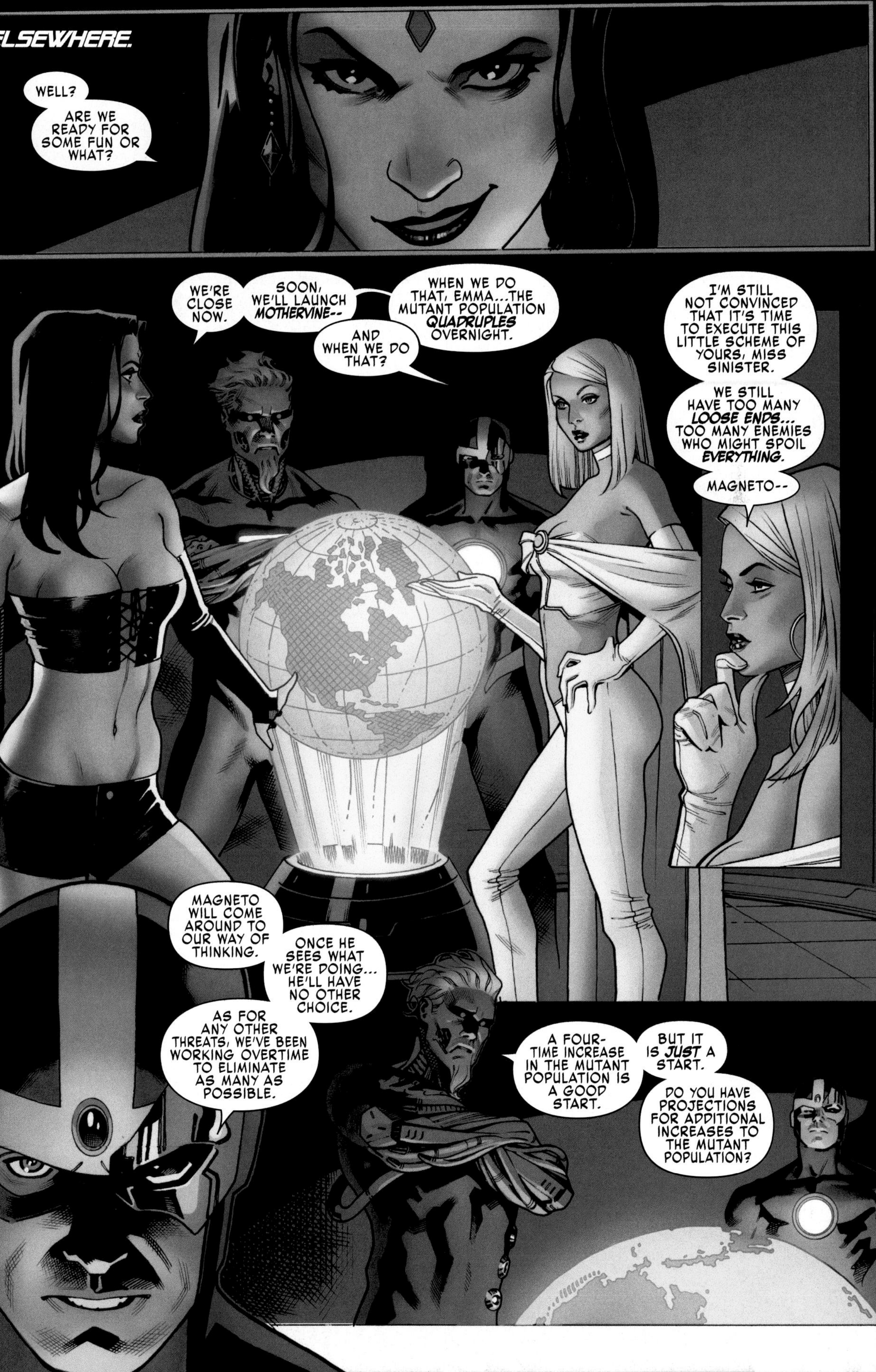
ELSEWHERE.
WELL?
ARE WE READY FOR SOME FUN OR WHAT?
WE'RE CLOSE NOW.
SOON, WE'LL LAUNCH MOTHERVINE--
WHEN WE DO THAT, EMMA...THE MUTANT POPULATION QUADRUPLES OVERNIGHT.
AND WHEN WE DO THAT?
I'M STILL NOT CONVINCED THAT IT'S TIME TO EXECUTE THIS LITTLE SCHEME OF YOURS, MISS SINISTER.
WE STILL HAVE TOO MANY LOOSE ENDS... TOO MANY ENEMIES WHO MIGHT SPOIL EVERYTHING.
MAGNETO--
MAGNETO WILL COME AROUND TO OUR WAY OF THINKING.
ONCE HE SEES WHAT WE'RE DOING... HE'LL HAVE NO OTHER CHOICE.
AS FOR ANY OTHER THREATS, WE'VE BEEN WORKING OVERTIME TO ELIMINATE AS MANY AS POSSIBLE.
A FOUR-TIME INCREASE IN THE MUTANT POPULATION IS A GOOD START.
BUT IT IS JUST A START.
DO YOU HAVE PROJECTIONS FOR ADDITIONAL INCREASES TO THE MUTANT POPULATION?

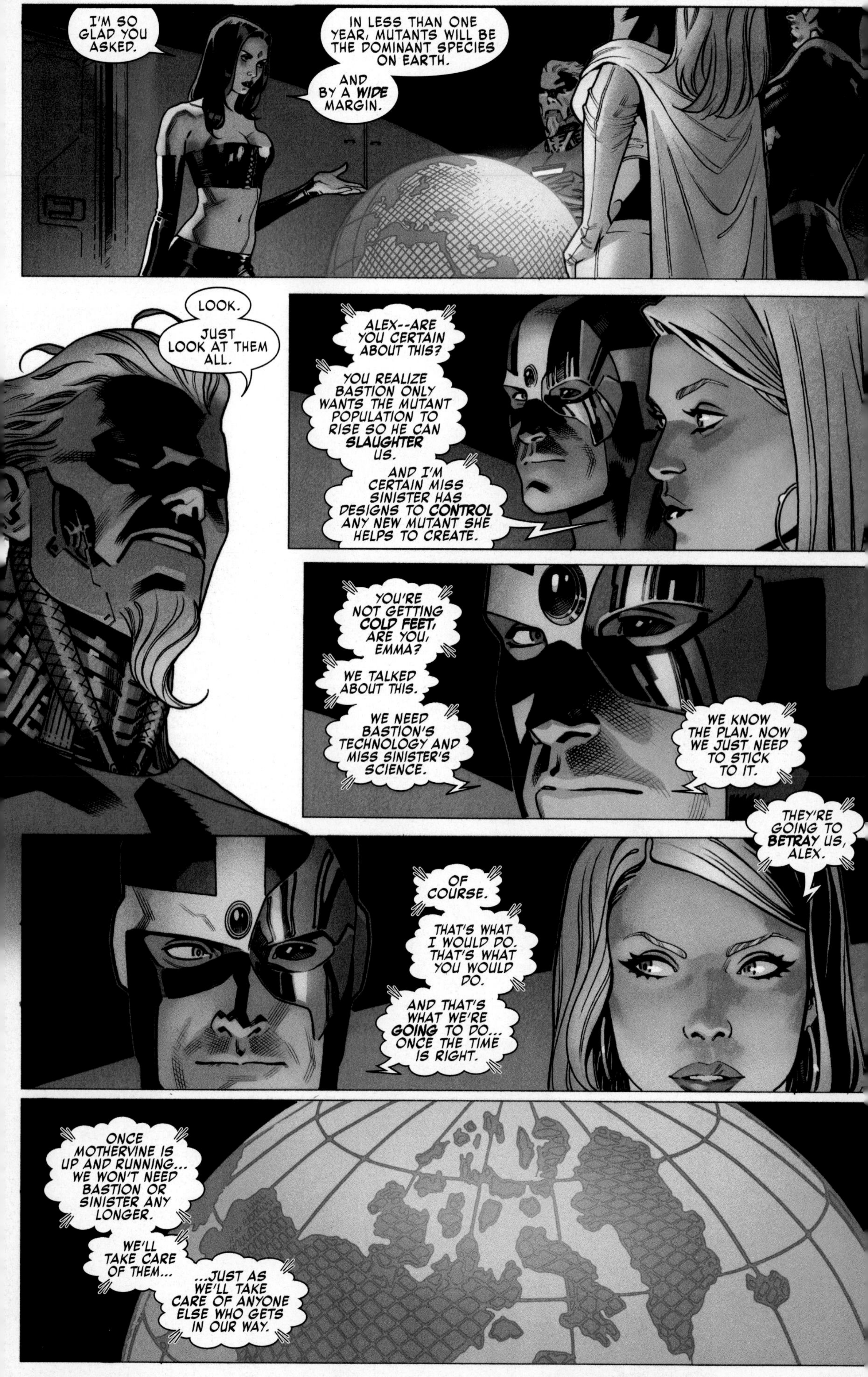
I'M SO GLAD YOU ASKED.
IN LESS THAN ONE YEAR, MUTANTS WILL BE THE DOMINANT SPECIES ON EARTH.
AND BY A WIDE MARGIN.
LOOK.
JUST LOOK AT THEM ALL.
ALEX--ARE YOU CERTAIN ABOUT THIS?
YOU REALIZE BASTION ONLY WANTS THE MUTANT POPULATION TO RISE SO HE CAN SLAUGHTER US.
AND I'M CERTAIN MISS SINISTER HAS DESIGNS TO CONTROL ANY NEW MUTANT SHE HELPS TO CREATE.
YOU'RE NOT GETTING COLD FEET, ARE YOU, EMMA?
WE TALKED ABOUT THIS.
WE NEED BASTION'S TECHNOLOGY AND MISS SINISTER'S SCIENCE.
WE KNOW THE PLAN. NOW WE JUST NEED TO STICK TO IT.
THEY'RE GOING TO BETRAY US, ALEX.
OF COURSE.
THAT'S WHAT I WOULD DO. THAT'S WHAT YOU WOULD DO.
AND THAT'S WHAT WE'RE GOING TO DO... ONCE THE TIME IS RIGHT.
ONCE MOTHERVINE IS UP AND RUNNING... WE WON'T NEED BASTION OR SINISTER ANY LONGER.
WE'LL TAKE CARE OF THEM...
...JUST AS WE'LL TAKE CARE OF ANYONE ELSE WHO GETS IN OUR WAY.

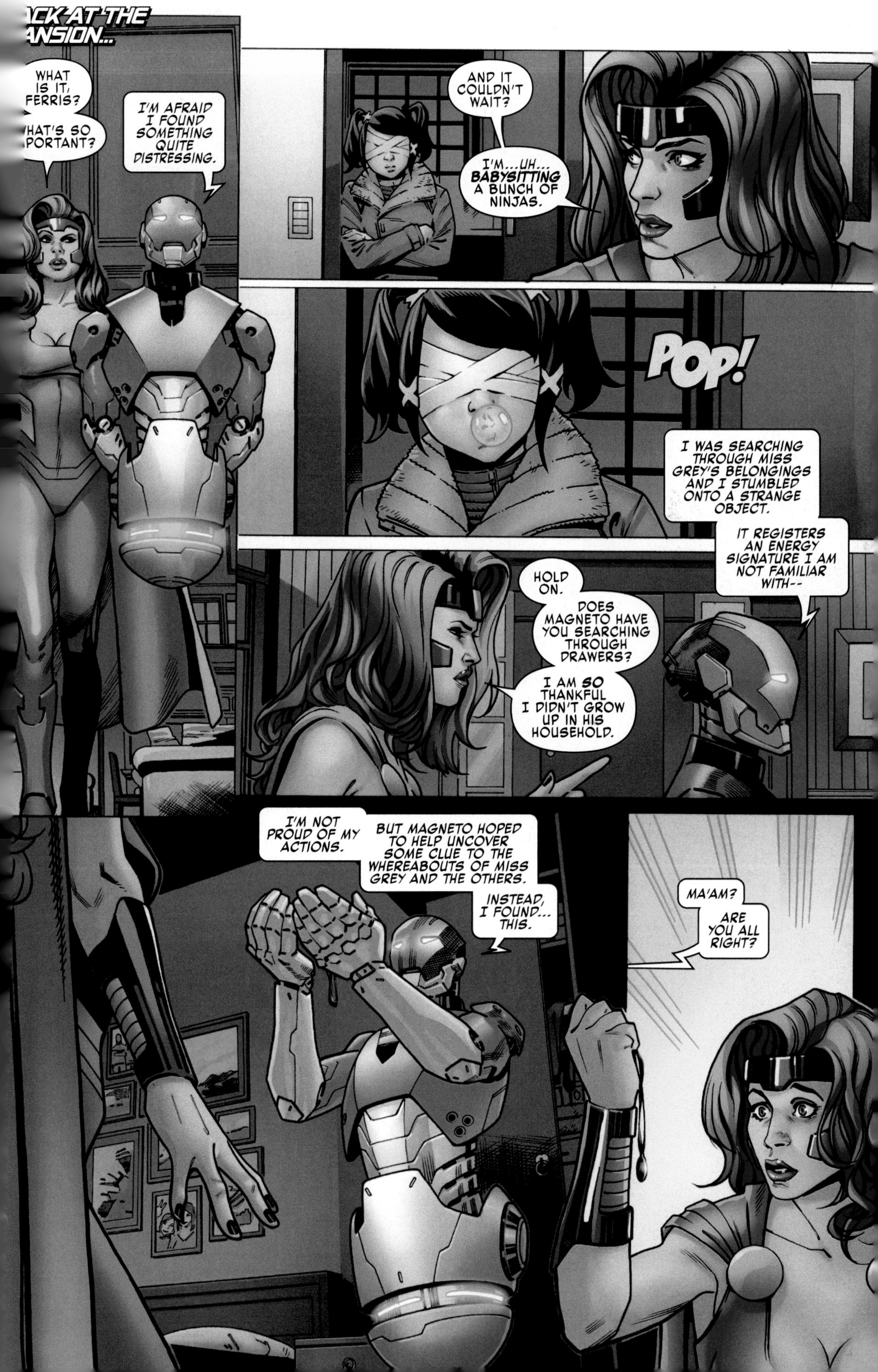

ACK AT THE ANSION...
WHAT IS IT, FERRIS?
WHAT'S SO PORTANT?
I'M AFRAID I FOUND SOMETHING QUITE DISTRESSING.
AND IT COULDN'T WAIT?
I'M...UH... BABYSITTING A BUNCH OF NINJAS.
POP!
I WAS SEARCHING THROUGH MISS GREY'S BELONGINGS AND I STUMBLED ONTO A STRANGE OBJECT.
IT REGISTERS AN ENERGY SIGNATURE I AM NOT FAMILIAR WITH--
HOLD ON.
DOES MAGNETO HAVE YOU SEARCHING THROUGH DRAWERS?
I AM SO THANKFUL I DIDN'T GROW UP IN HIS HOUSEHOLD.
I'M NOT PROUD OF MY ACTIONS.
BUT MAGNETO HOPED TO HELP UNCOVER SOME CLUE TO THE WHEREABOUTS OF MISS GREY AND THE OTHERS.
INSTEAD, I FOUND... THIS.
MA'AM?
ARE YOU ALL RIGHT?

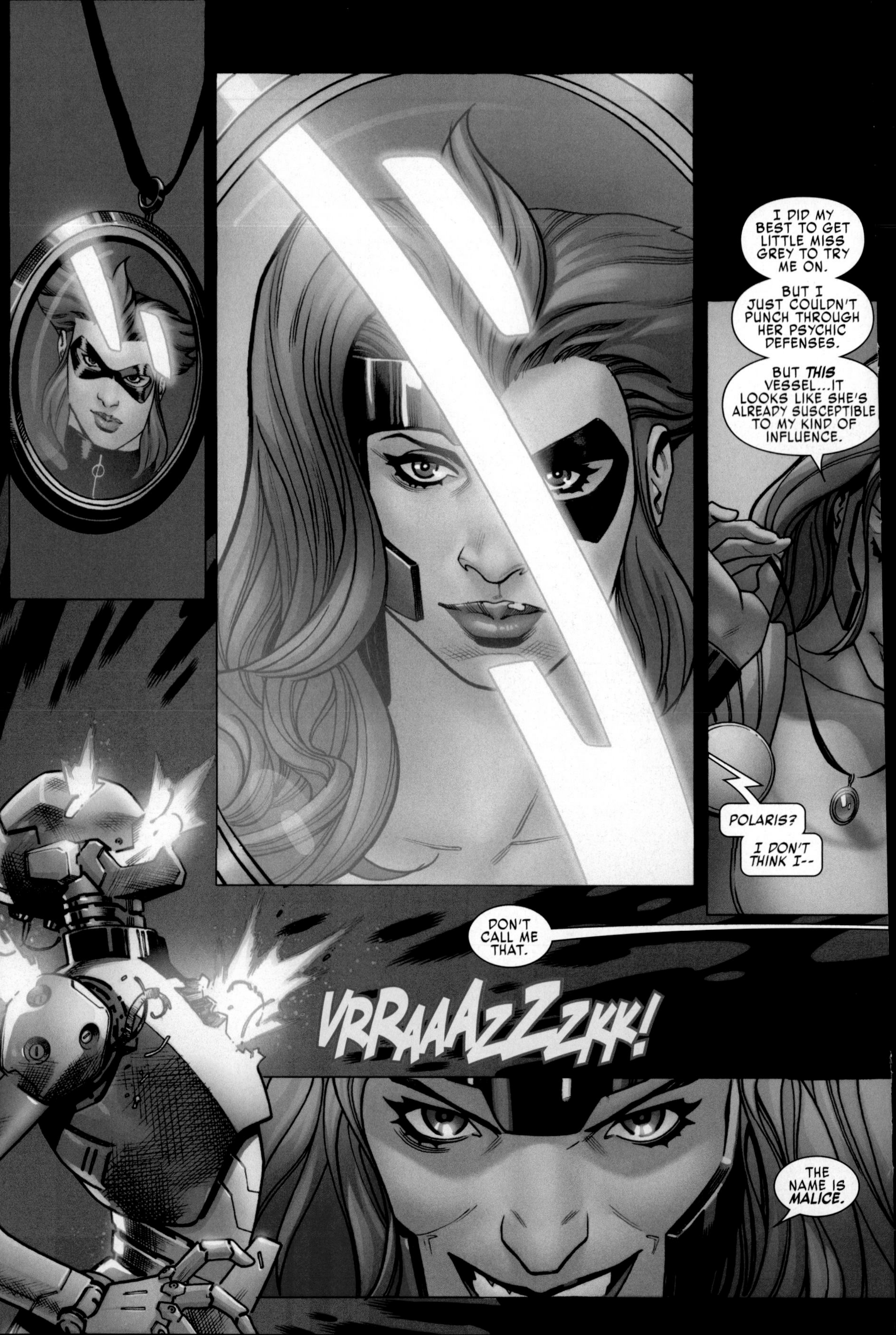
I DID MY BEST TO GET LITTLE MISS GREY TO TRY ME ON.
BUT I JUST COULDN'T PUNCH THROUGH HER PSYCHIC DEFENSES.
BUT *THIS* VESSEL...IT LOOKS LIKE SHE'S ALREADY SUSCEPTIBLE TO MY KIND OF INFLUENCE.
POLARIS?
I DON'T THINK I--
DON'T CALL ME THAT.
VRRAAAZZZKK!
THE NAME IS *MALICE.*

#23 NEW MUTANTS VARIANT BY **CLAYTON CRAIN**

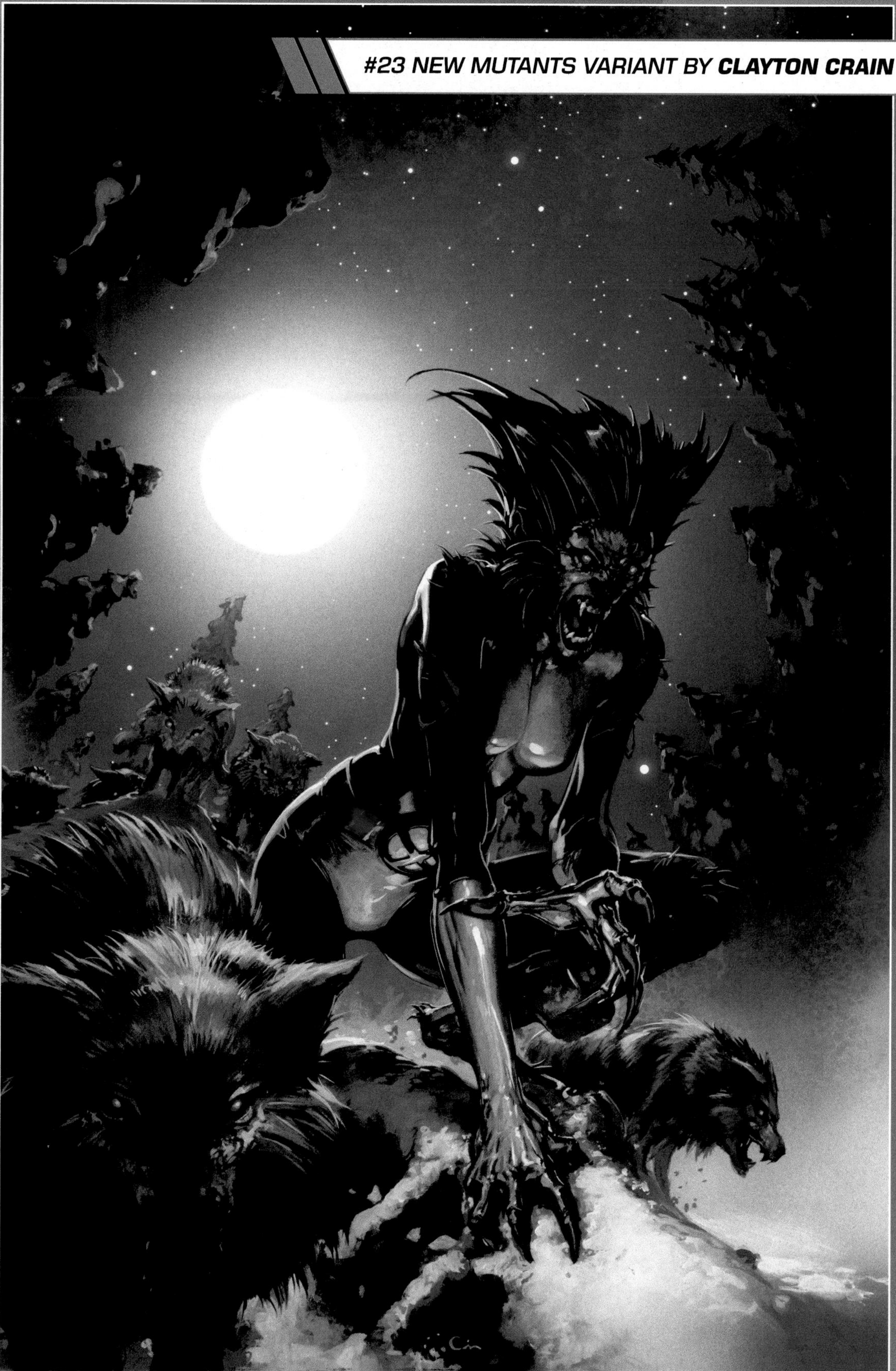

24

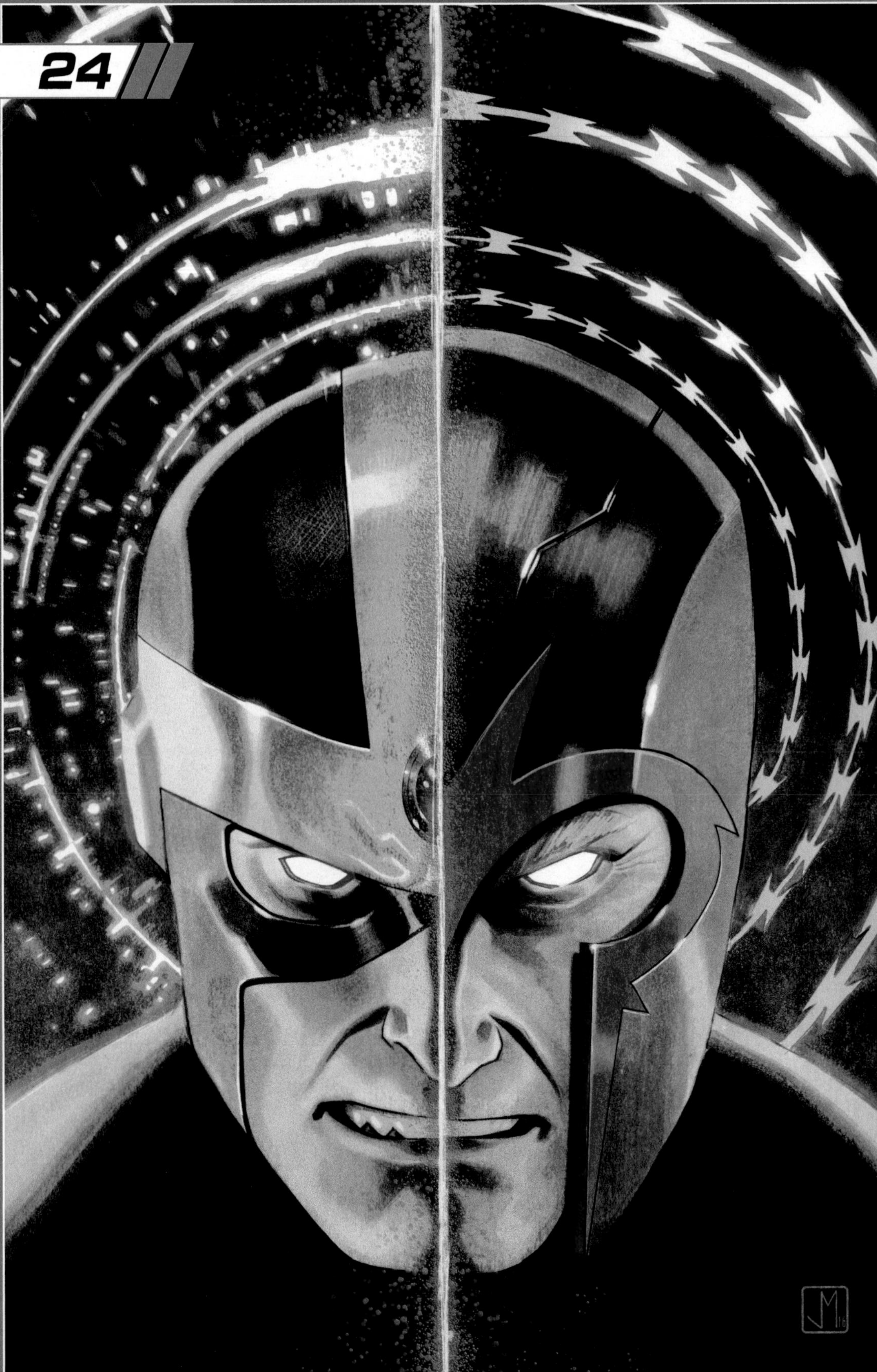

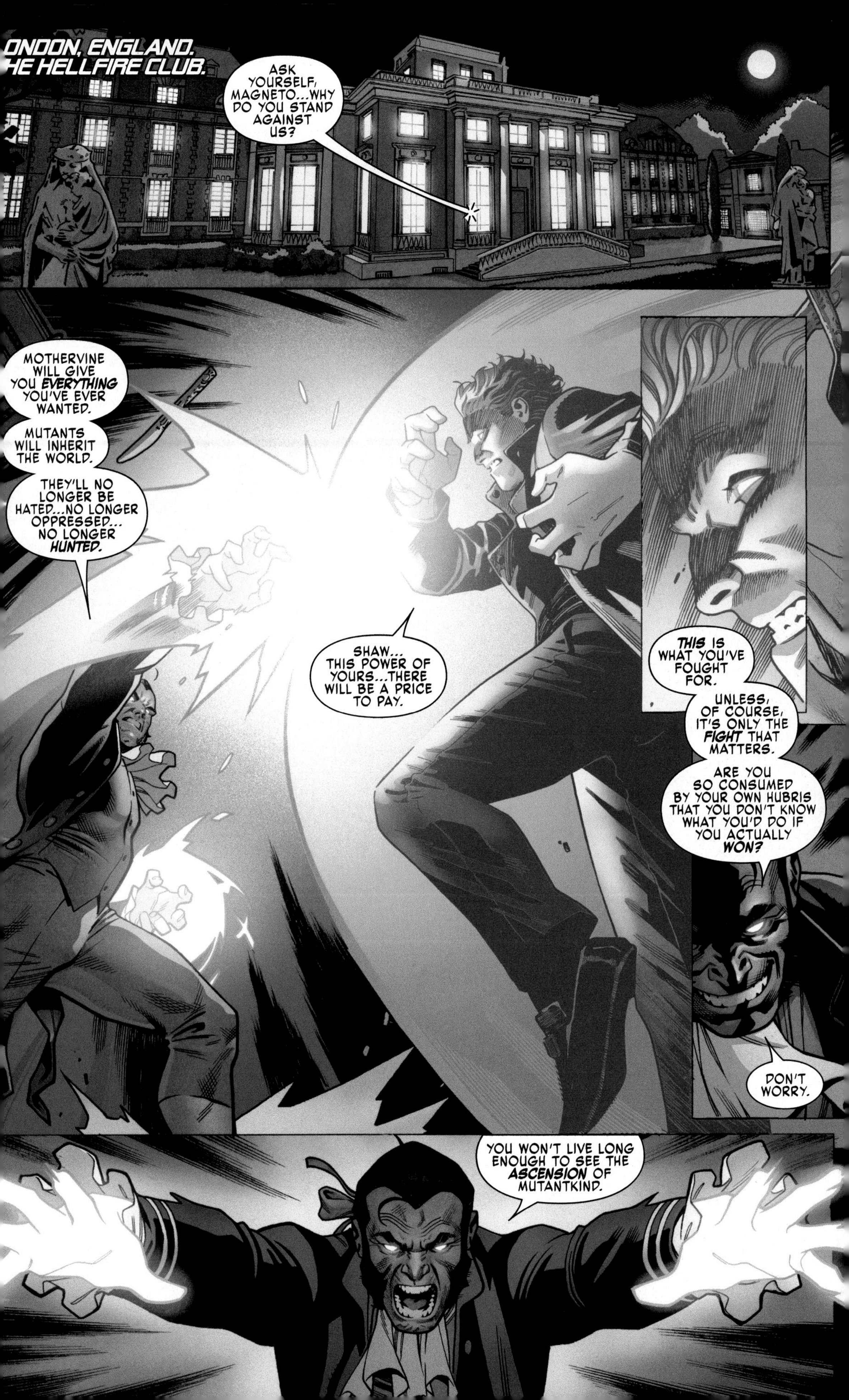

ONDON, ENGLAND. HE HELLFIRE CLUB.
ASK YOURSELF, MAGNETO...WHY DO YOU STAND AGAINST US?
MOTHERVINE WILL GIVE YOU EVERYTHING YOU'VE EVER WANTED.
MUTANTS WILL INHERIT THE WORLD.
THEY'LL NO LONGER BE HATED...NO LONGER OPPRESSED... NO LONGER HUNTED.
SHAW... THIS POWER OF YOURS...THERE WILL BE A PRICE TO PAY.
THIS IS WHAT YOU'VE FOUGHT FOR.
UNLESS, OF COURSE, IT'S ONLY THE FIGHT THAT MATTERS.
ARE YOU SO CONSUMED BY YOUR OWN HUBRIS THAT YOU DON'T KNOW WHAT YOU'D DO IF YOU ACTUALLY WON?
DON'T WORRY.
YOU WON'T LIVE LONG ENOUGH TO SEE THE ASCENSION OF MUTANTKIND.

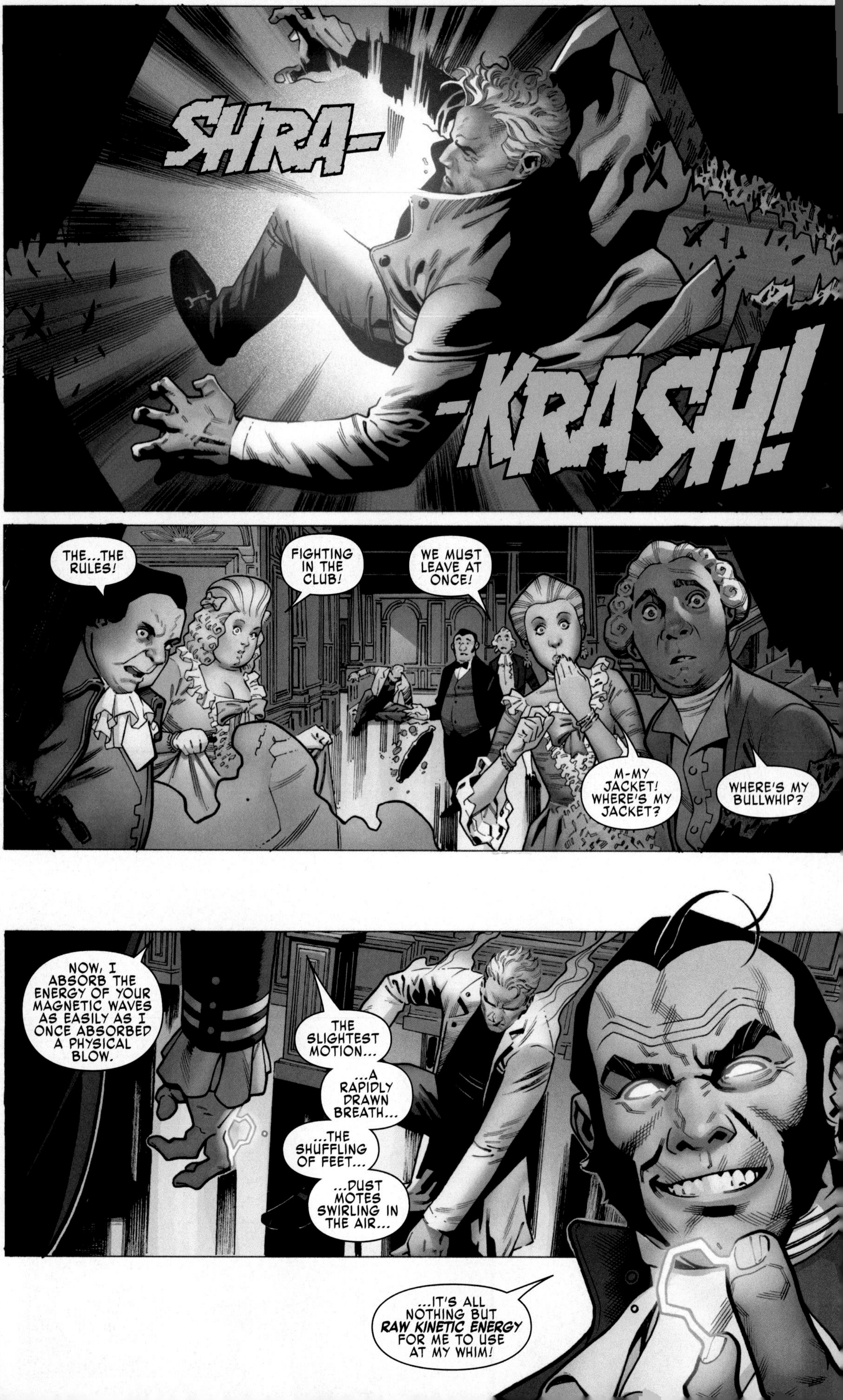
SHRA-
-KRASH!
THE...THE RULES!
FIGHTING IN THE CLUB!
WE MUST LEAVE AT ONCE!
M-MY JACKET! WHERE'S MY JACKET?
WHERE'S MY BULLWHIP?
NOW, I ABSORB THE ENERGY OF YOUR MAGNETIC WAVES AS EASILY AS I ONCE ABSORBED A PHYSICAL BLOW.
THE SLIGHTEST MOTION...
...A RAPIDLY DRAWN BREATH...
...THE SHUFFLING OF FEET...
...DUST MOTES SWIRLING IN THE AIR...
...IT'S ALL NOTHING BUT *RAW KINETIC ENERGY* FOR ME TO USE AT MY WHIM!

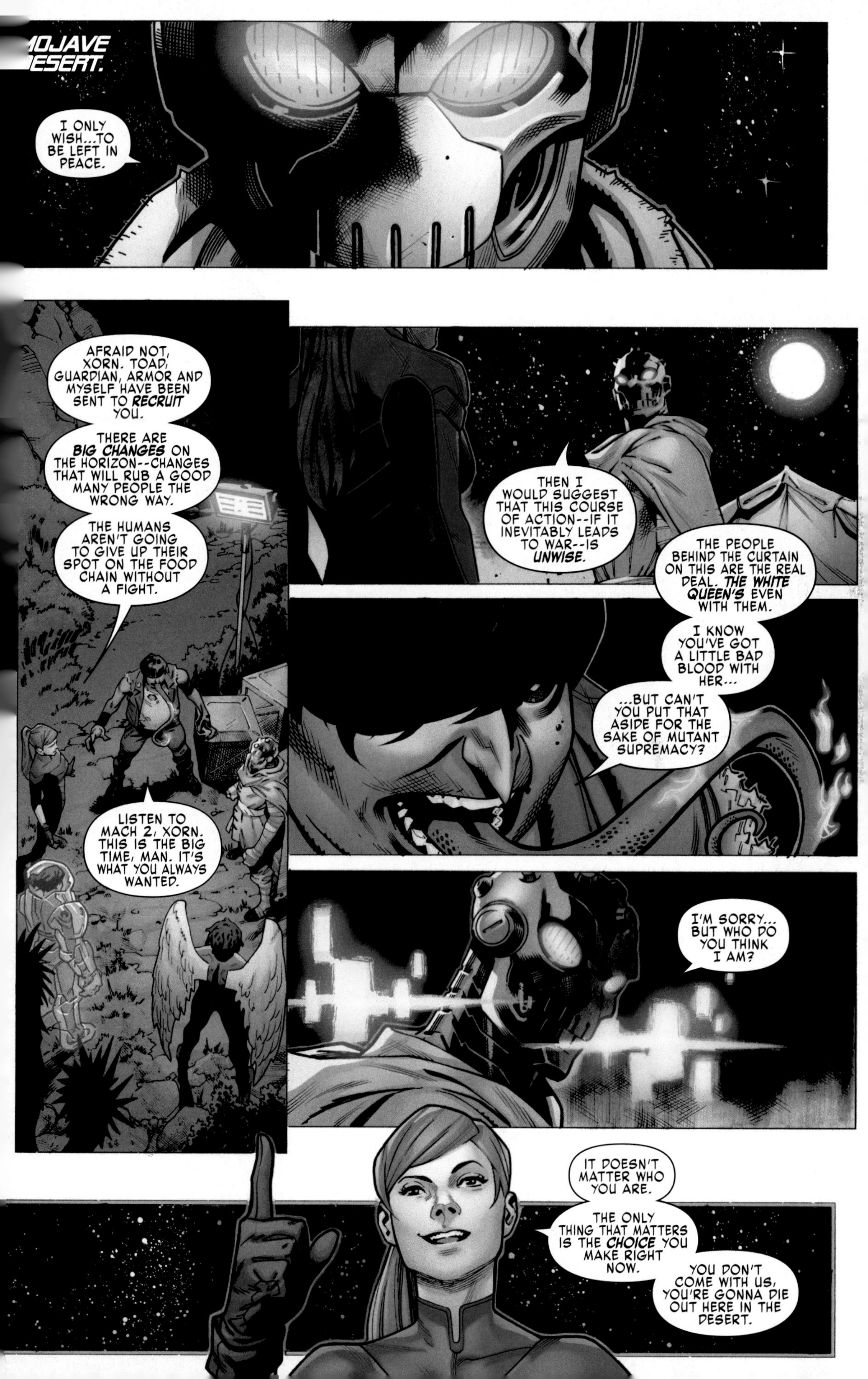
MOJAVE DESERT.
I ONLY WISH...TO BE LEFT IN PEACE.
AFRAID NOT, XORN. TOAD, GUARDIAN, ARMOR AND MYSELF HAVE BEEN SENT TO RECRUIT YOU.
THERE ARE BIG CHANGES ON THE HORIZON--CHANGES THAT WILL RUB A GOOD MANY PEOPLE THE WRONG WAY.
THE HUMANS AREN'T GOING TO GIVE UP THEIR SPOT ON THE FOOD CHAIN WITHOUT A FIGHT.
LISTEN TO MACH 2, XORN. THIS IS THE BIG TIME, MAN. IT'S WHAT YOU ALWAYS WANTED.
THEN I WOULD SUGGEST THAT THIS COURSE OF ACTION--IF IT INEVITABLY LEADS TO WAR--IS UNWISE.
THE PEOPLE BEHIND THE CURTAIN ON THIS ARE THE REAL DEAL. THE WHITE QUEEN'S EVEN WITH THEM.
I KNOW YOU'VE GOT A LITTLE BAD BLOOD WITH HER...
...BUT CAN'T YOU PUT THAT ASIDE FOR THE SAKE OF MUTANT SUPREMACY?
I'M SORRY... BUT WHO DO YOU THINK I AM?
IT DOESN'T MATTER WHO YOU ARE.
THE ONLY THING THAT MATTERS IS THE CHOICE YOU MAKE RIGHT NOW.
YOU DON'T COME WITH US, YOU'RE GONNA DIE OUT HERE IN THE DESERT.

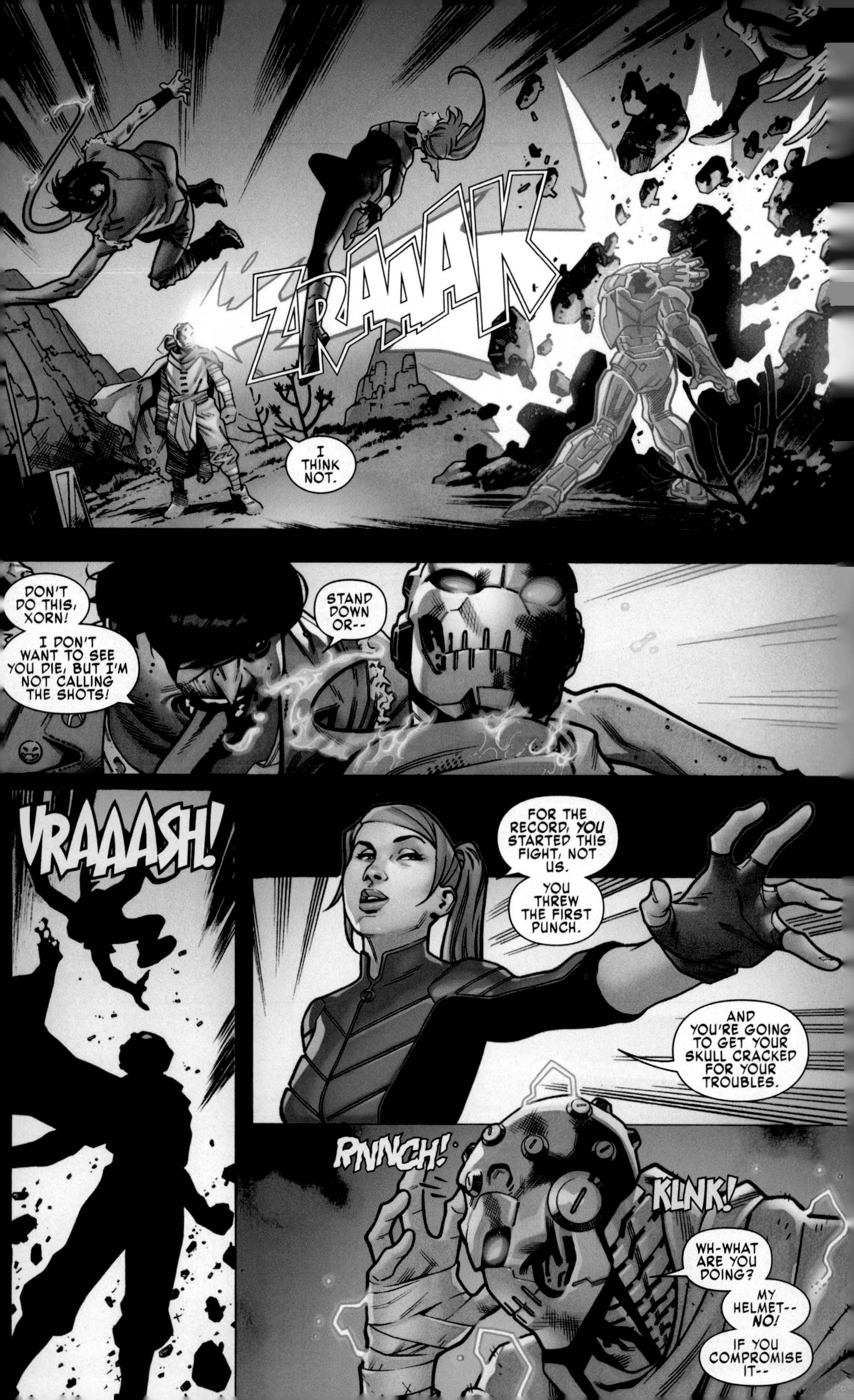
ZRAAAK
I THINK NOT.
DON'T DO THIS, XORN!
I DON'T WANT TO SEE YOU DIE, BUT I'M NOT CALLING THE SHOTS!
STAND DOWN OR--
VRAAASH!
FOR THE RECORD, YOU STARTED THIS FIGHT, NOT US.
YOU THREW THE FIRST PUNCH.
AND YOU'RE GOING TO GET YOUR SKULL CRACKED FOR YOUR TROUBLES.
RNNCH!
KLNK!
WH-WHAT ARE YOU DOING?
MY HELMET-- NO!
IF YOU COMPROMISE IT--

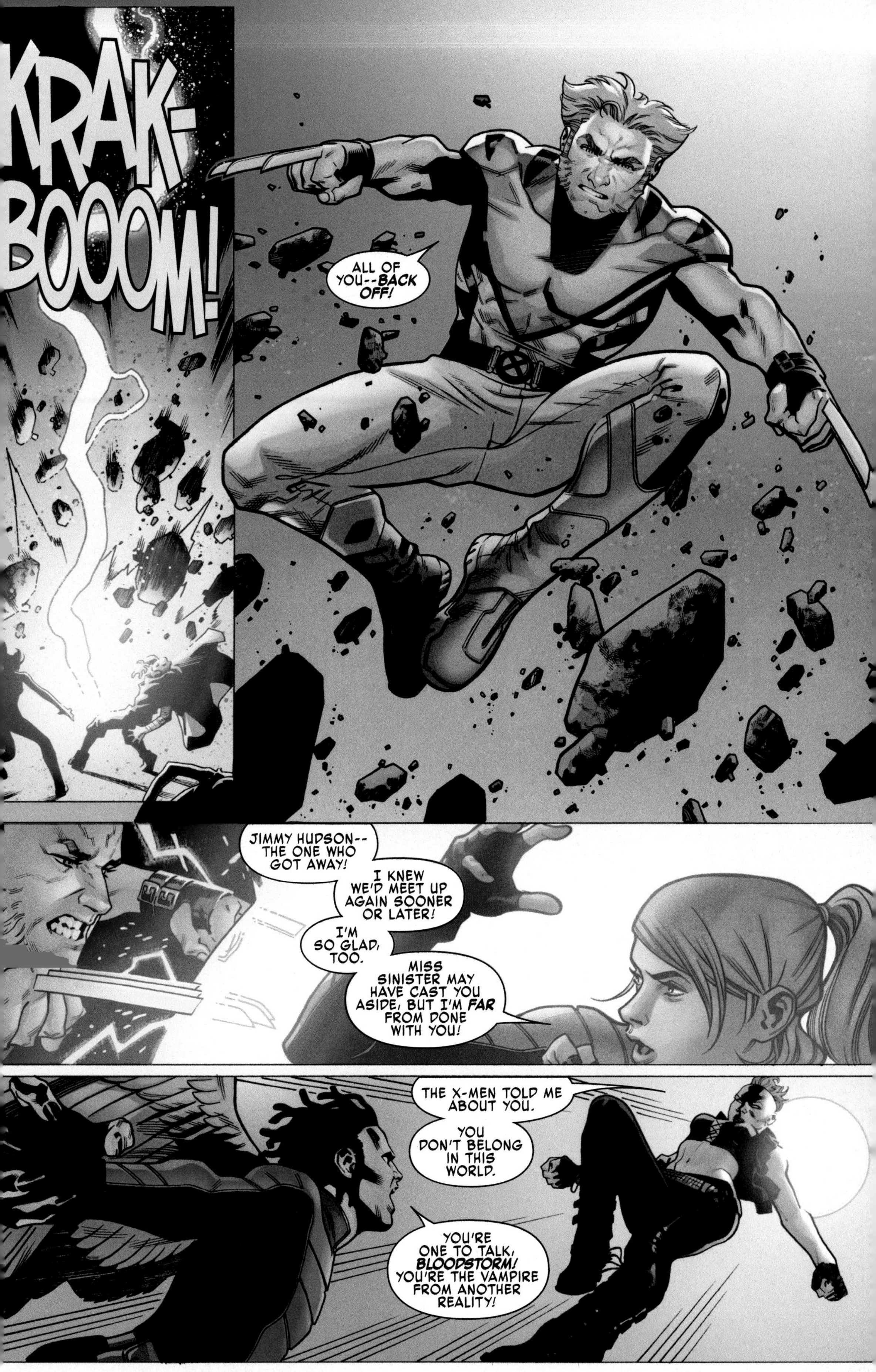
KRAK-BOOOM!
ALL OF YOU--BACK OFF!
JIMMY HUDSON--THE ONE WHO GOT AWAY!
I KNEW WE'D MEET UP AGAIN SOONER OR LATER!
I'M SO GLAD, TOO.
MISS SINISTER MAY HAVE CAST YOU ASIDE, BUT I'M FAR FROM DONE WITH YOU!
THE X-MEN TOLD ME ABOUT YOU.
YOU DON'T BELONG IN THIS WORLD.
YOU'RE ONE TO TALK, BLOODSTORM! YOU'RE THE VAMPIRE FROM ANOTHER REALITY!

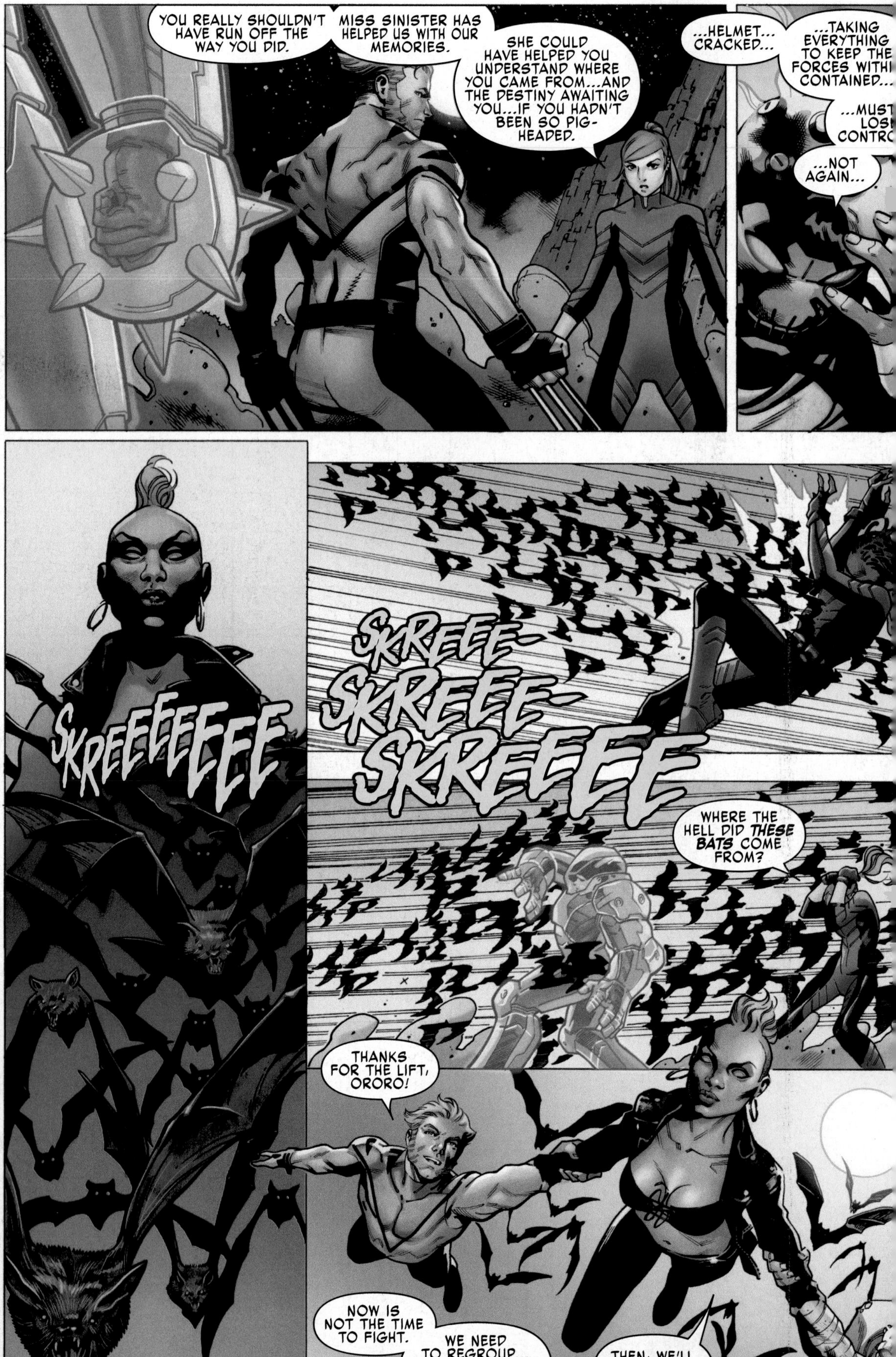

YOU REALLY SHOULDN'T HAVE RUN OFF THE WAY YOU DID.
MISS SINISTER HAS HELPED US WITH OUR MEMORIES.
SHE COULD HAVE HELPED YOU UNDERSTAND WHERE YOU CAME FROM...AND THE DESTINY AWAITING YOU...IF YOU HADN'T BEEN SO PIG-HEADED.
...HELMET... CRACKED...
...TAKING EVERYTHING TO KEEP THE FORCES WITHI CONTAINED...
...MUST LOS CONTRO
...NOT AGAIN...
SKREEEEEEEE
SKREEE-SKREEE-SKREEEEE
WHERE THE HELL DID THESE BATS COME FROM?
THANKS FOR THE LIFT, ORORO!
NOW IS NOT THE TIME TO FIGHT.
WE NEED TO REGROUP... TO GET OUR NEW FRIEND SOME ASSISTANCE.
THEN, WE'LL MEET THESE MARAUDERS AGAIN.

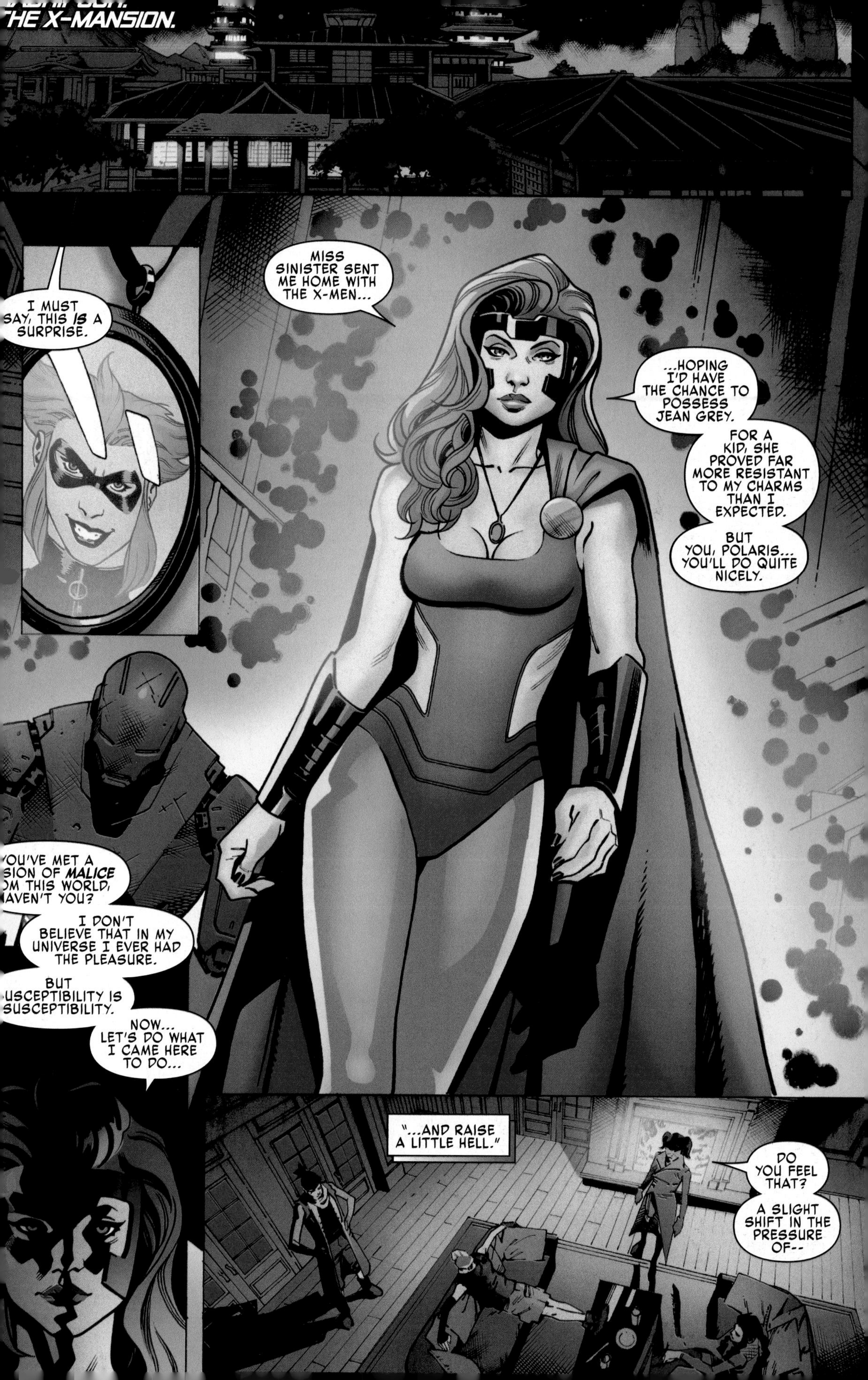
THE X-MANSION.
I MUST SAY, THIS IS A SURPRISE.
MISS SINISTER SENT ME HOME WITH THE X-MEN...
...HOPING I'D HAVE THE CHANCE TO POSSESS JEAN GREY.
FOR A KID, SHE PROVED FAR MORE RESISTANT TO MY CHARMS THAN I EXPECTED.
BUT YOU, POLARIS... YOU'LL DO QUITE NICELY.
YOU'VE MET A SION OF MALICE OM THIS WORLD, HAVEN'T YOU?
I DON'T BELIEVE THAT IN MY UNIVERSE I EVER HAD THE PLEASURE.
BUT USCEPTIBILITY IS SUSCEPTIBILITY.
NOW... LET'S DO WHAT I CAME HERE TO DO...
"...AND RAISE A LITTLE HELL."
DO YOU FEEL THAT?
A SLIGHT SHIFT IN THE PRESSURE OF--

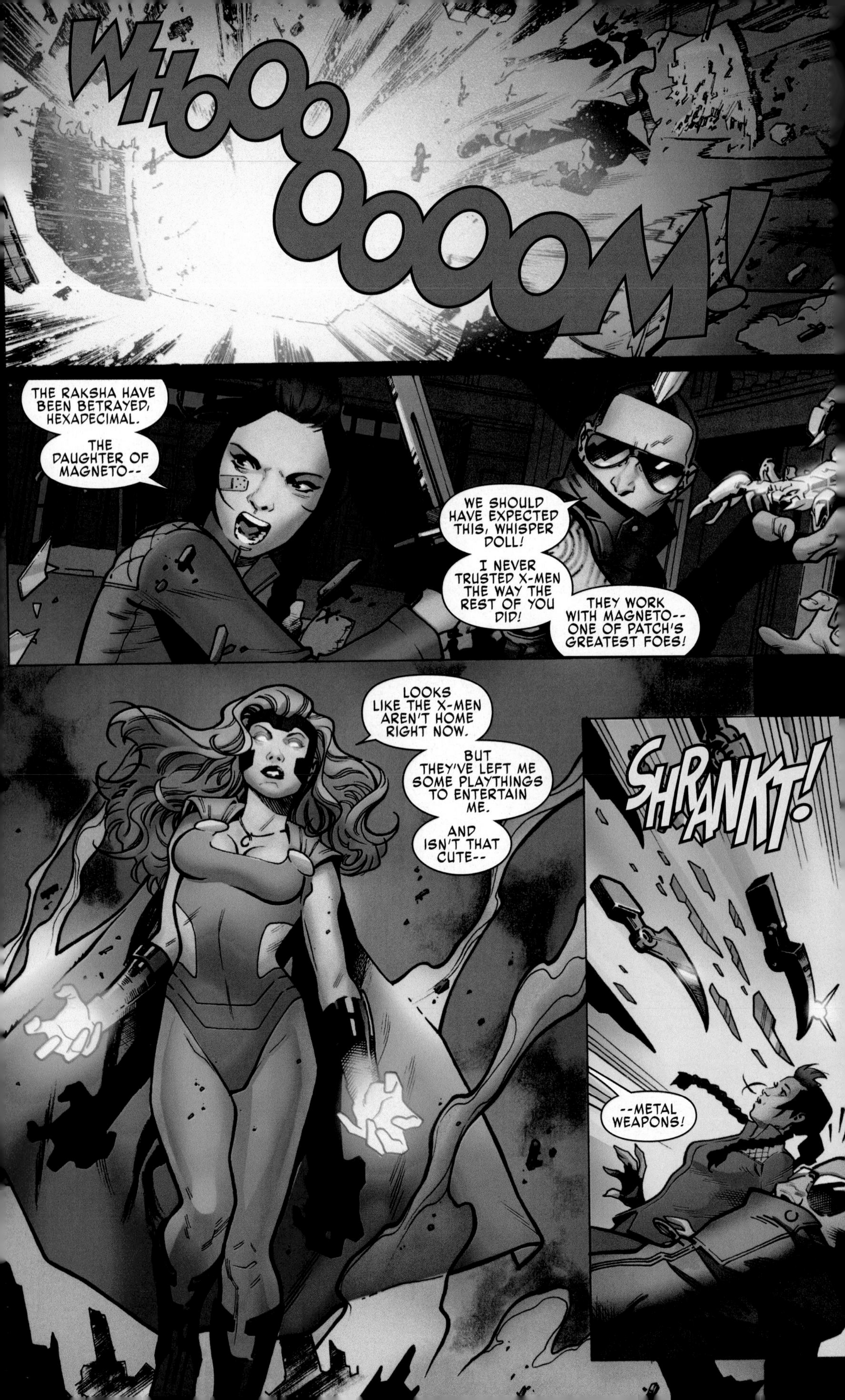
WHOOOOOOOOOM!
THE RAKSHA HAVE BEEN BETRAYED, HEXADECIMAL.
THE DAUGHTER OF MAGNETO--
WE SHOULD HAVE EXPECTED THIS, WHISPER DOLL!
I NEVER TRUSTED X-MEN THE WAY THE REST OF YOU DID!
THEY WORK WITH MAGNETO-- ONE OF PATCH'S GREATEST FOES!
LOOKS LIKE THE X-MEN AREN'T HOME RIGHT NOW.
BUT THEY'VE LEFT ME SOME PLAYTHINGS TO ENTERTAIN ME.
AND ISN'T THAT CUTE--
SHRANKT!
--METAL WEAPONS!

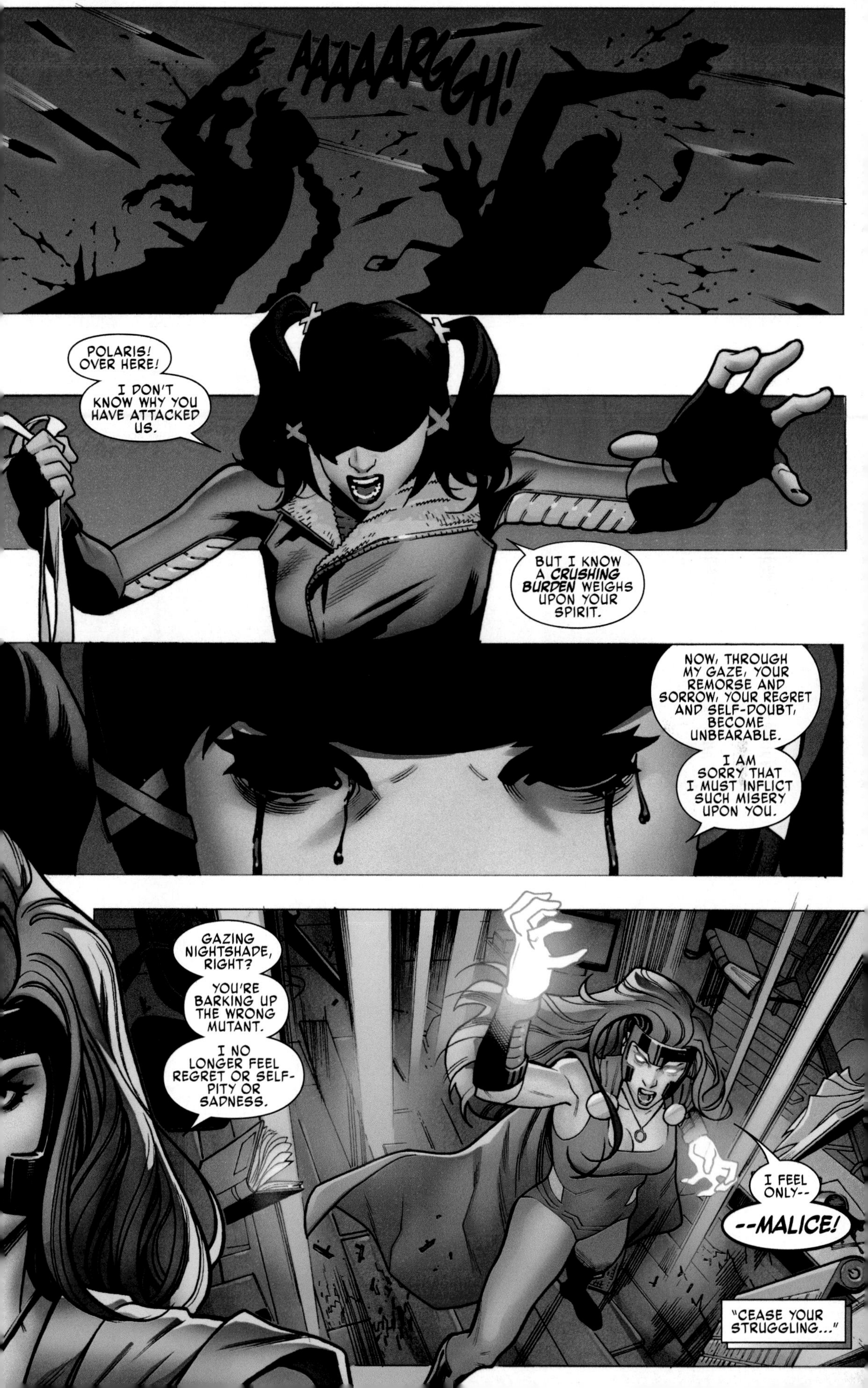
AAAAARGGH!
POLARIS! OVER HERE!
I DON'T KNOW WHY YOU HAVE ATTACKED US.
BUT I KNOW A **CRUSHING BURDEN** WEIGHS UPON YOUR SPIRIT.
NOW, THROUGH MY GAZE, YOUR REMORSE AND SORROW, YOUR REGRET AND SELF-DOUBT, BECOME UNBEARABLE.
I AM SORRY THAT I MUST INFLICT SUCH MISERY UPON YOU.
GAZING NIGHTSHADE, RIGHT?
YOU'RE BARKING UP THE WRONG MUTANT.
I NO LONGER FEEL REGRET OR SELF-PITY OR SADNESS.
I FEEL ONLY--
--MALICE!
"CEASE YOUR STRUGGLING..."

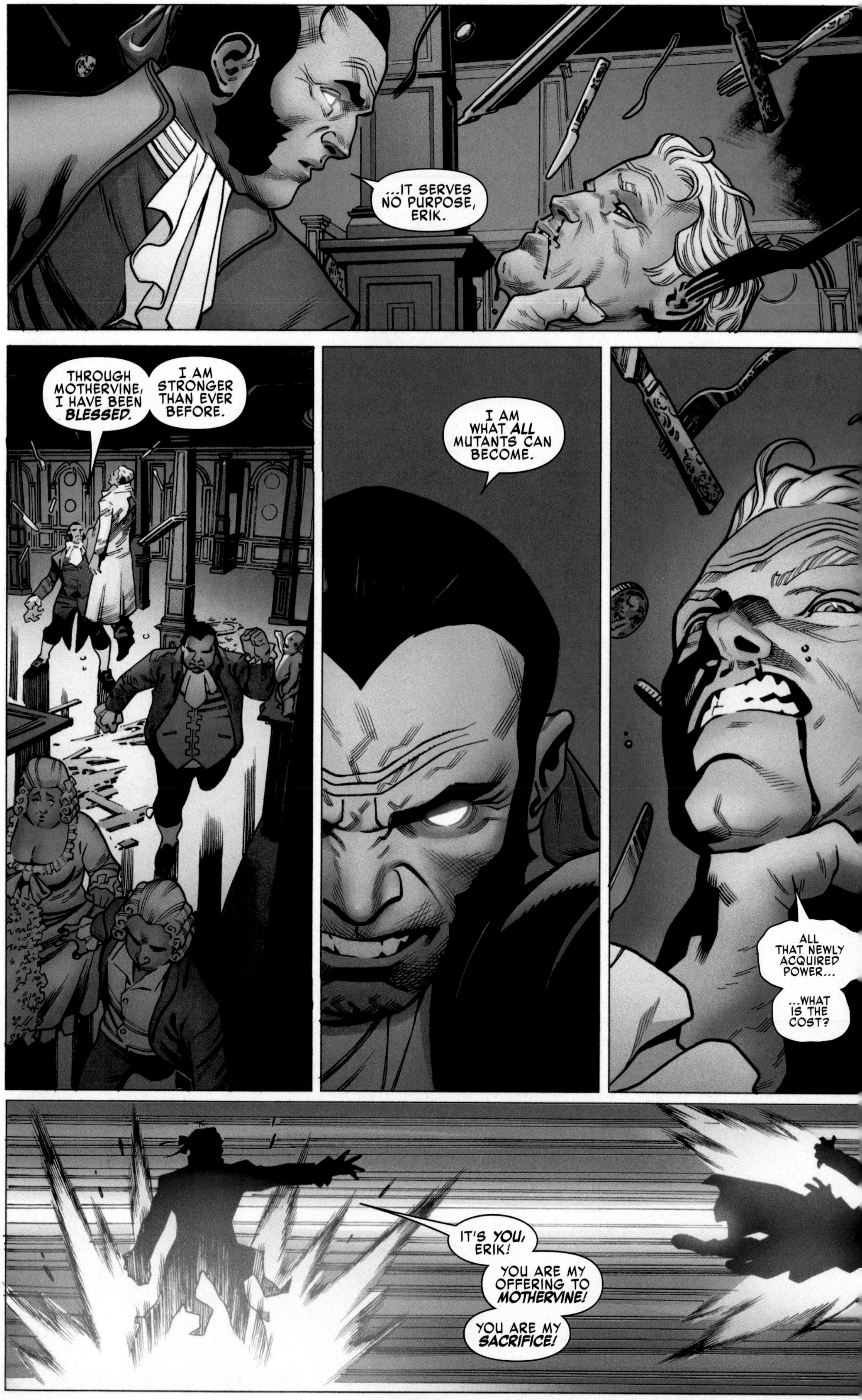
...IT SERVES NO PURPOSE, ERIK.
THROUGH MOTHERVINE, I HAVE BEEN BLESSED.
I AM STRONGER THAN EVER BEFORE.
I AM WHAT ALL MUTANTS CAN BECOME.
ALL THAT NEWLY ACQUIRED POWER...
...WHAT IS THE COST?
IT'S YOU, ERIK!
YOU ARE MY OFFERING TO MOTHERVINE!
YOU ARE MY SACRIFICE!

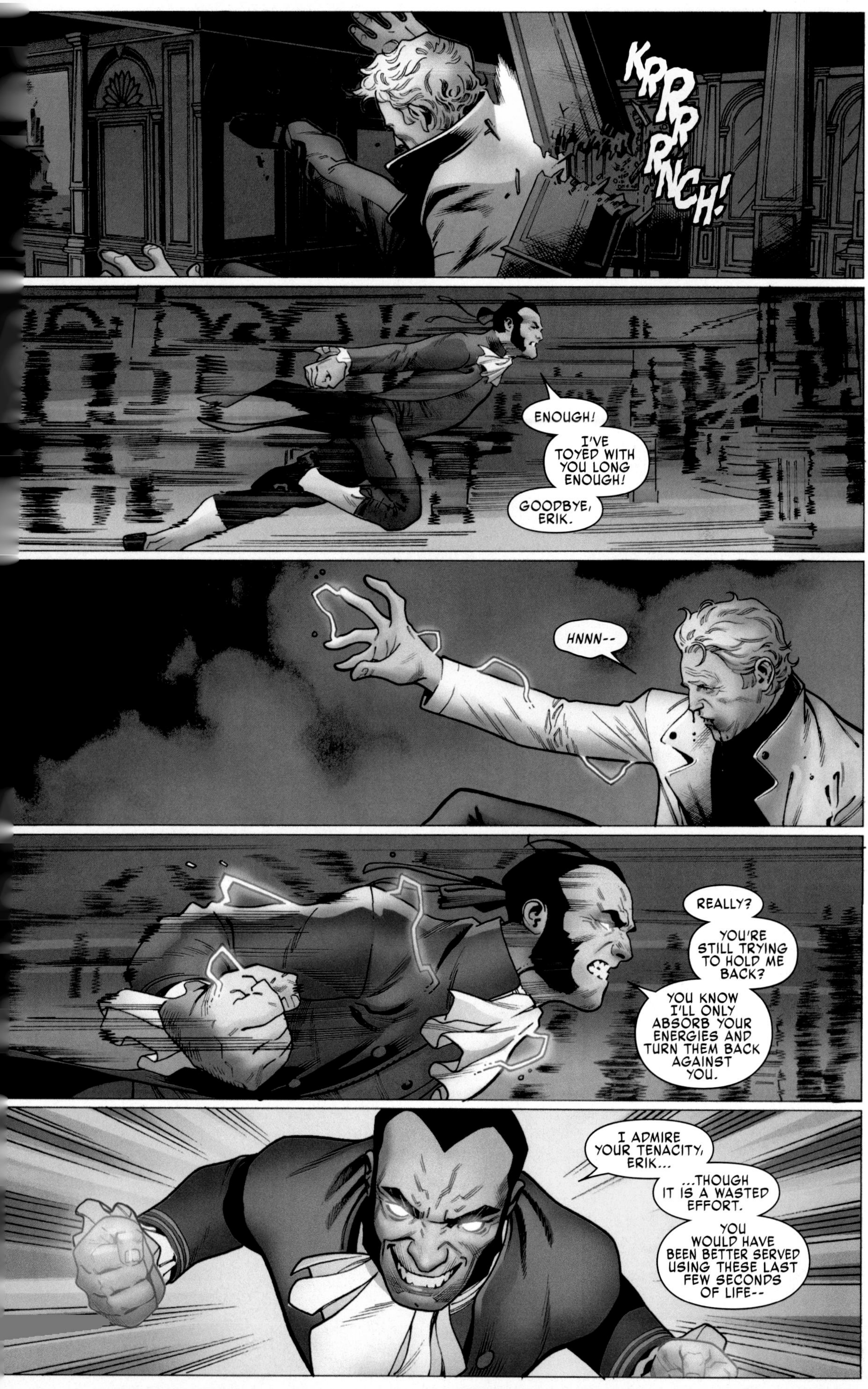
KRRRRNCH!
ENOUGH!
I'VE TOYED WITH YOU LONG ENOUGH!
GOODBYE, ERIK.
HNNN--
REALLY?
YOU'RE STILL TRYING TO HOLD ME BACK?
YOU KNOW I'LL ONLY ABSORB YOUR ENERGIES AND TURN THEM BACK AGAINST YOU.
I ADMIRE YOUR TENACITY, ERIK...
...THOUGH IT IS A WASTED EFFORT.
YOU WOULD HAVE BEEN BETTER SERVED USING THESE LAST FEW SECONDS OF LIFE--

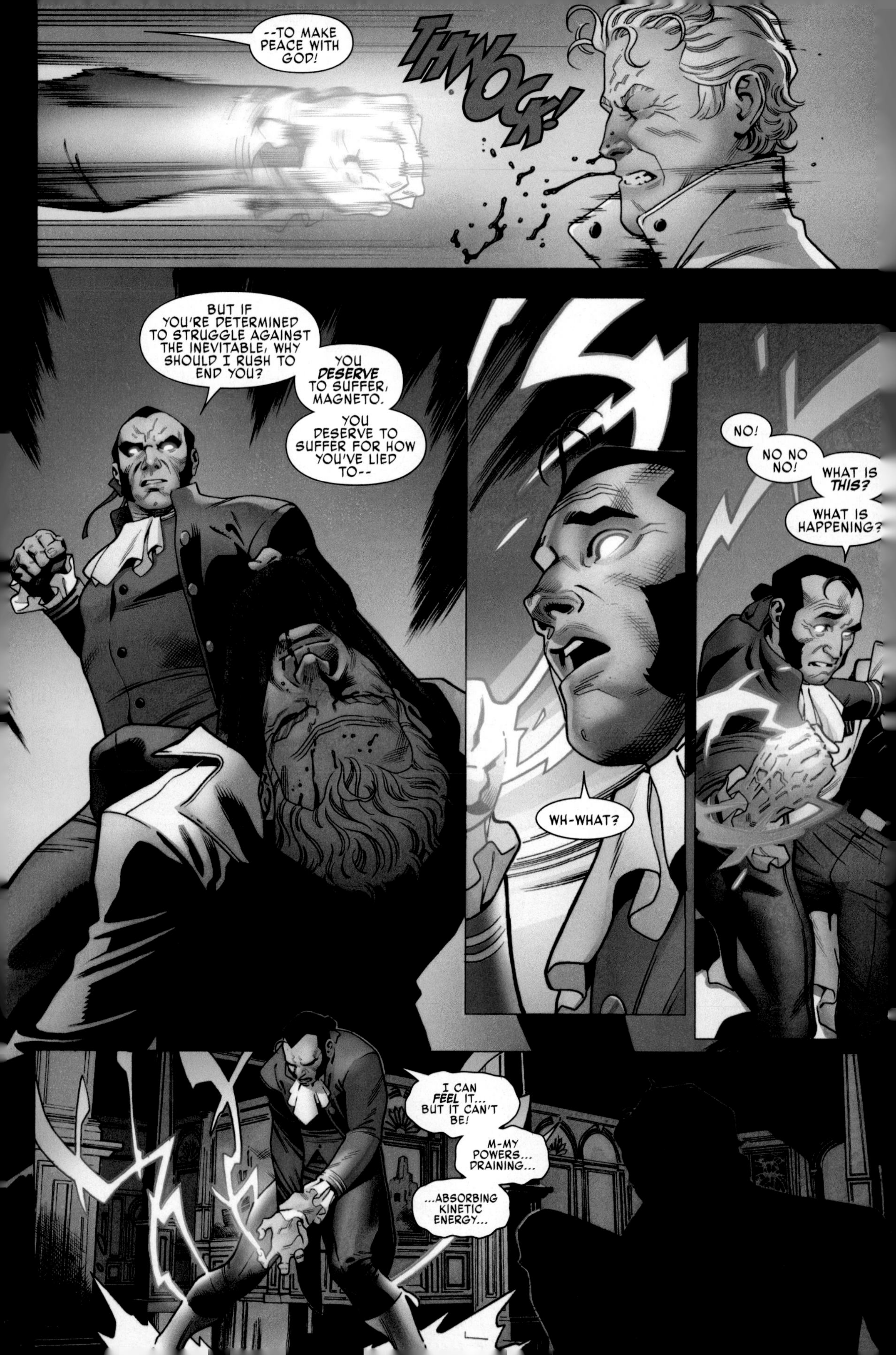
--TO MAKE PEACE WITH GOD!
THWOCK!
BUT IF YOU'RE DETERMINED TO STRUGGLE AGAINST THE INEVITABLE, WHY SHOULD I RUSH TO END YOU?
YOU *DESERVE* TO SUFFER, MAGNETO.
YOU DESERVE TO SUFFER FOR HOW YOU'VE LIED TO--
WH-WHAT?
NO!
NO NO NO!
WHAT IS *THIS?*
WHAT IS HAPPENING?
I CAN *FEEL* IT... BUT IT CAN'T BE!
M-MY POWERS... DRAINING...
...ABSORBING KINETIC ENERGY...

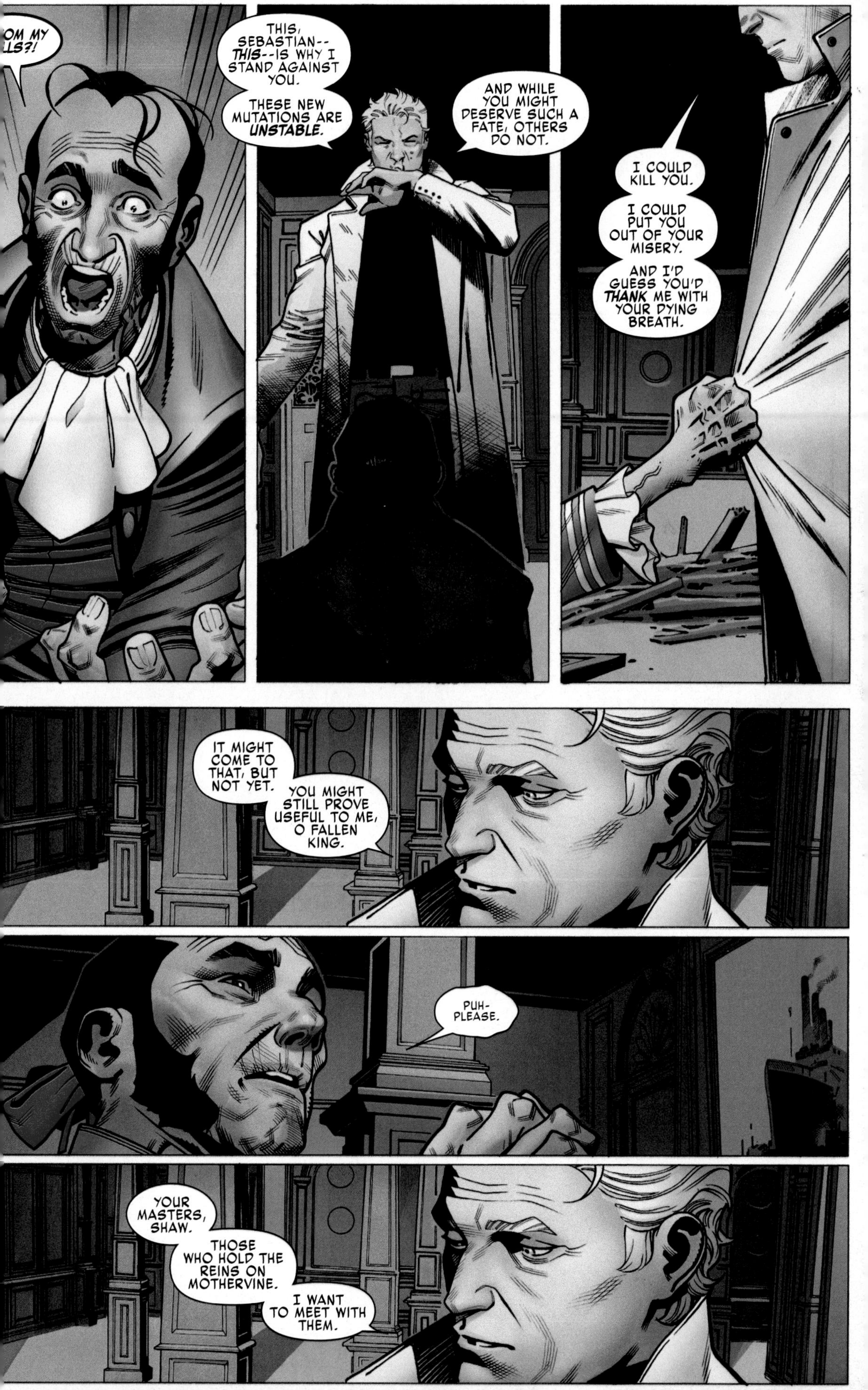
OM MY
LLS?!
THIS, SEBASTIAN-- THIS--IS WHY I STAND AGAINST YOU.
THESE NEW MUTATIONS ARE UNSTABLE.
AND WHILE YOU MIGHT DESERVE SUCH A FATE, OTHERS DO NOT.
I COULD KILL YOU.
I COULD PUT YOU OUT OF YOUR MISERY.
AND I'D GUESS YOU'D THANK ME WITH YOUR DYING BREATH.
IT MIGHT COME TO THAT, BUT NOT YET.
YOU MIGHT STILL PROVE USEFUL TO ME, O FALLEN KING.
PUH-PLEASE.
YOUR MASTERS, SHAW.
THOSE WHO HOLD THE REINS ON MOTHERVINE.
I WANT TO MEET WITH THEM.

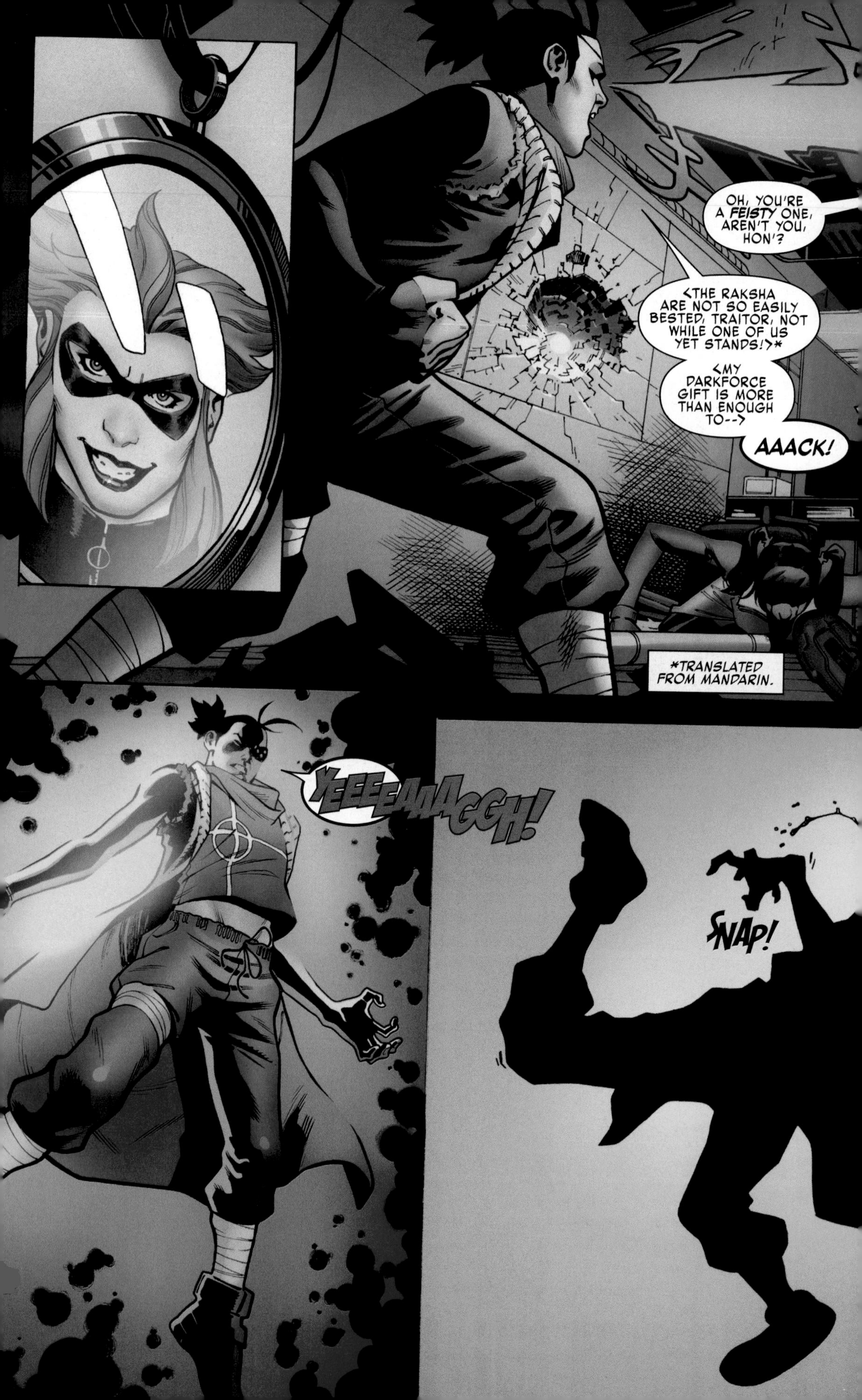
OH, YOU'RE A FEISTY ONE, AREN'T YOU, HON'?
<THE RAKSHA ARE NOT SO EASILY BESTED, TRAITOR, NOT WHILE ONE OF US YET STANDS!>*
<MY DARKFORCE GIFT IS MORE THAN ENOUGH TO-->
AAACK!
*TRANSLATED FROM MANDARIN.
YEEEEAAAGGH!
SNAP!

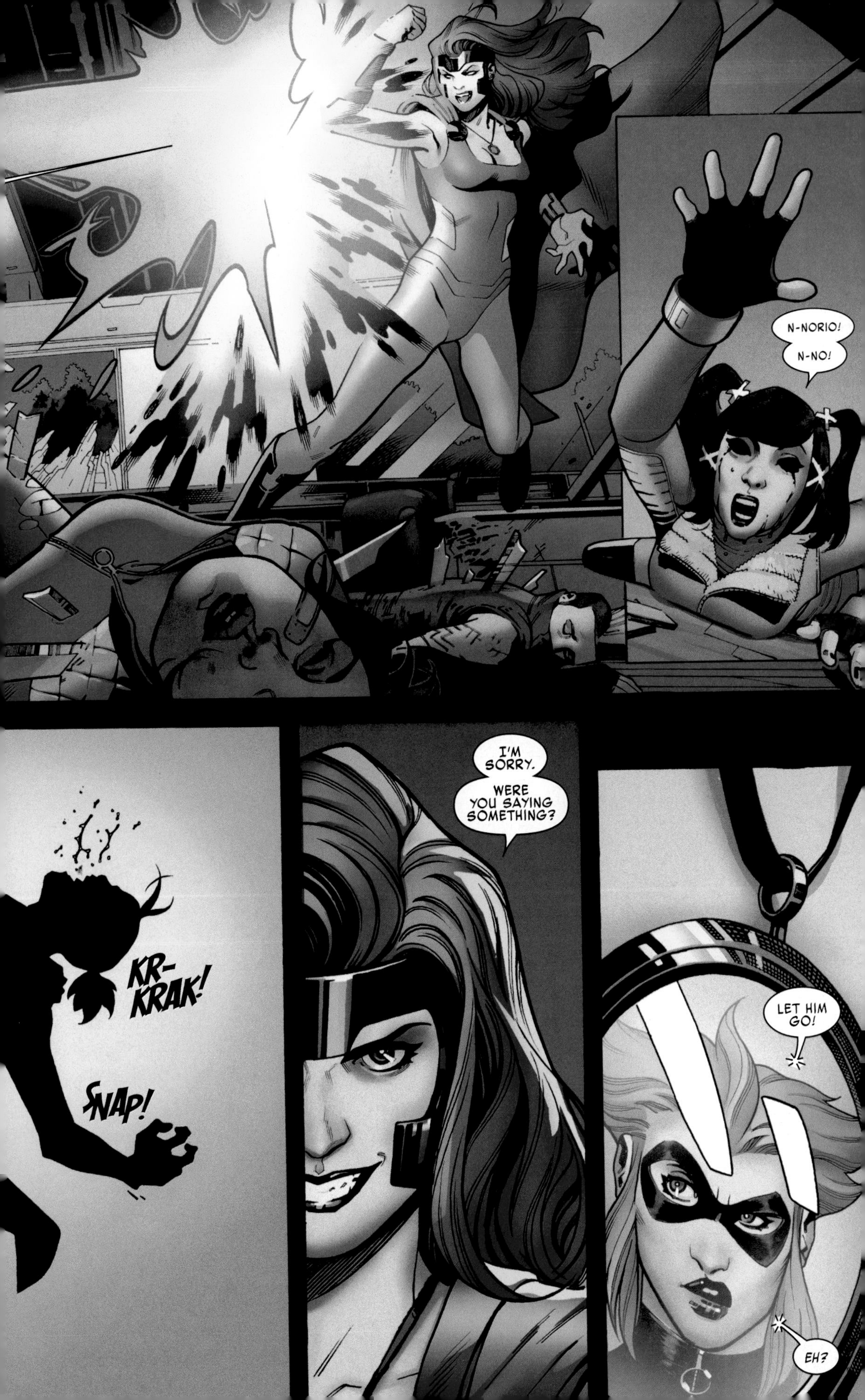
N-NORIO!
N-NO!
KR-KRAK!
SNAP!
I'M SORRY.
WERE YOU SAYING SOMETHING?
LET HIM GO!
EH?

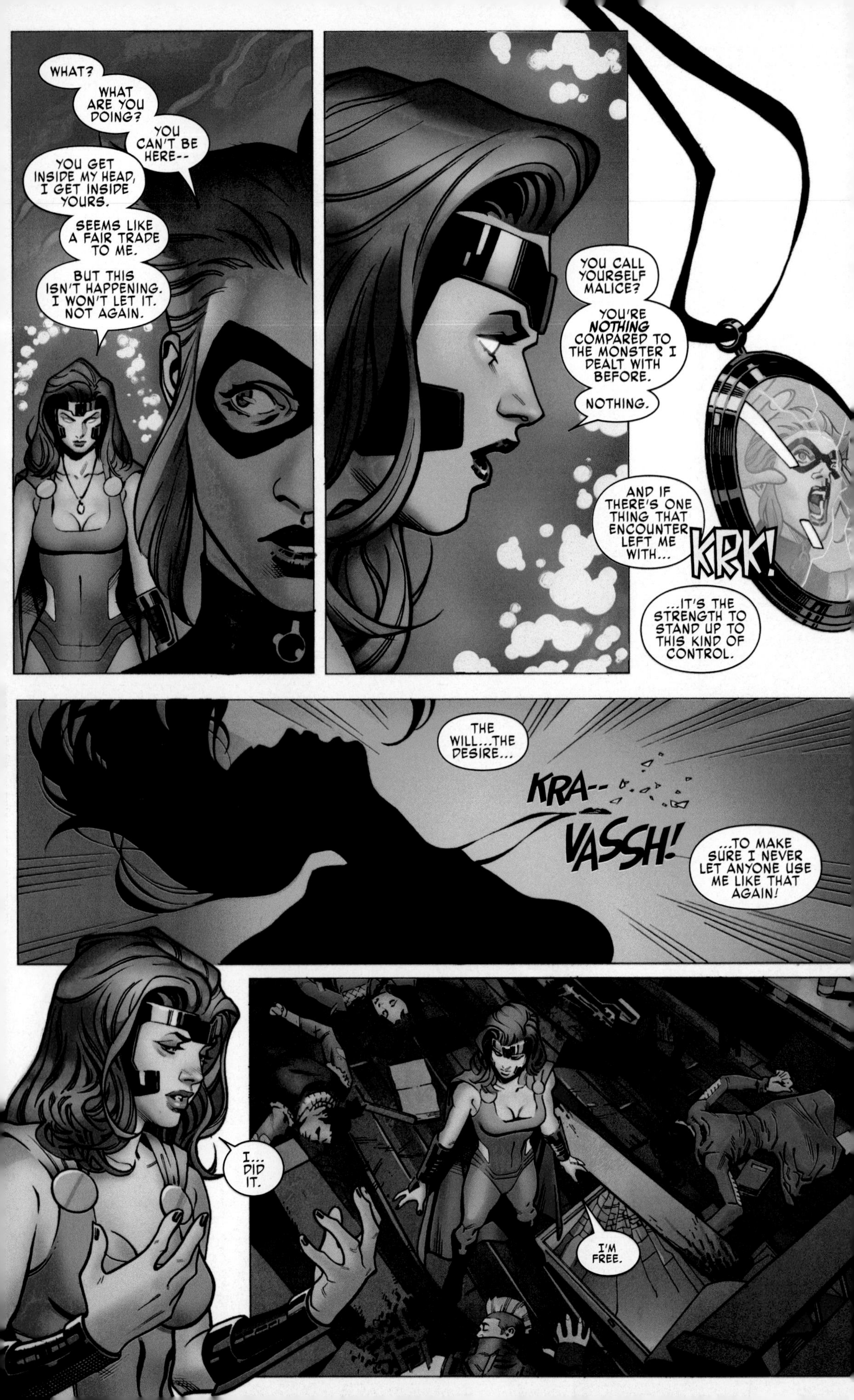
WHAT?
WHAT ARE YOU DOING?
YOU CAN'T BE HERE--
YOU GET INSIDE MY HEAD, I GET INSIDE YOURS.
SEEMS LIKE A FAIR TRADE TO ME.
BUT THIS ISN'T HAPPENING. I WON'T LET IT. NOT AGAIN.
YOU CALL YOURSELF MALICE?
YOU'RE NOTHING COMPARED TO THE MONSTER I DEALT WITH BEFORE.
NOTHING.
AND IF THERE'S ONE THING THAT ENCOUNTER LEFT ME WITH...
KRK!
...IT'S THE STRENGTH TO STAND UP TO THIS KIND OF CONTROL.
THE WILL...THE DESIRE...
KRA--VASSH!
...TO MAKE SURE I NEVER LET ANYONE USE ME LIKE THAT AGAIN!
I... DID IT.
I'M FREE.

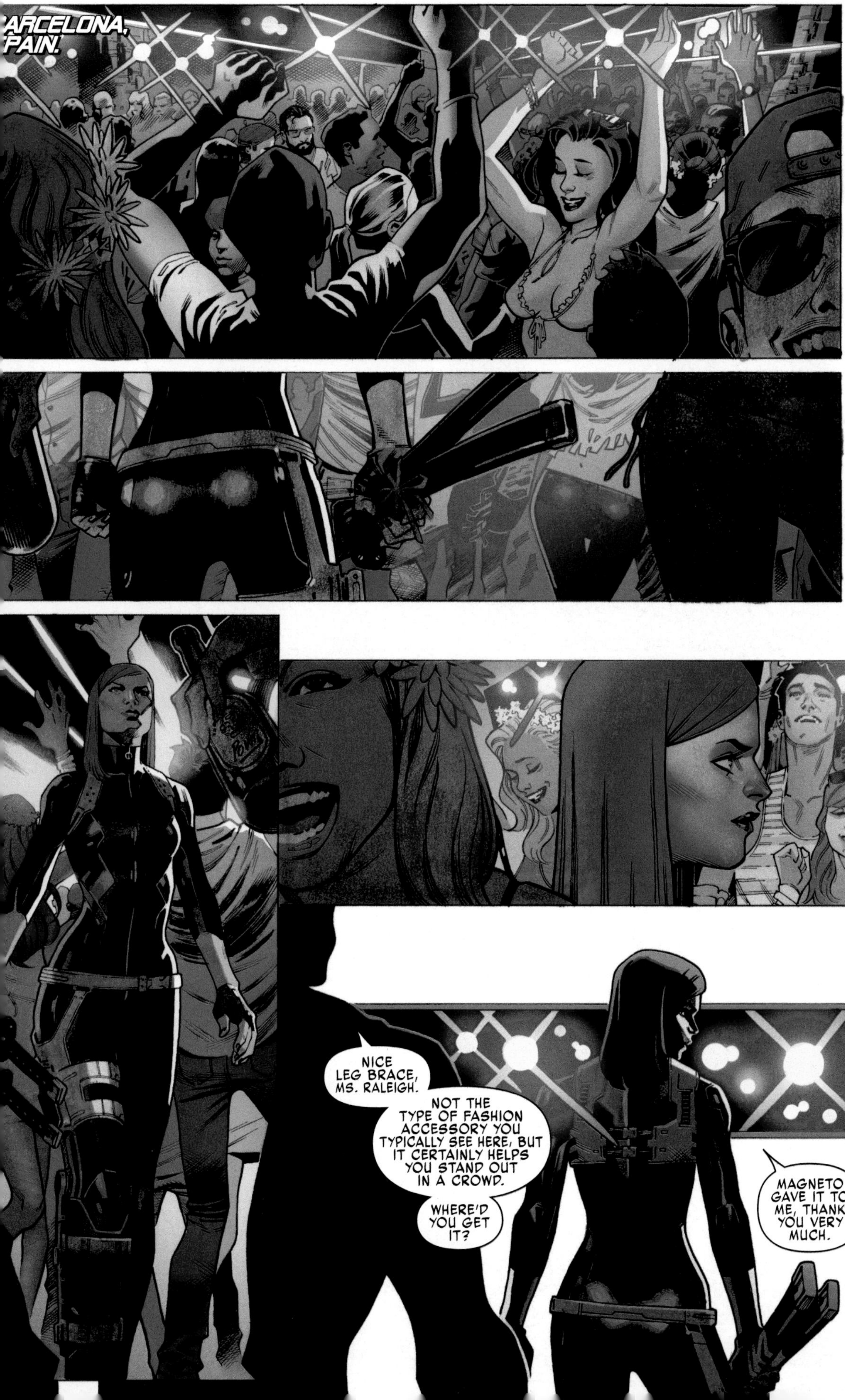
ARCELONA,
PAIN.
NICE LEG BRACE, MS. RALEIGH.
NOT THE TYPE OF FASHION ACCESSORY YOU TYPICALLY SEE HERE, BUT IT CERTAINLY HELPS YOU STAND OUT IN A CROWD.
WHERE'D YOU GET IT?
MAGNETO GAVE IT TO ME, THANK YOU VERY MUCH.

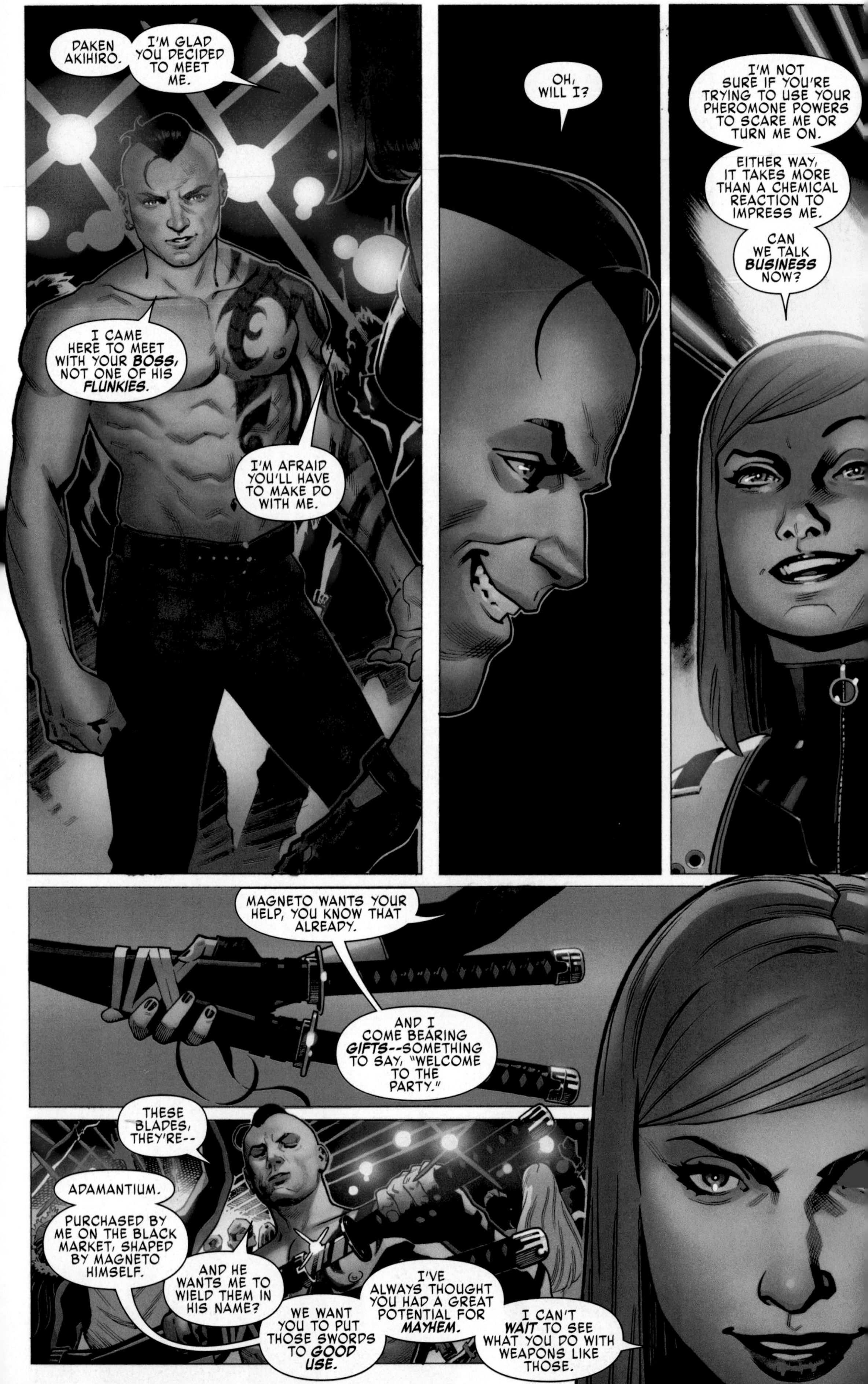
DAKEN AKIHIRO.
I'M GLAD YOU DECIDED TO MEET ME.
I CAME HERE TO MEET WITH YOUR BOSS, NOT ONE OF HIS FLUNKIES.
I'M AFRAID YOU'LL HAVE TO MAKE DO WITH ME.
OH, WILL I?
I'M NOT SURE IF YOU'RE TRYING TO USE YOUR PHEROMONE POWERS TO SCARE ME OR TURN ME ON.
EITHER WAY, IT TAKES MORE THAN A CHEMICAL REACTION TO IMPRESS ME.
CAN WE TALK BUSINESS NOW?
MAGNETO WANTS YOUR HELP, YOU KNOW THAT ALREADY.
AND I COME BEARING GIFTS--SOMETHING TO SAY, "WELCOME TO THE PARTY."
THESE BLADES, THEY'RE--
ADAMANTIUM.
PURCHASED BY ME ON THE BLACK MARKET, SHAPED BY MAGNETO HIMSELF.
AND HE WANTS ME TO WIELD THEM IN HIS NAME?
WE WANT YOU TO PUT THOSE SWORDS TO GOOD USE.
I'VE ALWAYS THOUGHT YOU HAD A GREAT POTENTIAL FOR MAYHEM.
I CAN'T WAIT TO SEE WHAT YOU DO WITH WEAPONS LIKE THOSE.

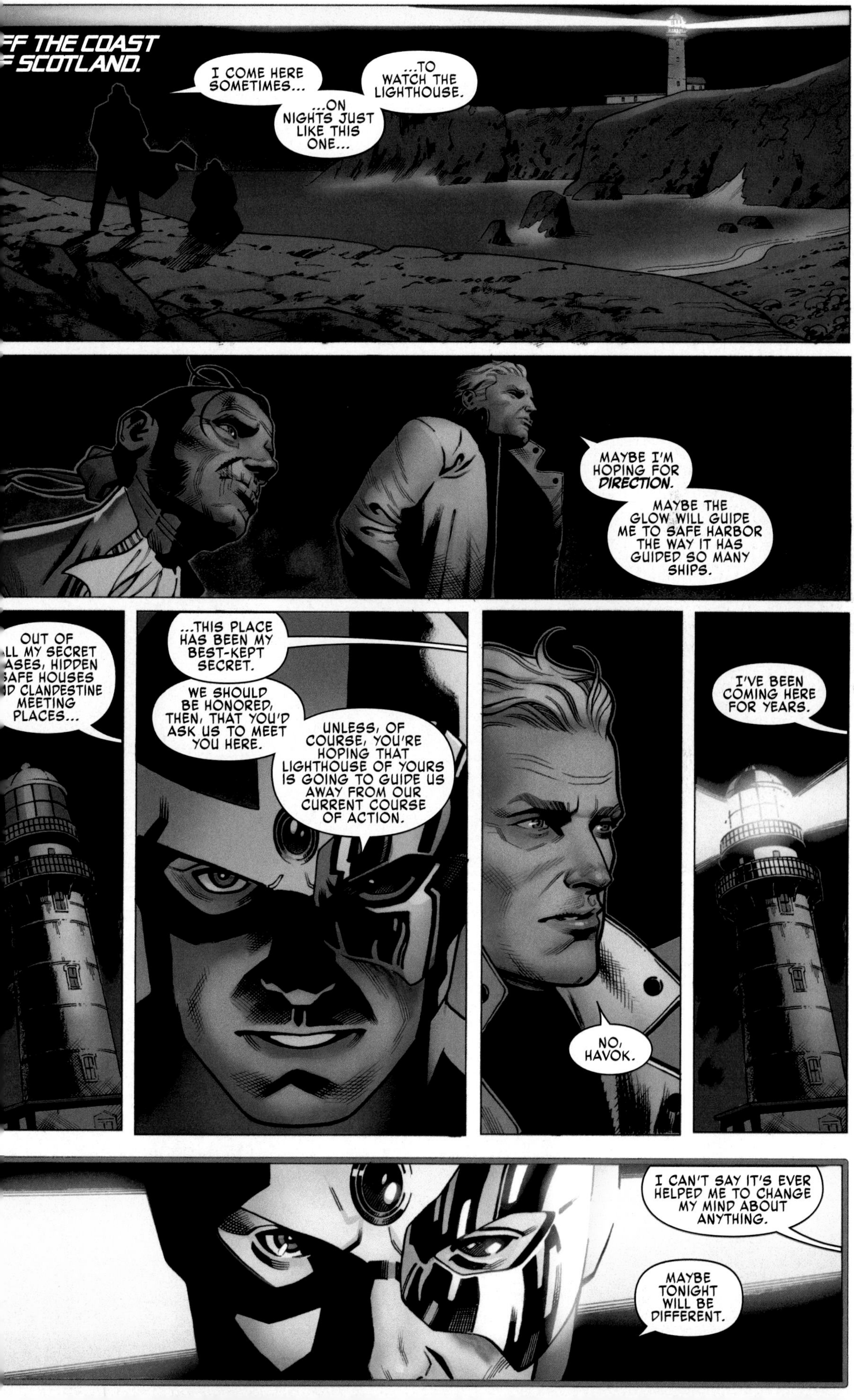

...FF THE COAST
...F SCOTLAND.
I COME HERE SOMETIMES...
...ON NIGHTS JUST LIKE THIS ONE...
...TO WATCH THE LIGHTHOUSE.
MAYBE I'M HOPING FOR DIRECTION.
MAYBE THE GLOW WILL GUIDE ME TO SAFE HARBOR THE WAY IT HAS GUIDED SO MANY SHIPS.
OUT OF ...LL MY SECRET ...ASES, HIDDEN ...AFE HOUSES ...D CLANDESTINE MEETING PLACES...
...THIS PLACE HAS BEEN MY BEST-KEPT SECRET.
WE SHOULD BE HONORED, THEN, THAT YOU'D ASK US TO MEET YOU HERE.
UNLESS, OF COURSE, YOU'RE HOPING THAT LIGHTHOUSE OF YOURS IS GOING TO GUIDE US AWAY FROM OUR CURRENT COURSE OF ACTION.
NO, HAVOK.
I'VE BEEN COMING HERE FOR YEARS.
I CAN'T SAY IT'S EVER HELPED ME TO CHANGE MY MIND ABOUT ANYTHING.
MAYBE TONIGHT WILL BE DIFFERENT.

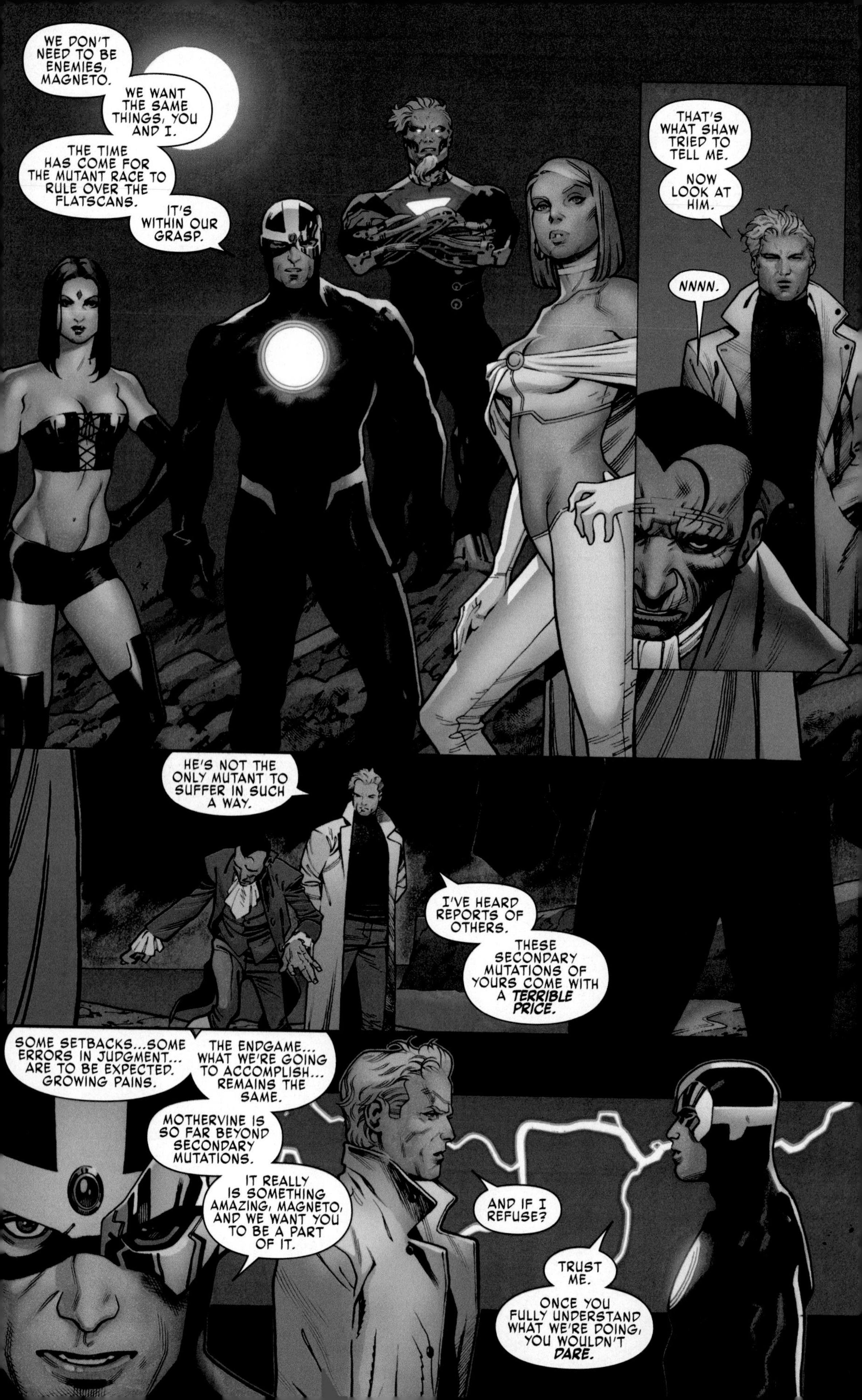
WE DON'T NEED TO BE ENEMIES, MAGNETO.
WE WANT THE SAME THINGS, YOU AND I.
THE TIME HAS COME FOR THE MUTANT RACE TO RULE OVER THE FLATSCANS.
IT'S WITHIN OUR GRASP.
THAT'S WHAT SHAW TRIED TO TELL ME.
NOW LOOK AT HIM.
NNNN.
HE'S NOT THE ONLY MUTANT TO SUFFER IN SUCH A WAY.
I'VE HEARD REPORTS OF OTHERS.
THESE SECONDARY MUTATIONS OF YOURS COME WITH A *TERRIBLE PRICE.*
SOME SETBACKS...SOME ERRORS IN JUDGMENT... ARE TO BE EXPECTED. GROWING PAINS.
THE ENDGAME... WHAT WE'RE GOING TO ACCOMPLISH... REMAINS THE SAME.
MOTHERVINE IS SO FAR BEYOND SECONDARY MUTATIONS.
IT REALLY IS SOMETHING AMAZING, MAGNETO, AND WE WANT YOU TO BE A PART OF IT.
AND IF I REFUSE?
TRUST ME.
ONCE YOU FULLY UNDERSTAND WHAT WE'RE DOING, YOU WOULDN'T *DARE.*

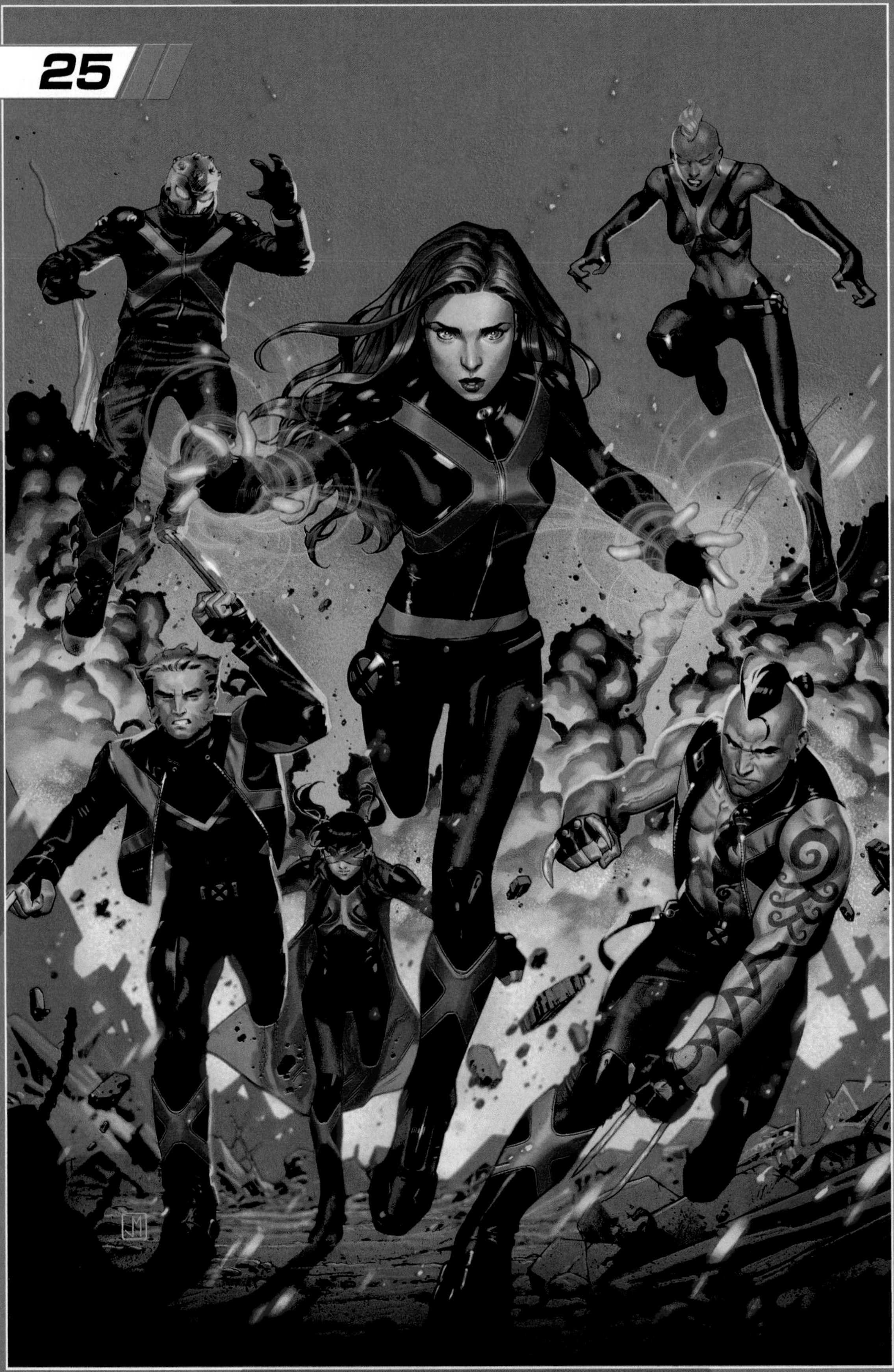
25

FREE.

THIS... VERSION OF MALICE...

IT'S SO WEIRD TO TALK ABOUT *VERSIONS* OF PEOPLE.

...SHE WASN'T FROM THIS WORLD.

I THINK SHE MIGHT HAVE BEEN FROM THE SAME UNIVERSE AS JIMMY.

SHE WASN'T AS STRONG AS THE MALICE I KNOW.

AT LEAST, SHE WAS *WEAKENED.* SHE WAS *CONFUSED.*

AND I *KILLED* HER.

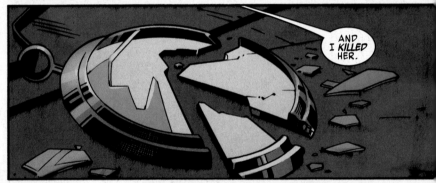

IF I MAY, MS. DANE...

...SHE GAVE YOU *LITTLE CHOICE.*

MISS SINISTER DID THIS, FERRIS. SHE SENT MALICE HERE.

SHE WANTED HER TO TAKE CONTROL OF JEAN.

SHE'S BEEN MANEUVERING AGAINST US ALL THIS TIME.

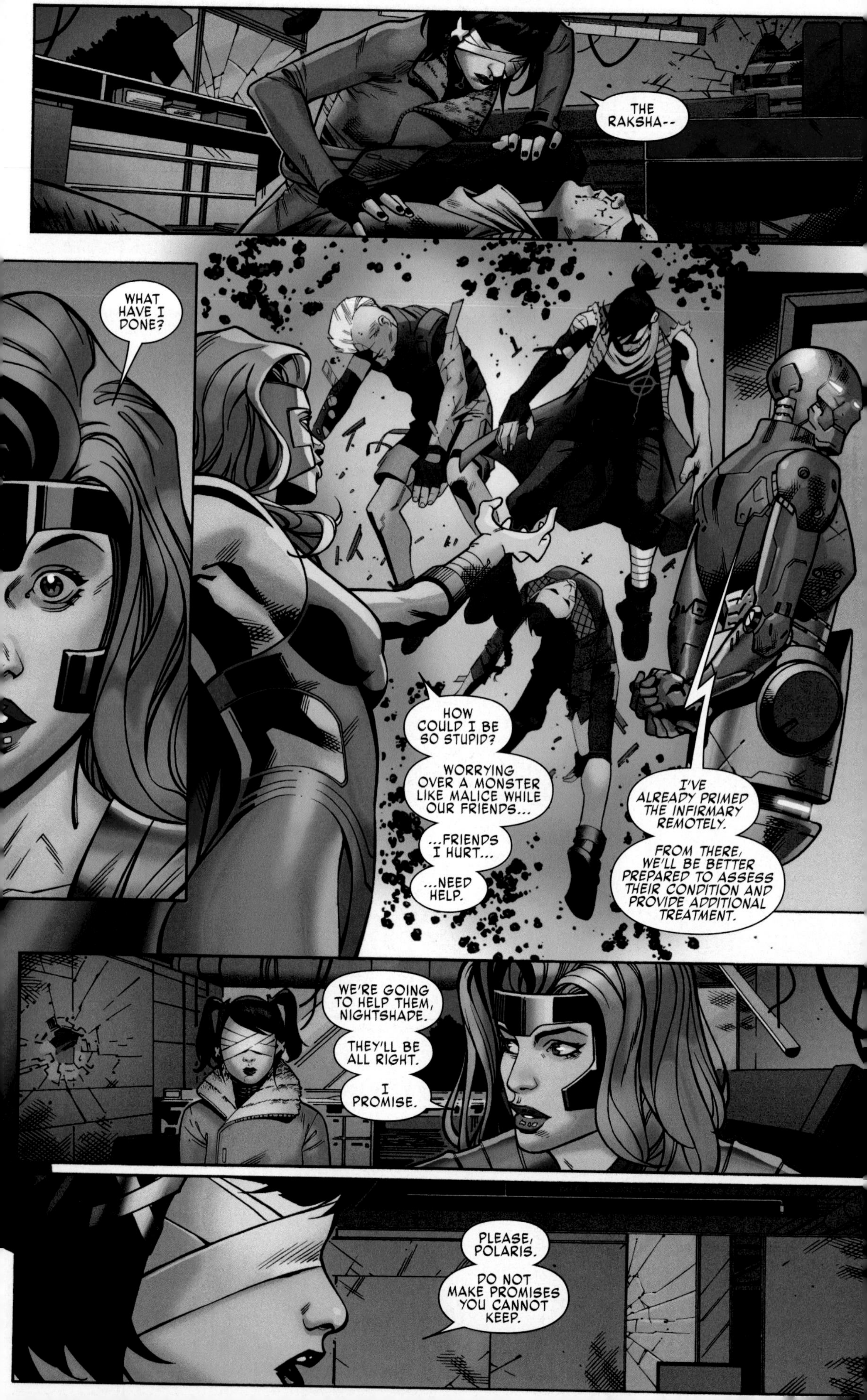
THE RAKSHA--
WHAT HAVE I DONE?
HOW COULD I BE SO STUPID?
WORRYING OVER A MONSTER LIKE MALICE WHILE OUR FRIENDS...
...FRIENDS I HURT...
...NEED HELP.
I'VE ALREADY PRIMED THE INFIRMARY REMOTELY.
FROM THERE, WE'LL BE BETTER PREPARED TO ASSESS THEIR CONDITION AND PROVIDE ADDITIONAL TREATMENT.
WE'RE GOING TO HELP THEM, NIGHTSHADE.
THEY'LL BE ALL RIGHT.
I PROMISE.
PLEASE, POLARIS.
DO NOT MAKE PROMISES YOU CANNOT KEEP.

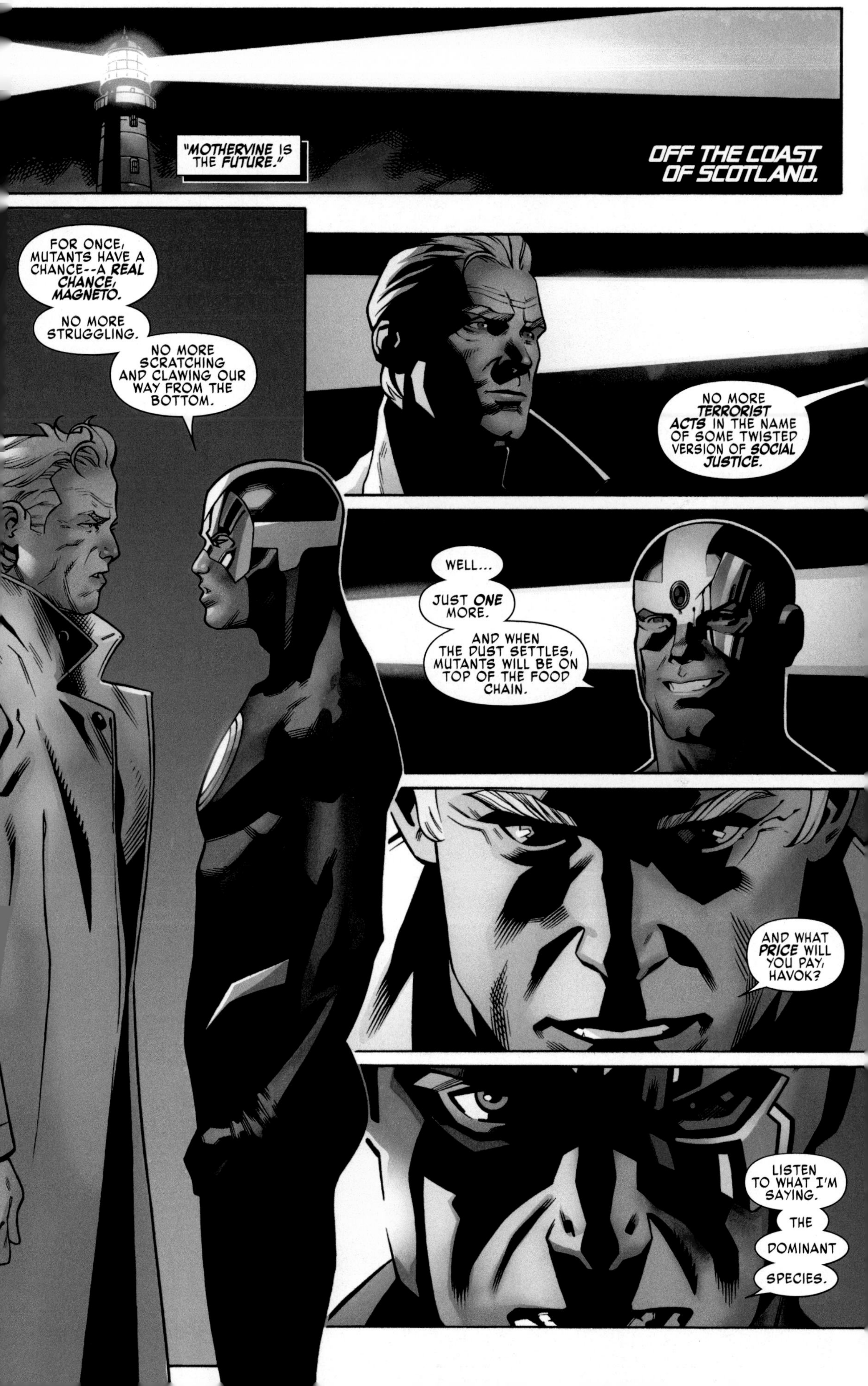
"MOTHERVINE IS THE FUTURE."
OFF THE COAST OF SCOTLAND.
FOR ONCE, MUTANTS HAVE A CHANCE--A REAL CHANCE, MAGNETO.
NO MORE STRUGGLING.
NO MORE SCRATCHING AND CLAWING OUR WAY FROM THE BOTTOM.
NO MORE TERRORIST ACTS IN THE NAME OF SOME TWISTED VERSION OF SOCIAL JUSTICE.
WELL...
JUST ONE MORE.
AND WHEN THE DUST SETTLES, MUTANTS WILL BE ON TOP OF THE FOOD CHAIN.
AND WHAT PRICE WILL YOU PAY, HAVOK?
LISTEN TO WHAT I'M SAYING.
THE
DOMINANT
SPECIES.

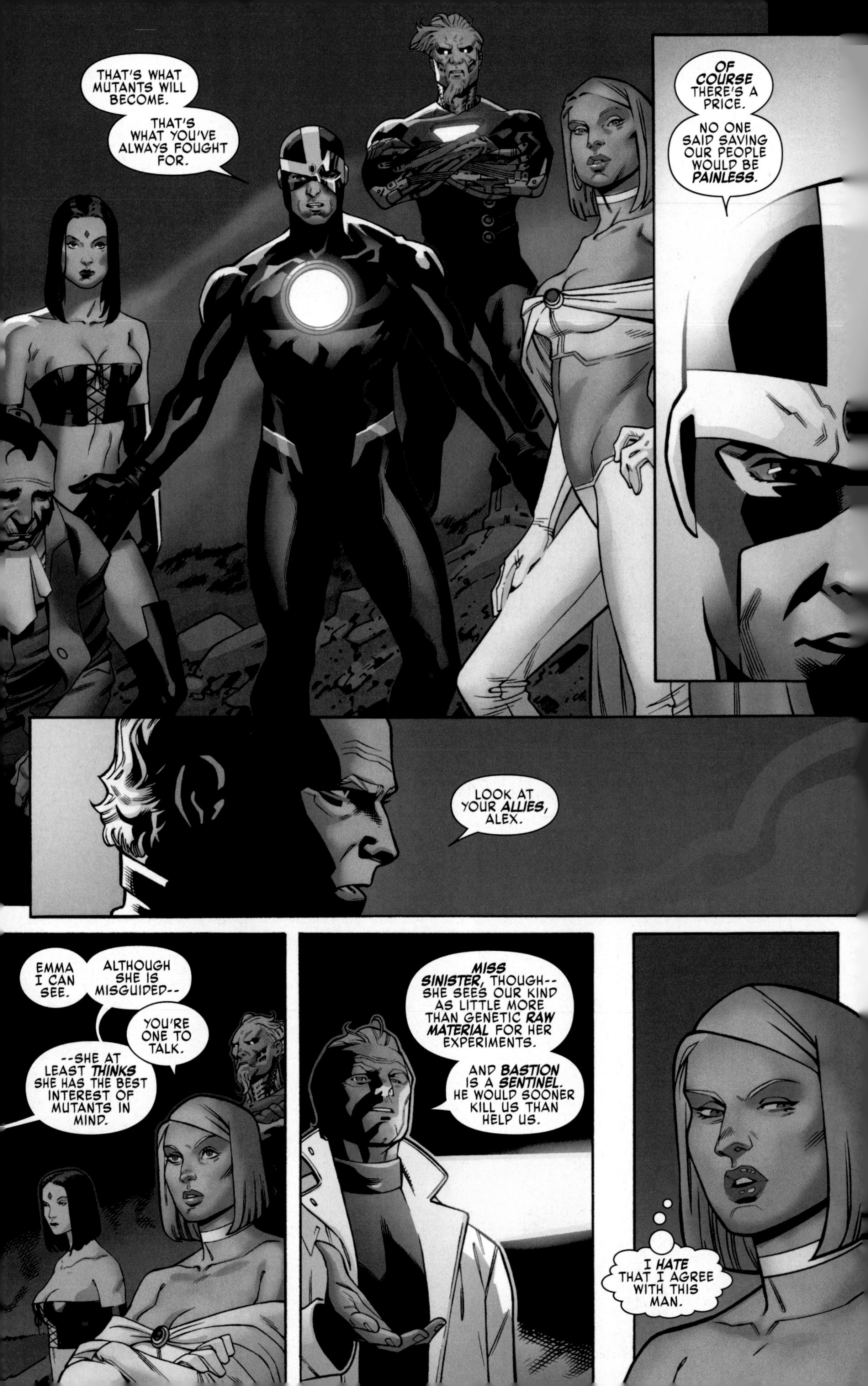
THAT'S WHAT MUTANTS WILL BECOME.
THAT'S WHAT YOU'VE ALWAYS FOUGHT FOR.
OF COURSE THERE'S A PRICE.
NO ONE SAID SAVING OUR PEOPLE WOULD BE PAINLESS.
LOOK AT YOUR ALLIES, ALEX.
EMMA I CAN SEE.
ALTHOUGH SHE IS MISGUIDED--
YOU'RE ONE TO TALK.
--SHE AT LEAST THINKS SHE HAS THE BEST INTEREST OF MUTANTS IN MIND.
MISS SINISTER, THOUGH-- SHE SEES OUR KIND AS LITTLE MORE THAN GENETIC RAW MATERIAL FOR HER EXPERIMENTS.
AND BASTION IS A SENTINEL. HE WOULD SOONER KILL US THAN HELP US.
I HATE THAT I AGREE WITH THIS MAN.

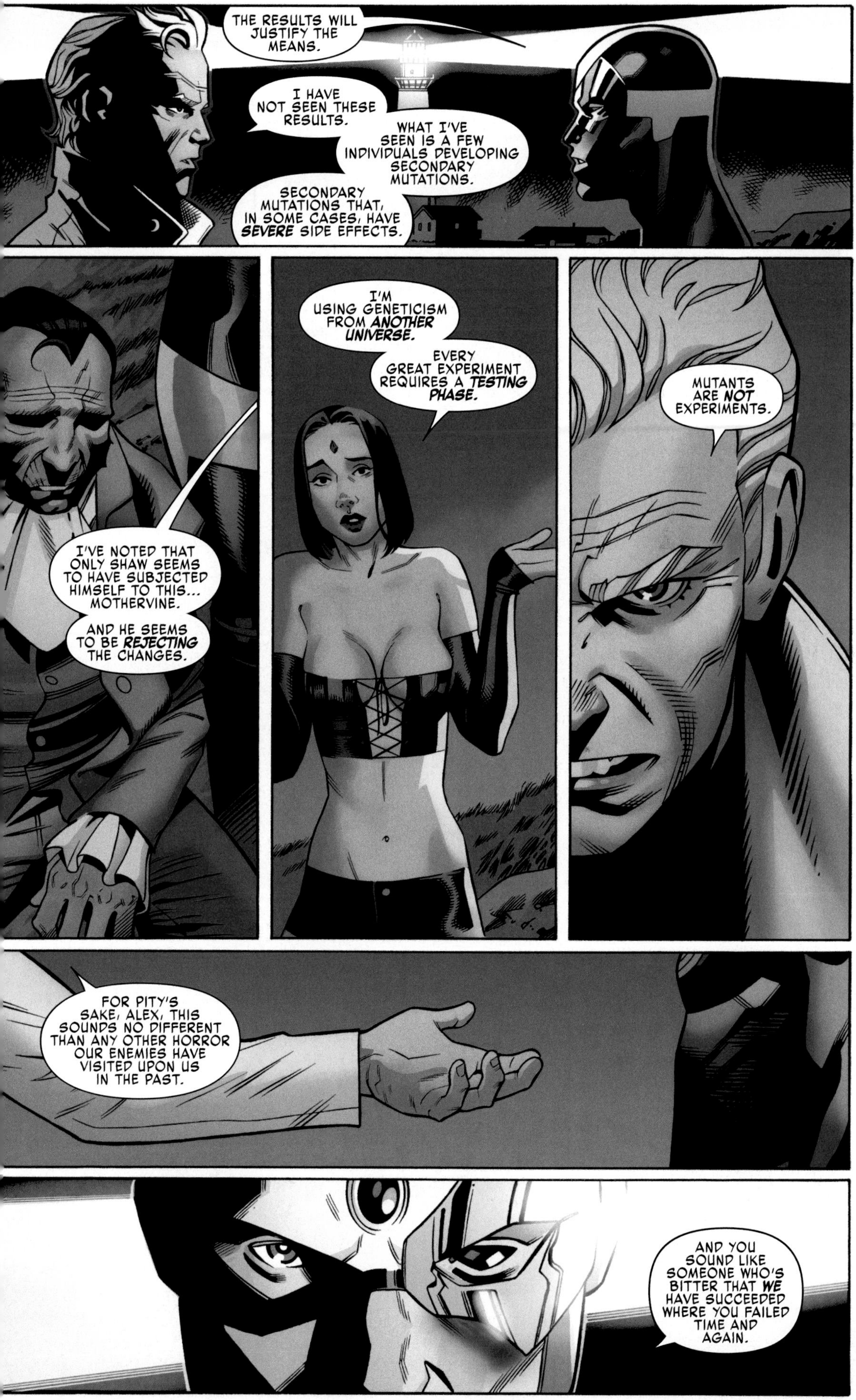
THE RESULTS WILL JUSTIFY THE MEANS.
I HAVE NOT SEEN THESE RESULTS.
WHAT I'VE SEEN IS A FEW INDIVIDUALS DEVELOPING SECONDARY MUTATIONS.
SECONDARY MUTATIONS THAT, IN SOME CASES, HAVE *SEVERE* SIDE EFFECTS.
I'VE NOTED THAT ONLY SHAW SEEMS TO HAVE SUBJECTED HIMSELF TO THIS... MOTHERVINE.
AND HE SEEMS TO BE *REJECTING* THE CHANGES.
I'M USING GENETICISM FROM *ANOTHER UNIVERSE.*
EVERY GREAT EXPERIMENT REQUIRES A *TESTING PHASE.*
MUTANTS ARE *NOT* EXPERIMENTS.
FOR PITY'S SAKE, ALEX, THIS SOUNDS NO DIFFERENT THAN ANY OTHER HORROR OUR ENEMIES HAVE VISITED UPON US IN THE PAST.
AND YOU SOUND LIKE SOMEONE WHO'S BITTER THAT *WE* HAVE SUCCEEDED WHERE YOU FAILED TIME AND AGAIN.

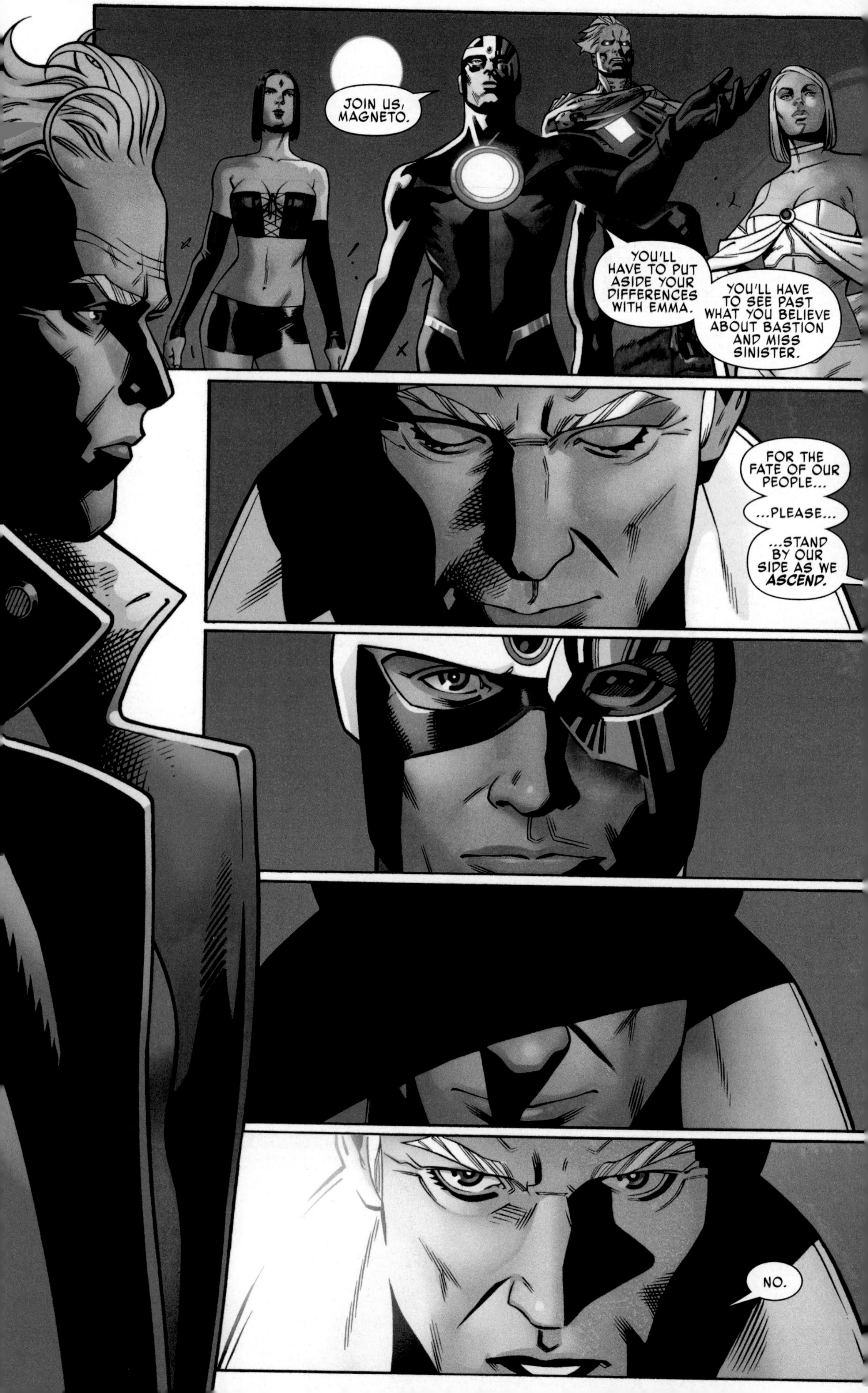
JOIN US, MAGNETO.
YOU'LL HAVE TO PUT ASIDE YOUR DIFFERENCES WITH EMMA.
YOU'LL HAVE TO SEE PAST WHAT YOU BELIEVE ABOUT BASTION AND MISS SINISTER.
FOR THE FATE OF OUR PEOPLE...
...PLEASE...
...STAND BY OUR SIDE AS WE *ASCEND.*
NO.

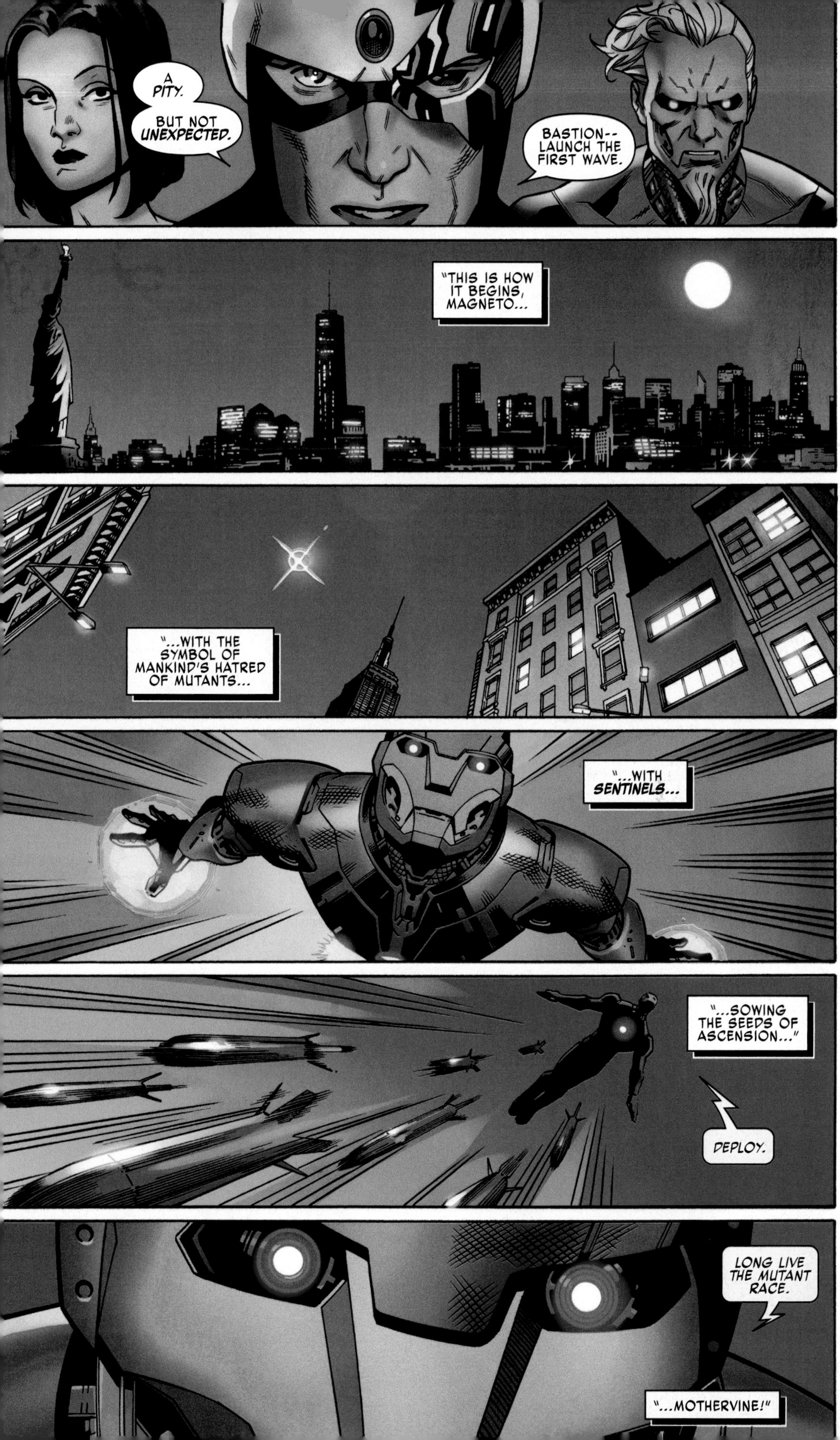
A PITY.
BUT NOT *UNEXPECTED.*
BASTION-- LAUNCH THE FIRST WAVE.
"THIS IS HOW IT BEGINS, MAGNETO...
"...WITH THE SYMBOL OF MANKIND'S HATRED OF MUTANTS...
"...WITH *SENTINELS*...
"...SOWING THE SEEDS OF ASCENSION..."
DEPLOY.
LONG LIVE THE MUTANT RACE.
"...MOTHERVINE!"

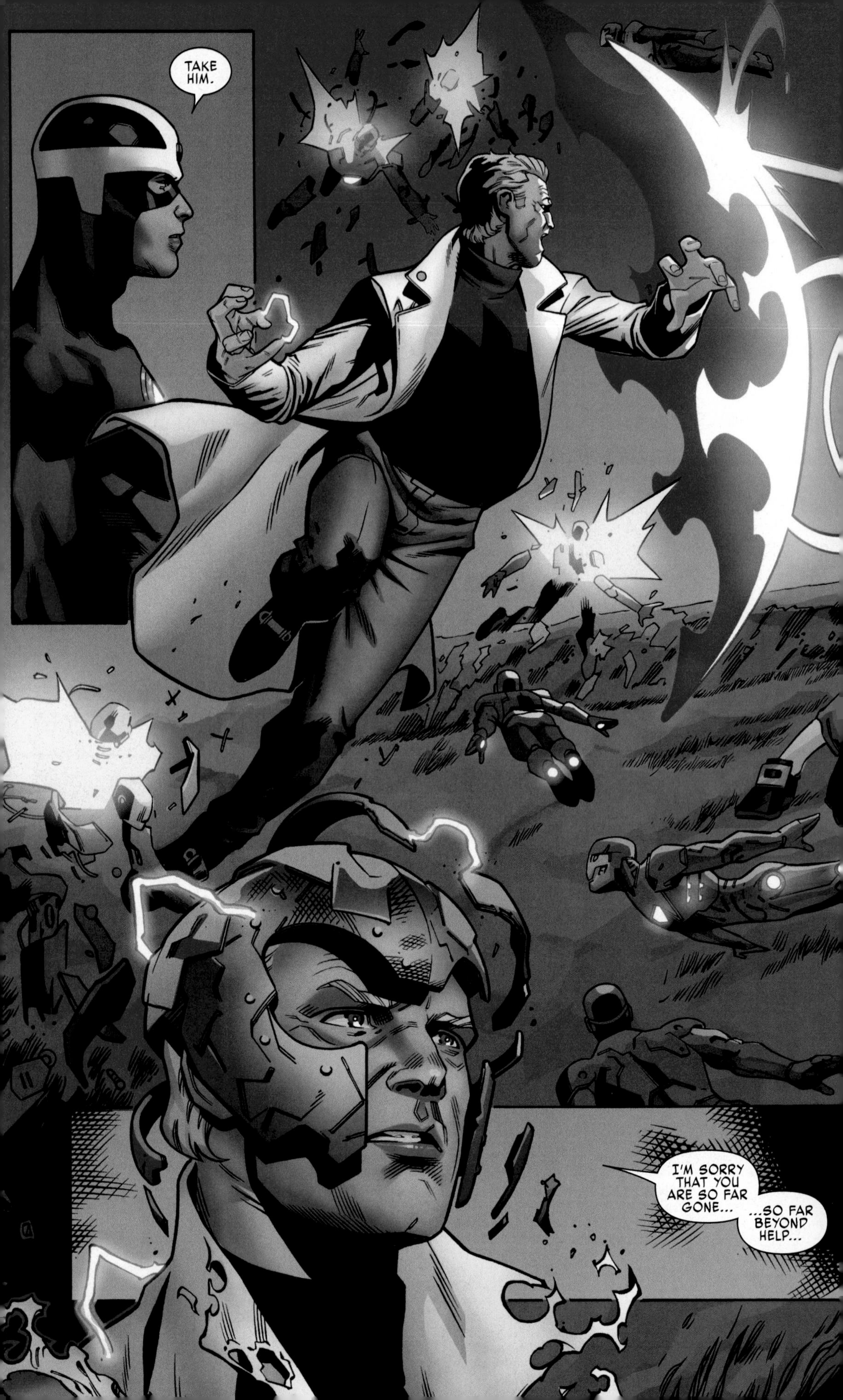
TAKE HIM.
I'M SORRY THAT YOU ARE SO FAR GONE...
...SO FAR BEYOND HELP...

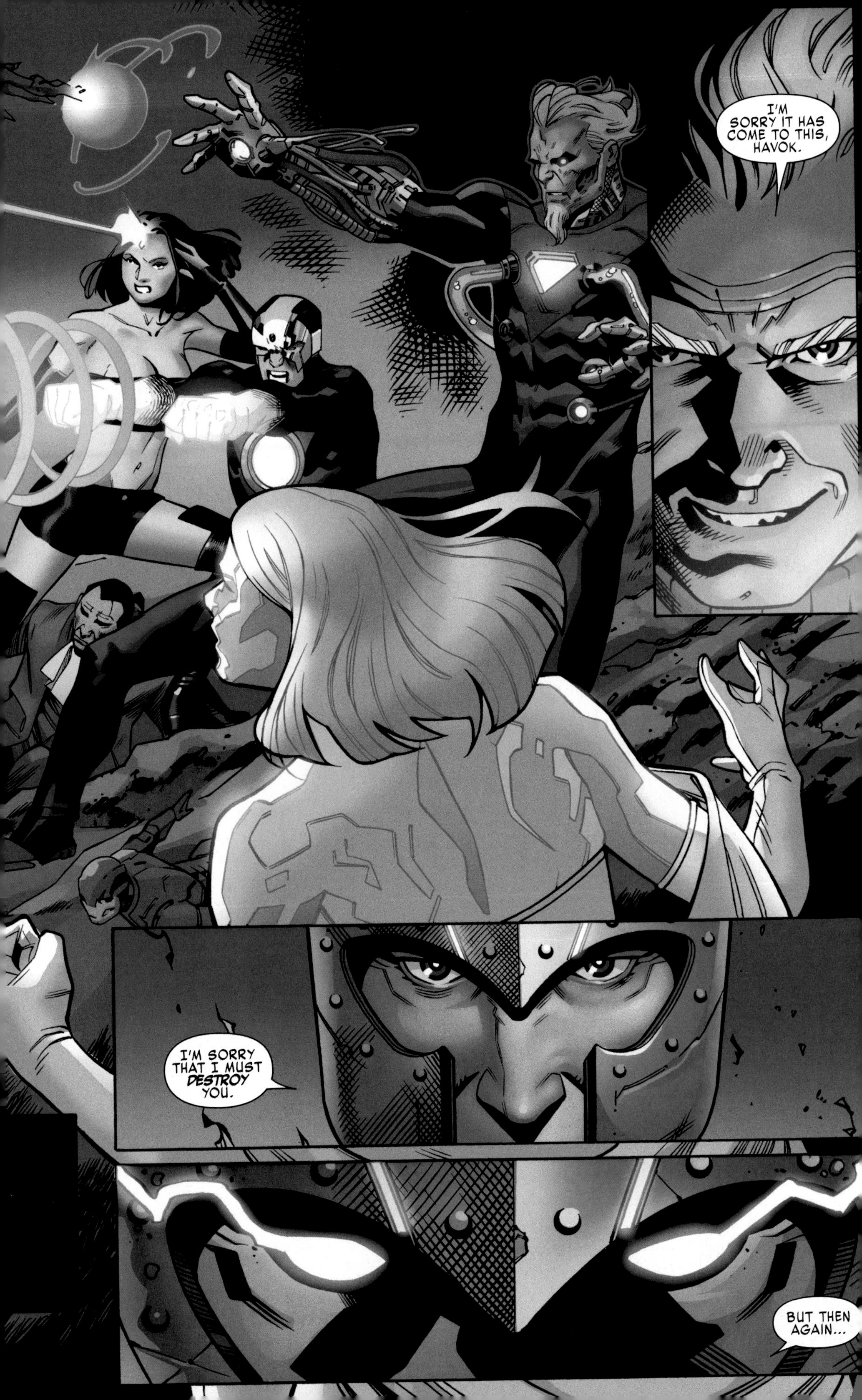
I'M SORRY IT HAS COME TO THIS, HAVOK.
I'M SORRY THAT I MUST DESTROY YOU.
BUT THEN AGAIN...

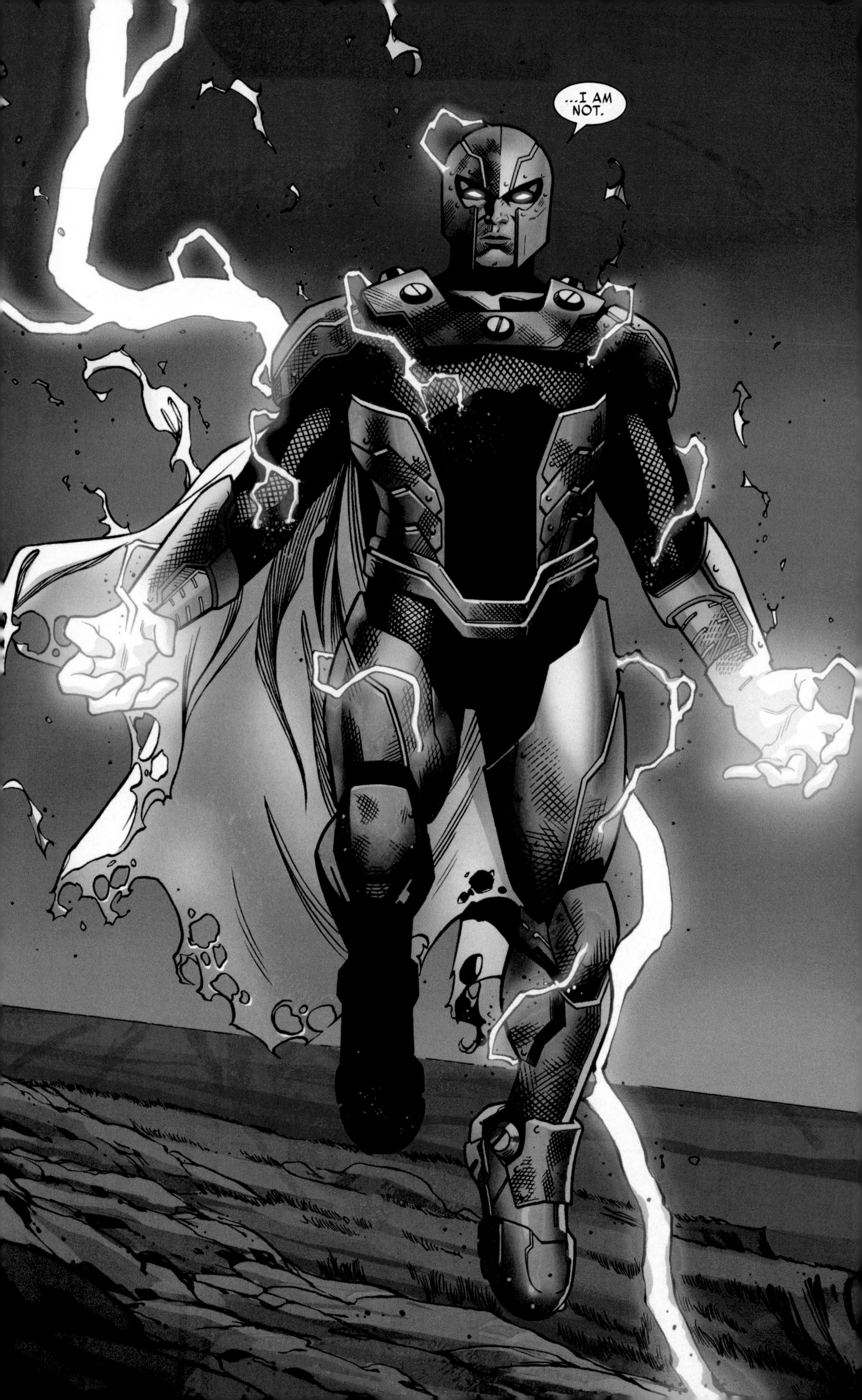
...I AM NOT.

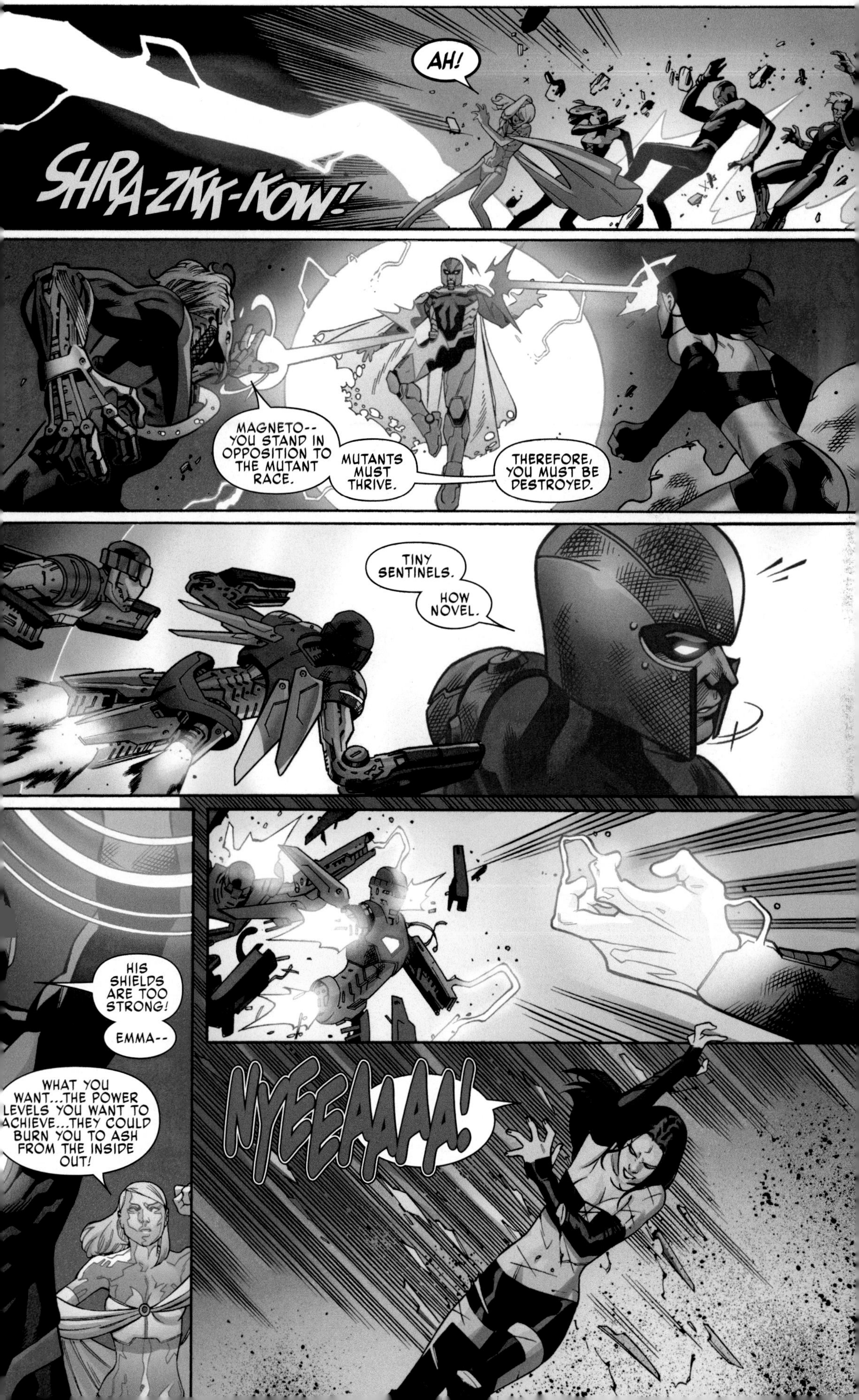
AH!
SHRA-ZKK-KOW!
MAGNETO-- YOU STAND IN OPPOSITION TO THE MUTANT RACE.
MUTANTS MUST THRIVE.
THEREFORE, YOU MUST BE DESTROYED.
TINY SENTINELS.
HOW NOVEL.
HIS SHIELDS ARE TOO STRONG!
EMMA--
WHAT YOU WANT...THE POWER LEVELS YOU WANT TO ACHIEVE...THEY COULD BURN YOU TO ASH FROM THE INSIDE OUT!
NYEEAAAA!

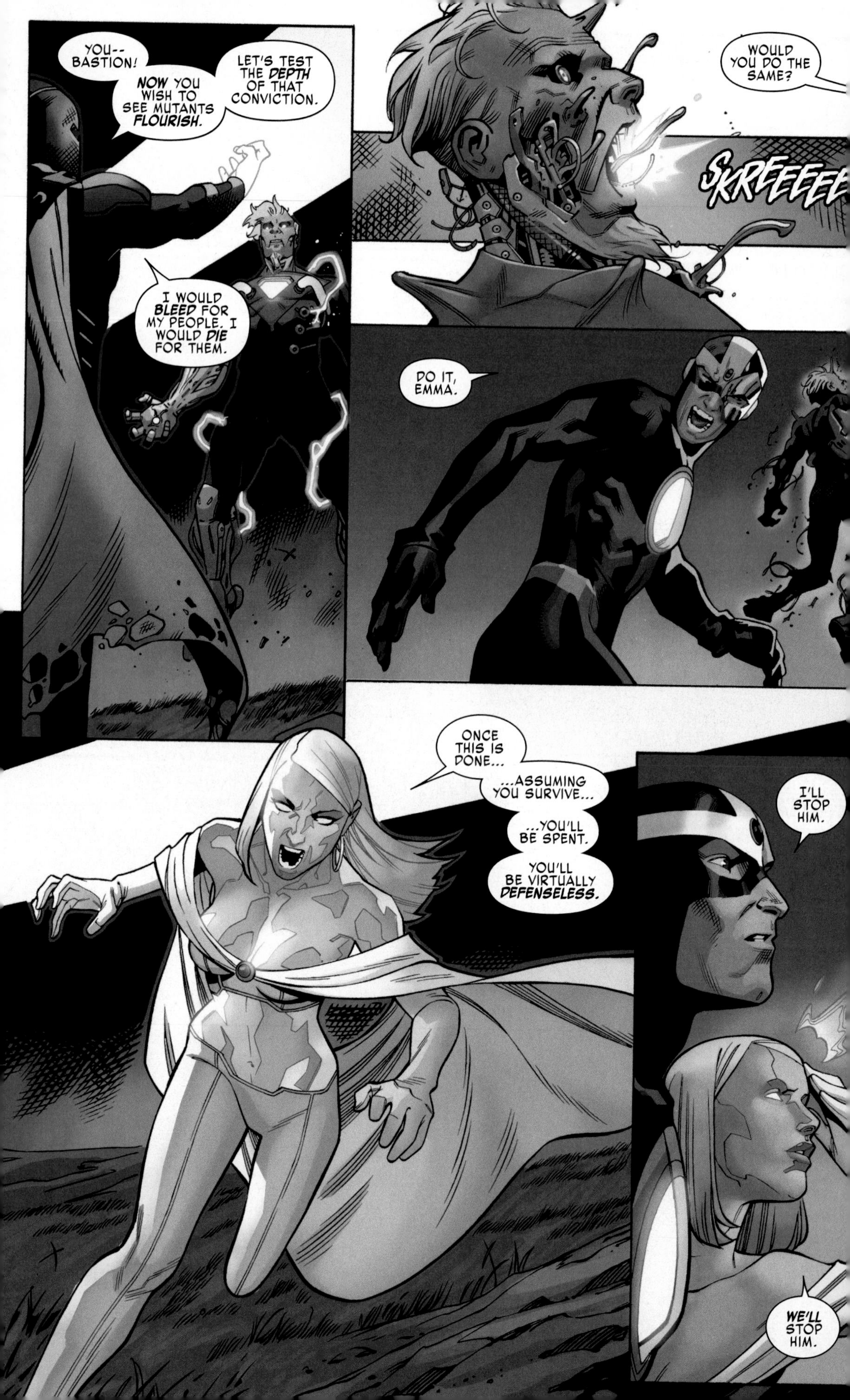
YOU--
BASTION!
NOW YOU WISH TO SEE MUTANTS FLOURISH.
LET'S TEST THE DEPTH OF THAT CONVICTION.
I WOULD BLEED FOR MY PEOPLE. I WOULD DIE FOR THEM.
WOULD YOU DO THE SAME?
SKREEEEE
DO IT, EMMA.
ONCE THIS IS DONE...
...ASSUMING YOU SURVIVE...
...YOU'LL BE SPENT.
YOU'LL BE VIRTUALLY DEFENSELESS.
I'LL STOP HIM.
WE'LL STOP HIM.

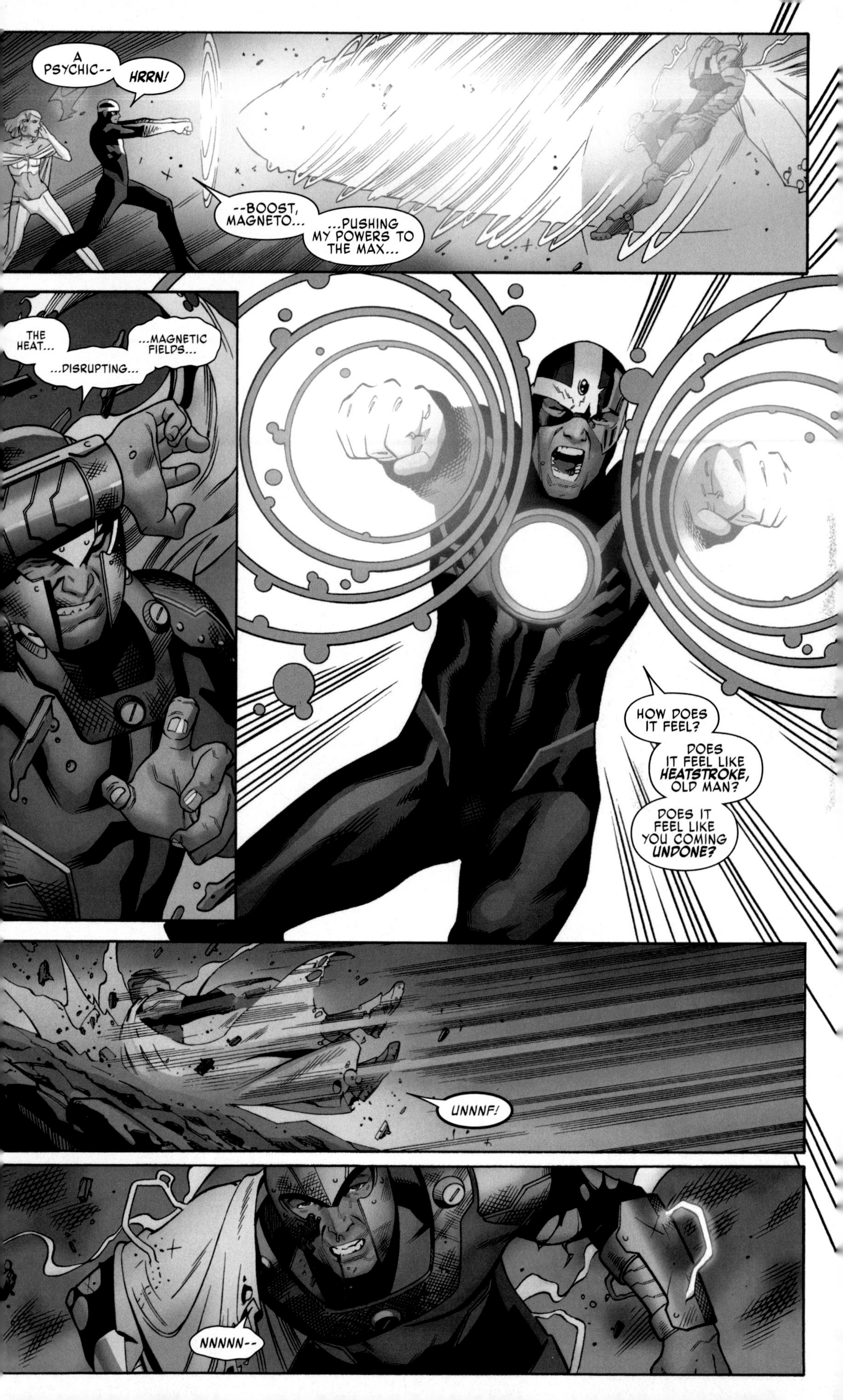
A PSYCHIC--
HRRN!
--BOOST, MAGNETO...
...PUSHING MY POWERS TO THE MAX...
THE HEAT...
...DISRUPTING...
...MAGNETIC FIELDS...
HOW DOES IT FEEL?
DOES IT FEEL LIKE HEATSTROKE, OLD MAN?
DOES IT FEEL LIKE YOU COMING UNDONE?
UNNNF!
NNNNN--

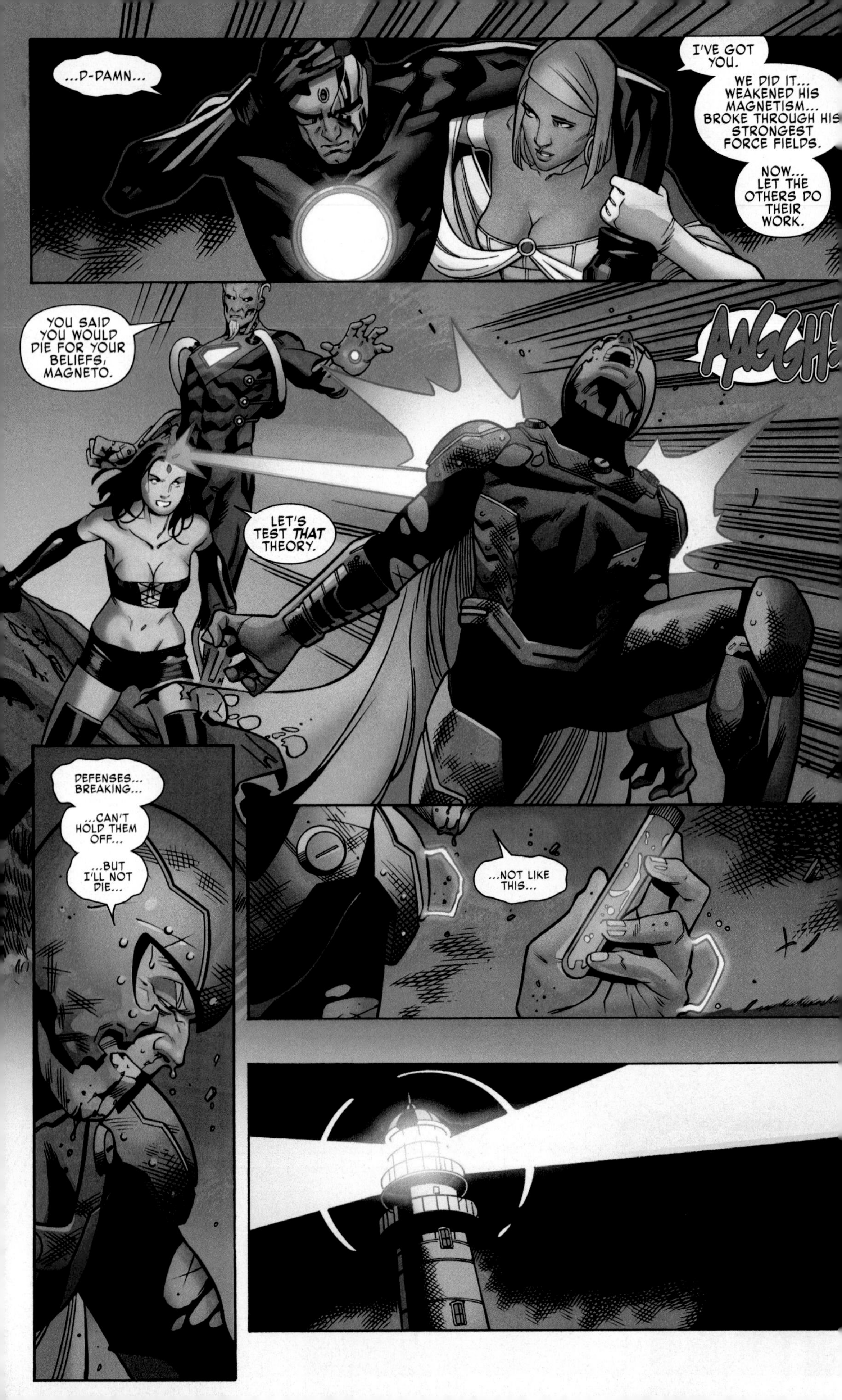

...D-DAMN...
I'VE GOT YOU.
WE DID IT... WEAKENED HIS MAGNETISM... BROKE THROUGH HIS STRONGEST FORCE FIELDS.
NOW... LET THE OTHERS DO THEIR WORK.
YOU SAID YOU WOULD DIE FOR YOUR BELIEFS, MAGNETO.
AAGGH!
LET'S TEST THAT THEORY.
DEFENSES... BREAKING...
...CAN'T HOLD THEM OFF...
...BUT I'LL NOT DIE...
...NOT LIKE THIS...

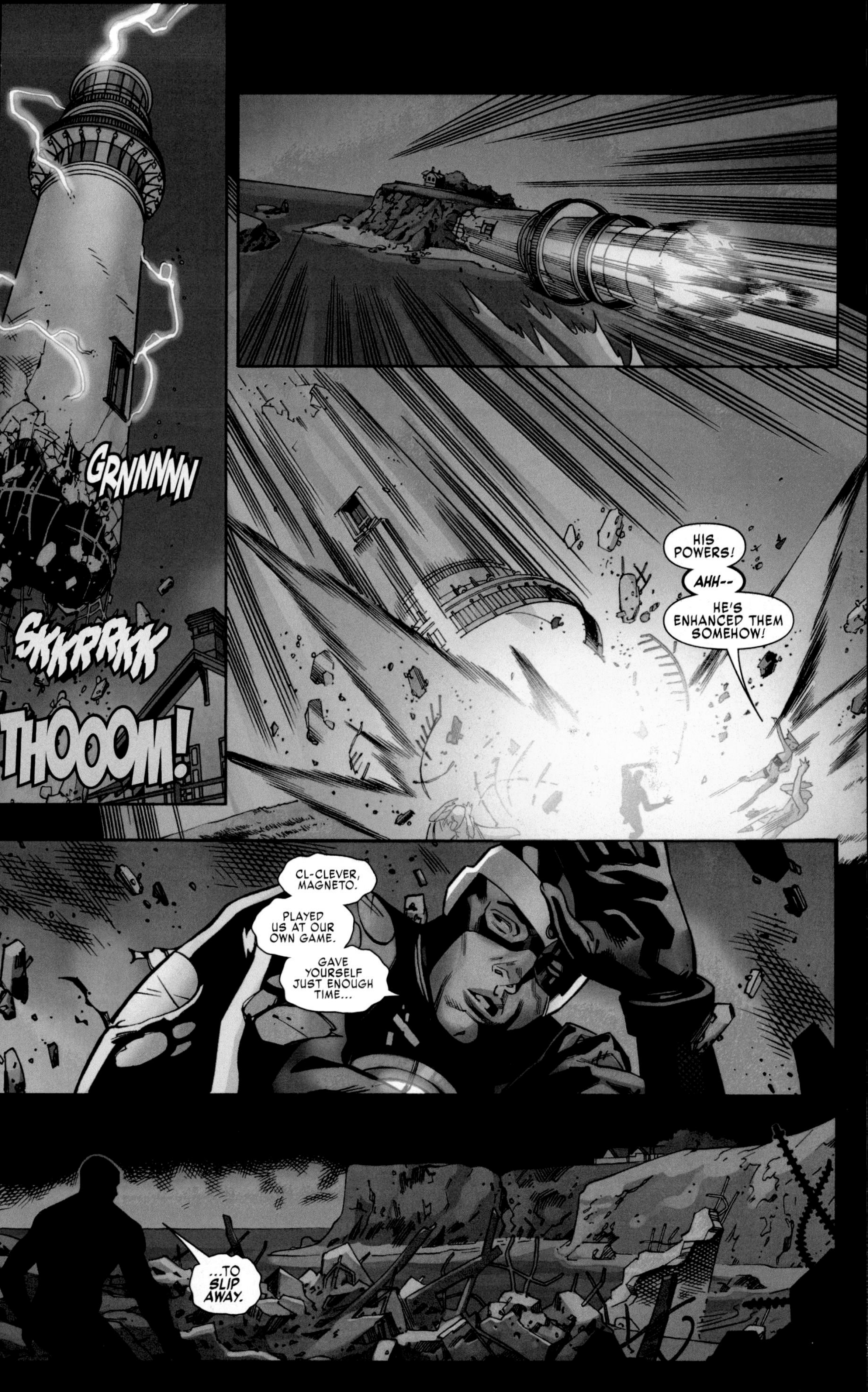
GRNNNNN
SKKRRKK
THOOOM!
HIS POWERS!
AHH--
HE'S ENHANCED THEM SOMEHOW!
CL-CLEVER, MAGNETO.
PLAYED US AT OUR OWN GAME.
GAVE YOURSELF JUST ENOUGH TIME...
...TO SLIP AWAY.

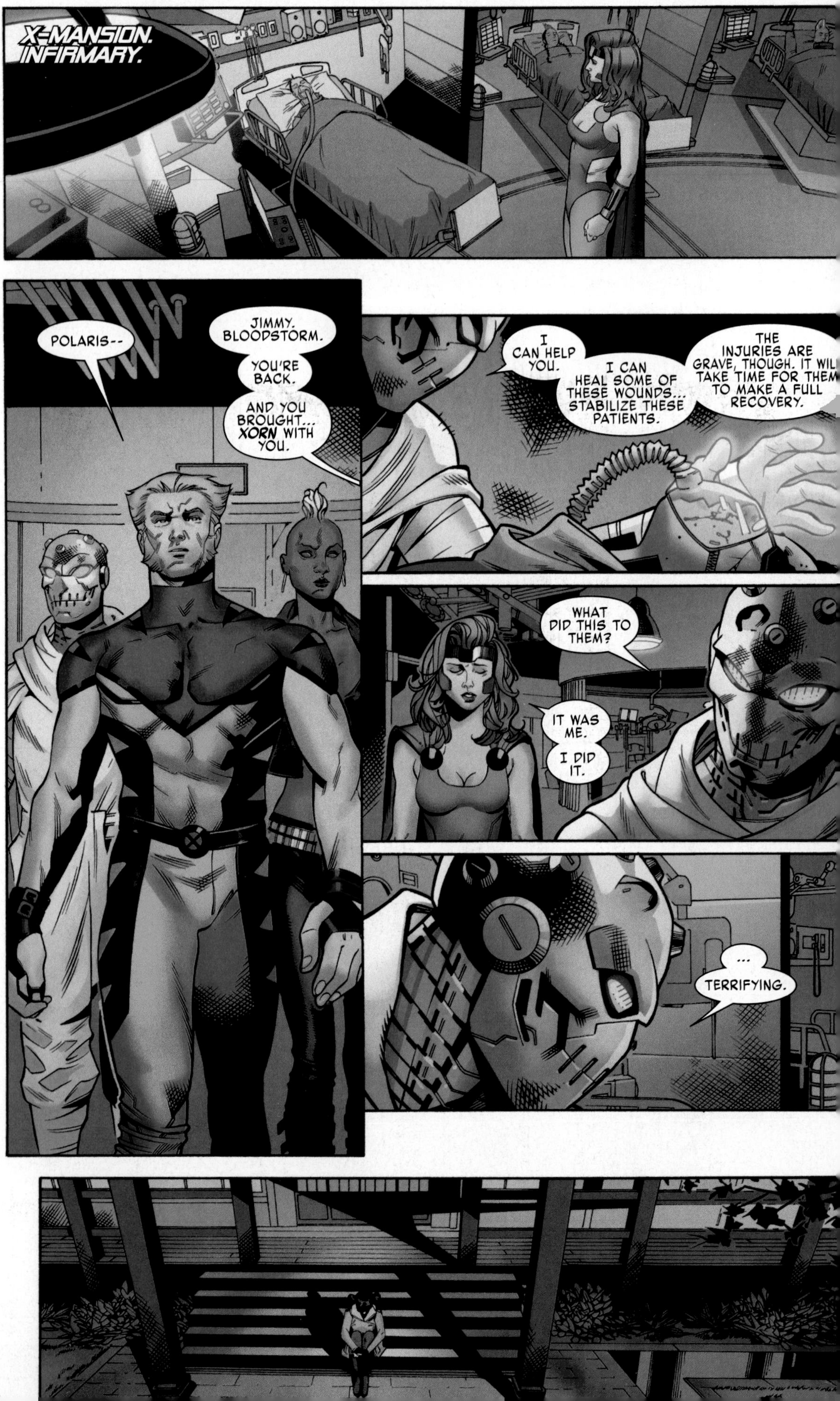
X-MANSION. INFIRMARY.
POLARIS--
JIMMY. BLOODSTORM.
YOU'RE BACK.
AND YOU BROUGHT... XORN WITH YOU.
I CAN HELP YOU.
I CAN HEAL SOME OF THESE WOUNDS... STABILIZE THESE PATIENTS.
THE INJURIES ARE GRAVE, THOUGH. IT WILL TAKE TIME FOR THEM TO MAKE A FULL RECOVERY.
WHAT DID THIS TO THEM?
IT WAS ME.
I DID IT.
...
TERRIFYING.

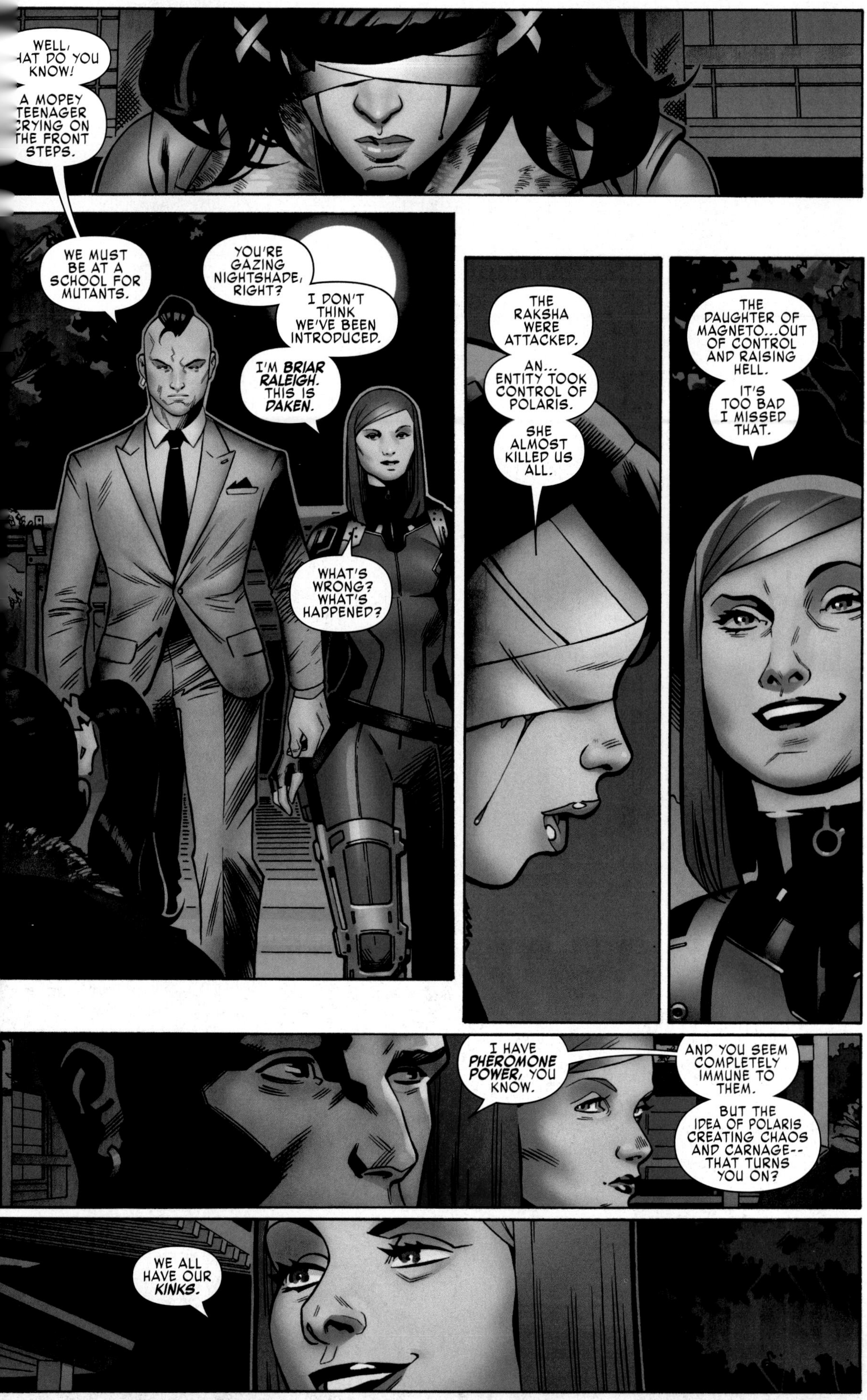
WELL, HAT DO YOU KNOW!
A MOPEY TEENAGER RYING ON THE FRONT STEPS.
WE MUST BE AT A SCHOOL FOR MUTANTS.
YOU'RE GAZING NIGHTSHADE, RIGHT?
I DON'T THINK WE'VE BEEN INTRODUCED.
I'M **BRIAR RALEIGH.** THIS IS ***DAKEN.***
WHAT'S WRONG? WHAT'S HAPPENED?
THE RAKSHA WERE ATTACKED.
AN... ENTITY TOOK CONTROL OF POLARIS.
SHE ALMOST KILLED US ALL.
THE DAUGHTER OF MAGNETO...OUT OF CONTROL AND RAISING HELL.
IT'S TOO BAD I MISSED THAT.
I HAVE ***PHEROMONE POWER,*** YOU KNOW.
AND YOU SEEM COMPLETELY IMMUNE TO THEM.
BUT THE IDEA OF POLARIS CREATING CHAOS AND CARNAGE-- THAT TURNS YOU ON?
WE ALL HAVE OUR ***KINKS.***

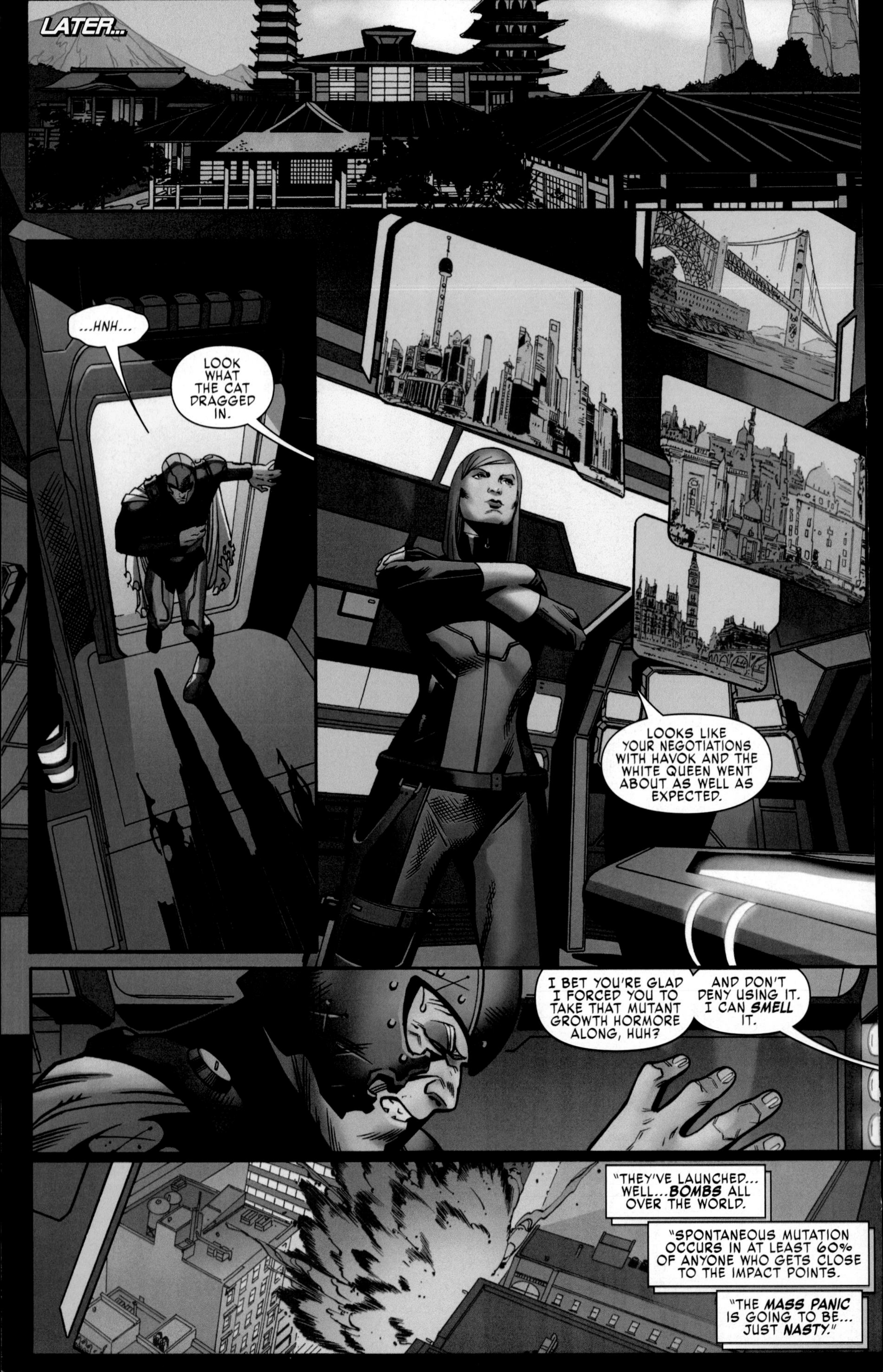
LATER...
...HNH...
LOOK WHAT THE CAT DRAGGED IN.
LOOKS LIKE YOUR NEGOTIATIONS WITH HAVOK AND THE WHITE QUEEN WENT ABOUT AS WELL AS EXPECTED.
I BET YOU'RE GLAD I FORCED YOU TO TAKE THAT MUTANT GROWTH HORMORE ALONG, HUH?
AND DON'T DENY USING IT. I CAN SMELL IT.
"THEY'VE LAUNCHED... WELL... BOMBS ALL OVER THE WORLD.
"SPONTANEOUS MUTATION OCCURS IN AT LEAST 60% OF ANYONE WHO GETS CLOSE TO THE IMPACT POINTS.
"THE MASS PANIC IS GOING TO BE... JUST NASTY."

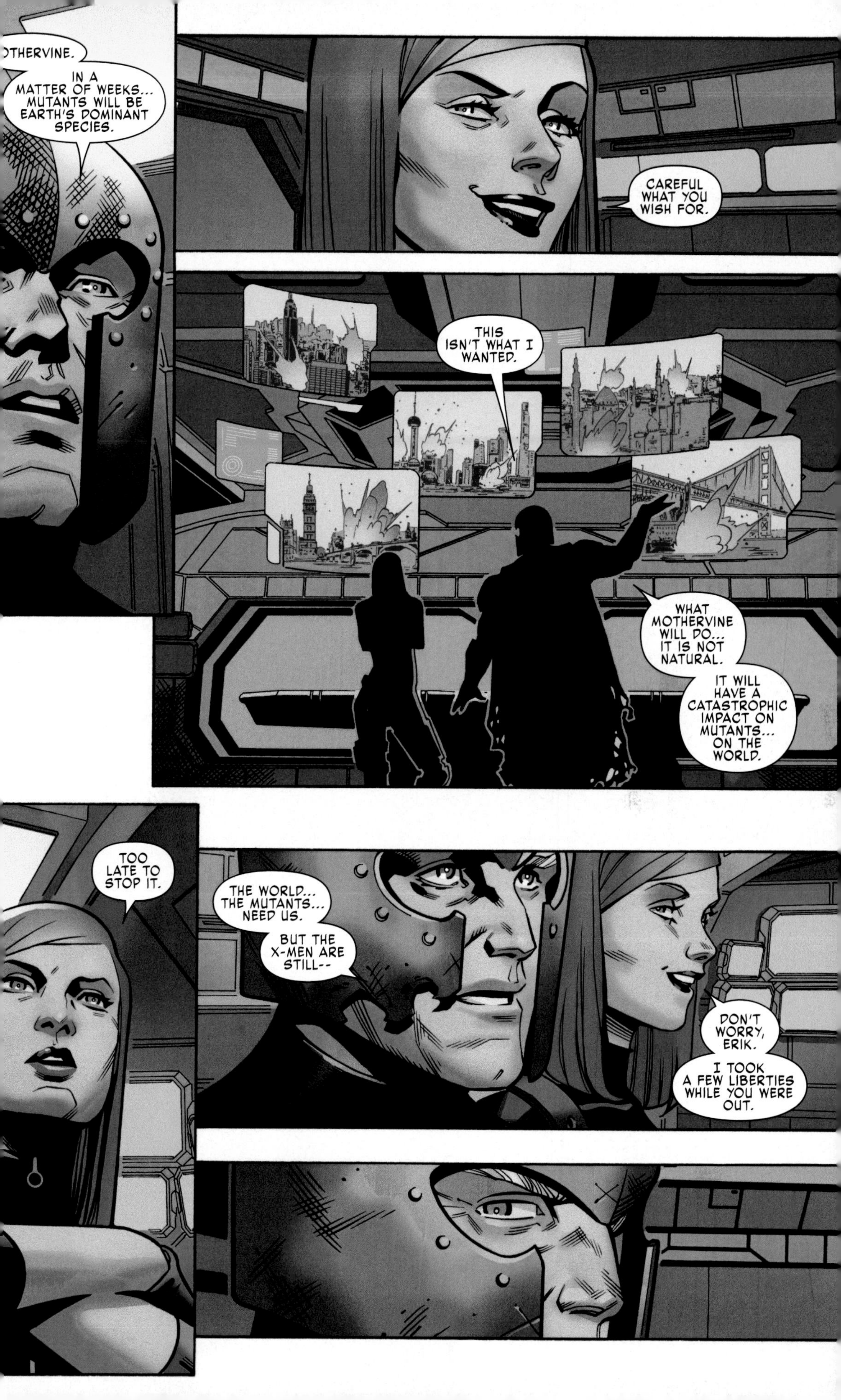
OTHERVINE.
IN A MATTER OF WEEKS... MUTANTS WILL BE EARTH'S DOMINANT SPECIES.
CAREFUL WHAT YOU WISH FOR.
THIS ISN'T WHAT I WANTED.
WHAT MOTHERVINE WILL DO... IT IS NOT NATURAL.
IT WILL HAVE A CATASTROPHIC IMPACT ON MUTANTS... ON THE WORLD.
TOO LATE TO STOP IT.
THE WORLD... THE MUTANTS... NEED US.
BUT THE X-MEN ARE STILL--
DON'T WORRY, ERIK.
I TOOK A FEW LIBERTIES WHILE YOU WERE OUT.

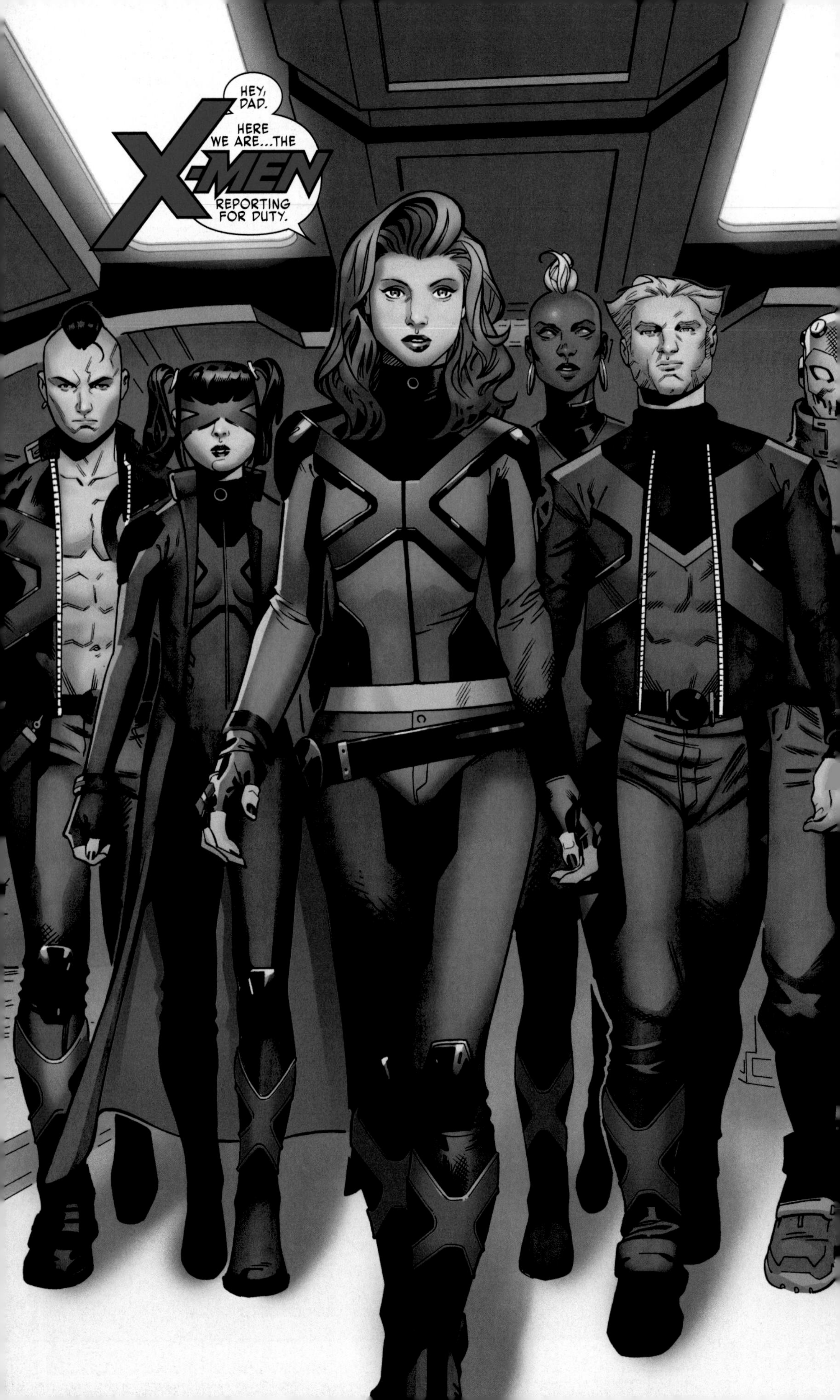
HEY, DAD.
HERE WE ARE...THE
X-MEN
REPORTING FOR DUTY.

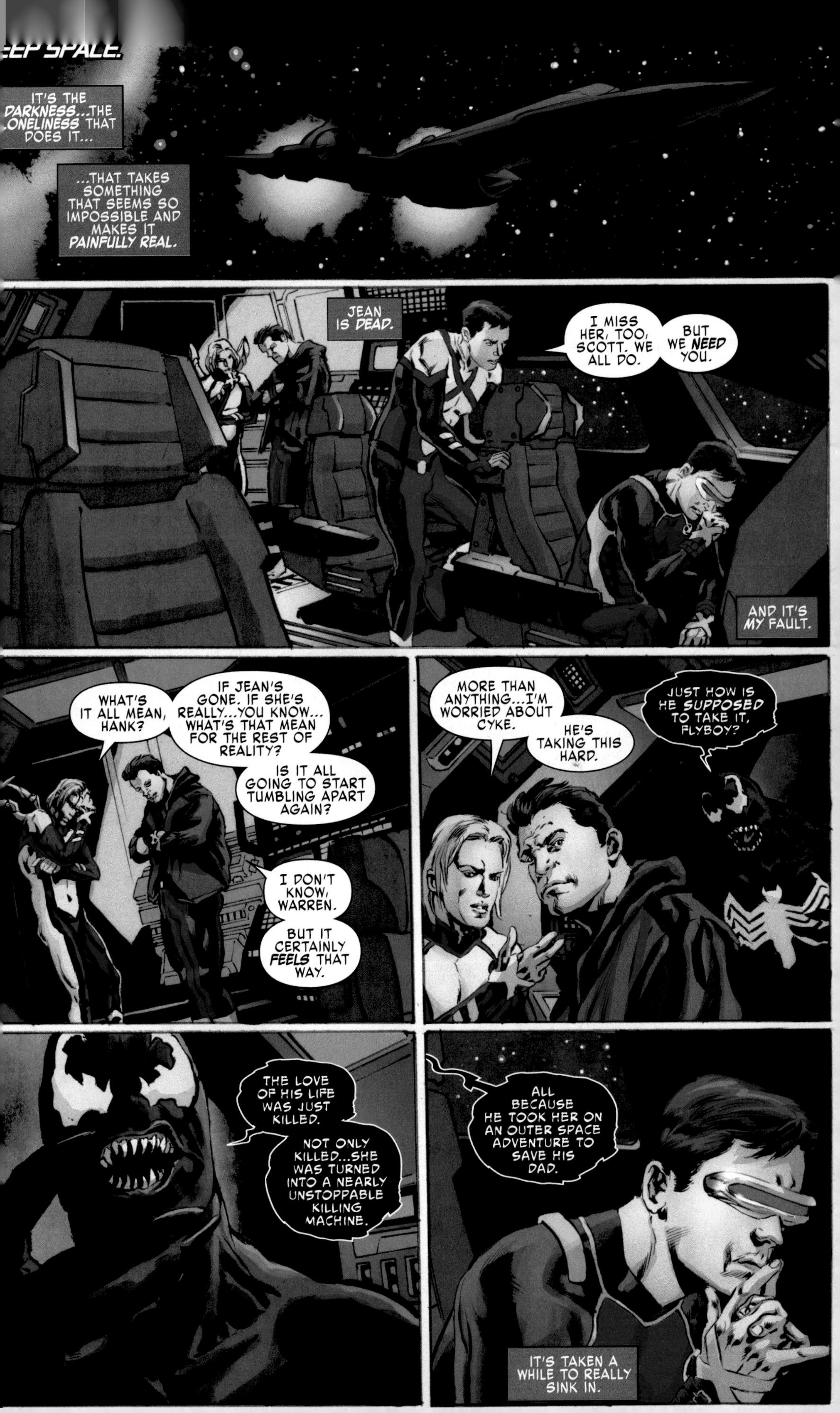

EEP SPACE.
IT'S THE DARKNESS...THE LONELINESS THAT DOES IT...
...THAT TAKES SOMETHING THAT SEEMS SO IMPOSSIBLE AND MAKES IT PAINFULLY REAL.
JEAN IS DEAD.
I MISS HER, TOO, SCOTT. WE ALL DO.
BUT WE NEED YOU.
AND IT'S MY FAULT.
WHAT'S IT ALL MEAN, HANK?
IF JEAN'S GONE. IF SHE'S REALLY...YOU KNOW... WHAT'S THAT MEAN FOR THE REST OF REALITY?
IS IT ALL GOING TO START TUMBLING APART AGAIN?
I DON'T KNOW, WARREN.
BUT IT CERTAINLY FEELS THAT WAY.
MORE THAN ANYTHING...I'M WORRIED ABOUT CYKE.
HE'S TAKING THIS HARD.
JUST HOW IS HE SUPPOSED TO TAKE IT, FLYBOY?
THE LOVE OF HIS LIFE WAS JUST KILLED.
NOT ONLY KILLED...SHE WAS TURNED INTO A NEARLY UNSTOPPABLE KILLING MACHINE.
ALL BECAUSE HE TOOK HER ON AN OUTER SPACE ADVENTURE TO SAVE HIS DAD.
IT'S TAKEN A WHILE TO REALLY SINK IN.

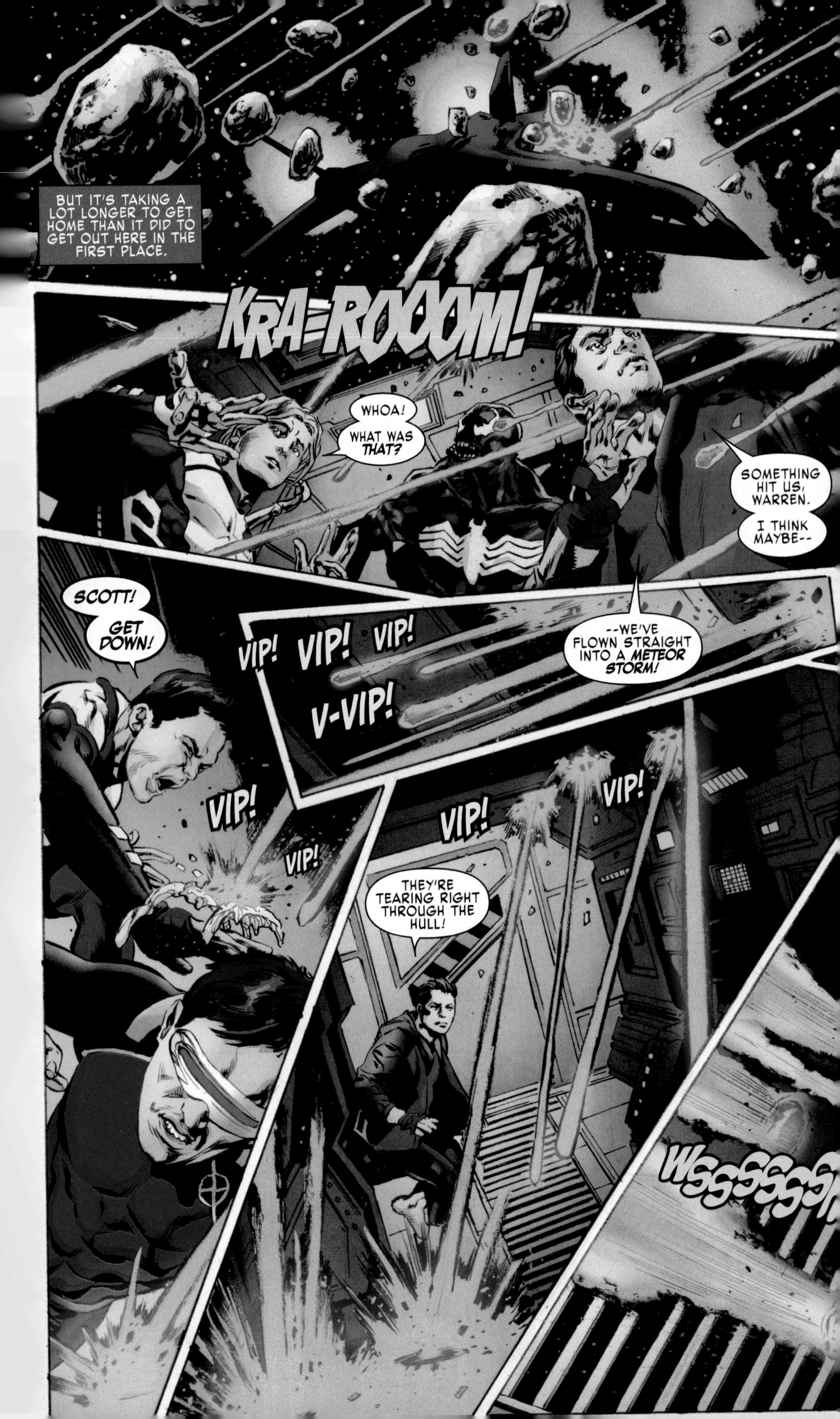
BUT IT'S TAKING A LOT LONGER TO GET HOME THAN IT DID TO GET OUT HERE IN THE FIRST PLACE.
KRA-ROOOM!
WHOA!
WHAT WAS *THAT?*
SOMETHING HIT US, WARREN.
I THINK MAYBE--
--WE'VE FLOWN STRAIGHT INTO A *METEOR STORM!*
SCOTT!
GET DOWN!
VIP! VIP! VIP!
V-VIP!
VIP!
VIP!
VIP!
VIP!
THEY'RE TEARING RIGHT THROUGH THE HULL!
WSSSSSS

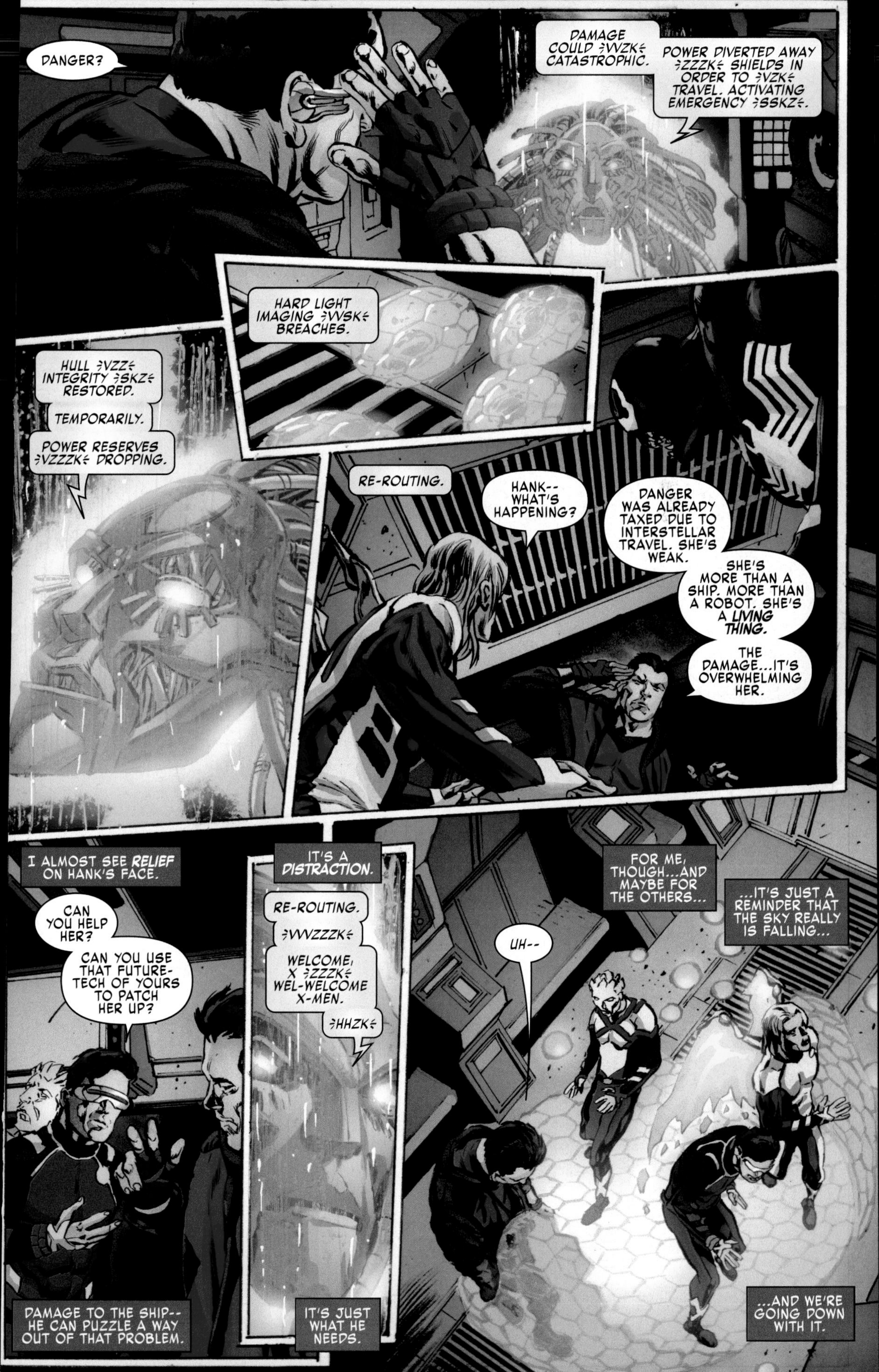
DANGER?
DAMAGE COULD ⋺VVZK⋲ CATASTROPHIC.
POWER DIVERTED AWAY ⋺ZZZK⋲ SHIELDS IN ORDER TO ⋺VZK⋲ TRAVEL. ACTIVATING EMERGENCY ⋺SSKZ⋲.
HARD LIGHT IMAGING ⋺VVSK⋲ BREACHES.
HULL ⋺VZZ⋲ INTEGRITY ⋺SKZ⋲ RESTORED.
TEMPORARILY.
POWER RESERVES ⋺VZZZK⋲ DROPPING.
RE-ROUTING.
HANK-- WHAT'S HAPPENING?
DANGER WAS ALREADY TAXED DUE TO INTERSTELLAR TRAVEL. SHE'S WEAK.
SHE'S MORE THAN A SHIP. MORE THAN A ROBOT. SHE'S A LIVING THING.
THE DAMAGE...IT'S OVERWHELMING HER.
I ALMOST SEE RELIEF ON HANK'S FACE.
CAN YOU HELP HER?
CAN YOU USE THAT FUTURE-TECH OF YOURS TO PATCH HER UP?
DAMAGE TO THE SHIP-- HE CAN PUZZLE A WAY OUT OF THAT PROBLEM.
IT'S A DISTRACTION.
RE-ROUTING.
⋺VVVZZZK⋲
WELCOME, X ⋺ZZZK⋲ WEL-WELCOME X-MEN.
⋺HHZK⋲
IT'S JUST WHAT HE NEEDS.
FOR ME, THOUGH...AND MAYBE FOR THE OTHERS...
...IT'S JUST A REMINDER THAT THE SKY REALLY IS FALLING...
UH--
...AND WE'RE GOING DOWN WITH IT.

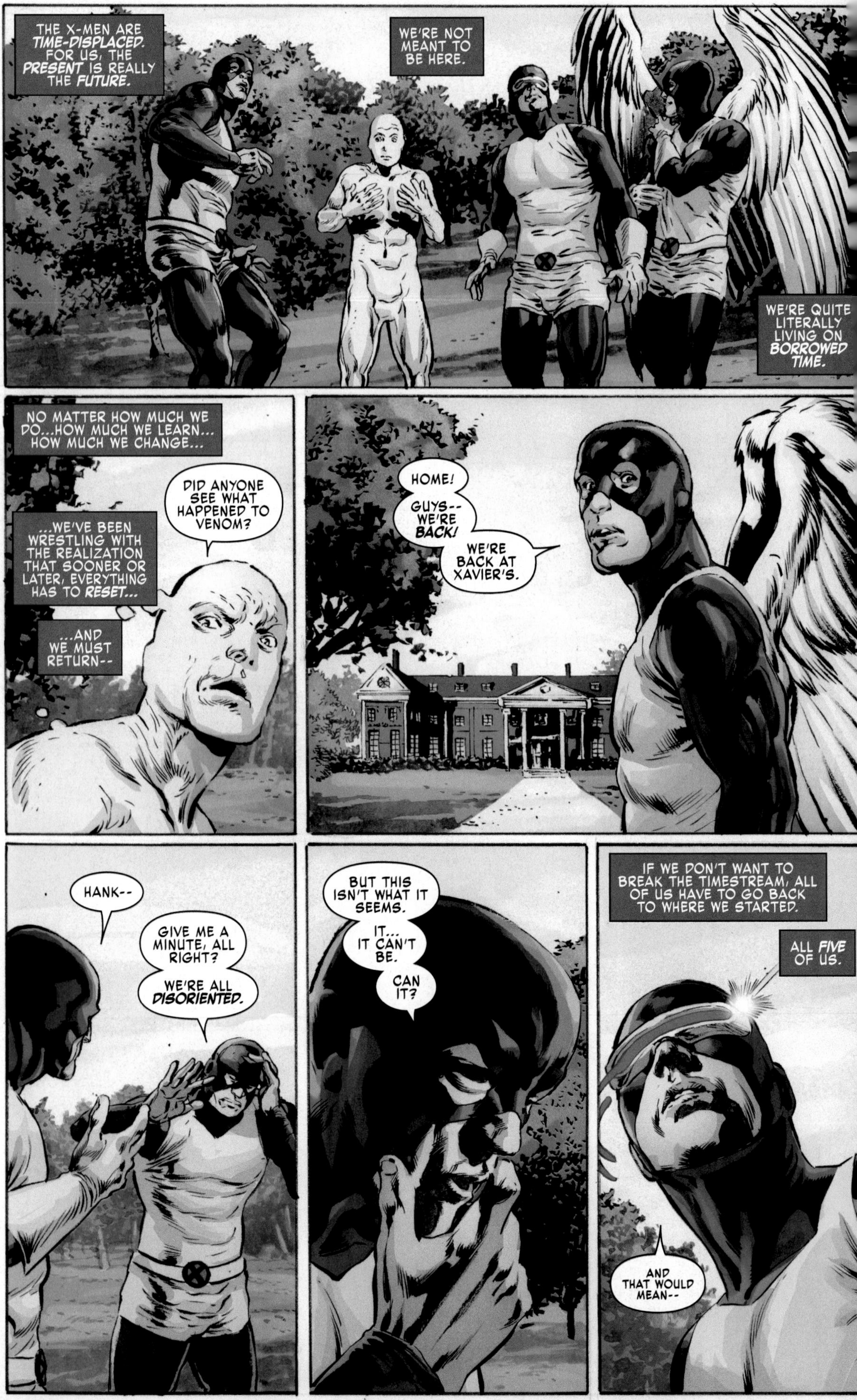
THE X-MEN ARE TIME-DISPLACED. FOR US, THE PRESENT IS REALLY THE FUTURE.
WE'RE NOT MEANT TO BE HERE.
WE'RE QUITE LITERALLY LIVING ON BORROWED TIME.
NO MATTER HOW MUCH WE DO...HOW MUCH WE LEARN... HOW MUCH WE CHANGE...
DID ANYONE SEE WHAT HAPPENED TO VENOM?
...WE'VE BEEN WRESTLING WITH THE REALIZATION THAT SOONER OR LATER, EVERYTHING HAS TO RESET...
...AND WE MUST RETURN--
HOME!
GUYS-- WE'RE BACK!
WE'RE BACK AT XAVIER'S.
HANK--
GIVE ME A MINUTE, ALL RIGHT?
WE'RE ALL DISORIENTED.
BUT THIS ISN'T WHAT IT SEEMS.
IT... IT CAN'T BE.
CAN IT?
IF WE DON'T WANT TO BREAK THE TIMESTREAM, ALL OF US HAVE TO GO BACK TO WHERE WE STARTED.
ALL FIVE OF US.
AND THAT WOULD MEAN--

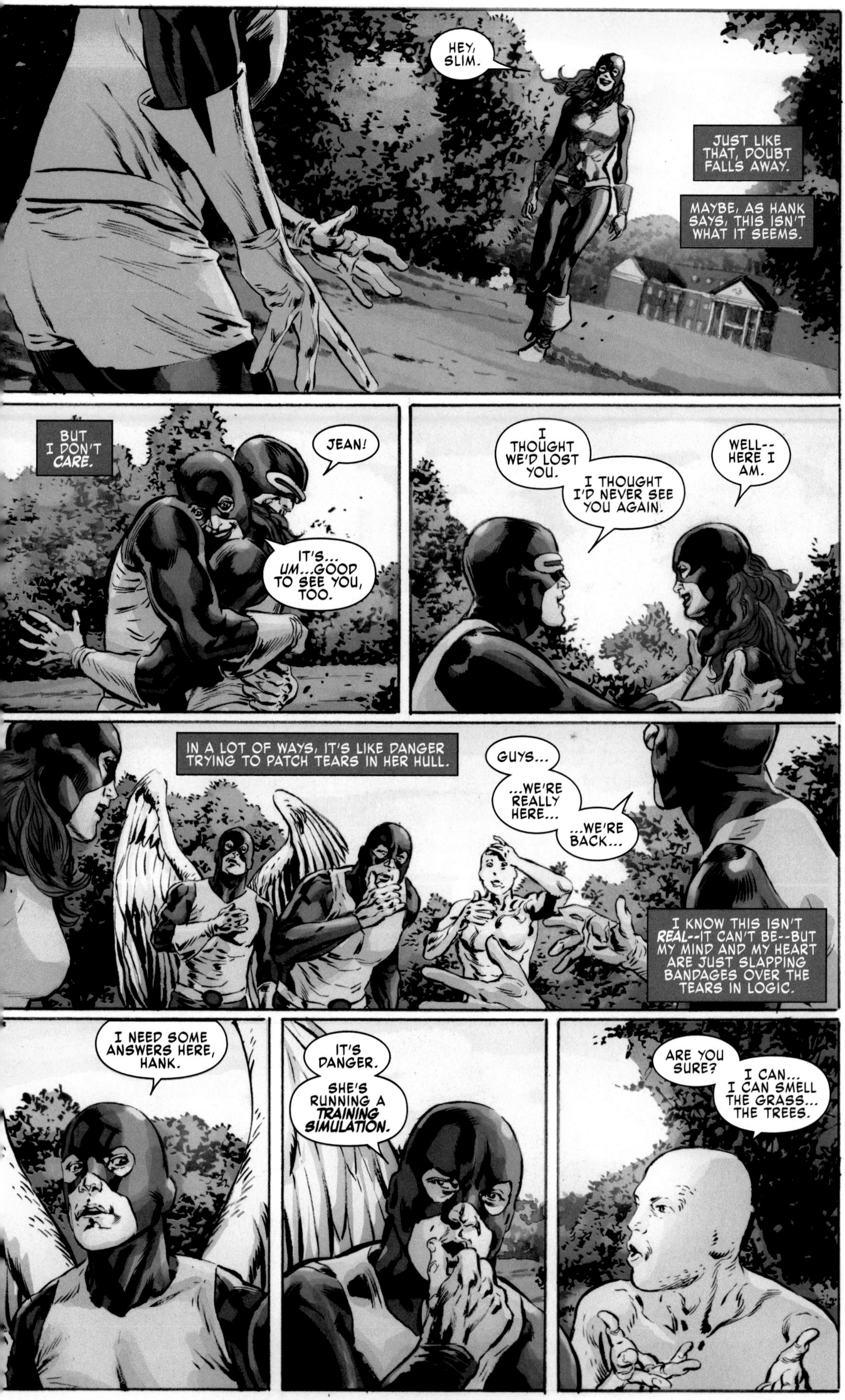
HEY, SLIM.
JUST LIKE THAT, DOUBT FALLS AWAY.
MAYBE, AS HANK SAYS, THIS ISN'T WHAT IT SEEMS.
BUT I DON'T CARE.
JEAN!
IT'S... UM...GOOD TO SEE YOU, TOO.
I THOUGHT WE'D LOST YOU.
I THOUGHT I'D NEVER SEE YOU AGAIN.
WELL-- HERE I AM.
IN A LOT OF WAYS, IT'S LIKE DANGER TRYING TO PATCH TEARS IN HER HULL.
GUYS...
...WE'RE REALLY HERE...
...WE'RE BACK...
I KNOW THIS ISN'T REAL--IT CAN'T BE--BUT MY MIND AND MY HEART ARE JUST SLAPPING BANDAGES OVER THE TEARS IN LOGIC.
I NEED SOME ANSWERS HERE, HANK.
IT'S DANGER.
SHE'S RUNNING A TRAINING SIMULATION.
ARE YOU SURE?
I CAN... I CAN SMELL THE GRASS... THE TREES.

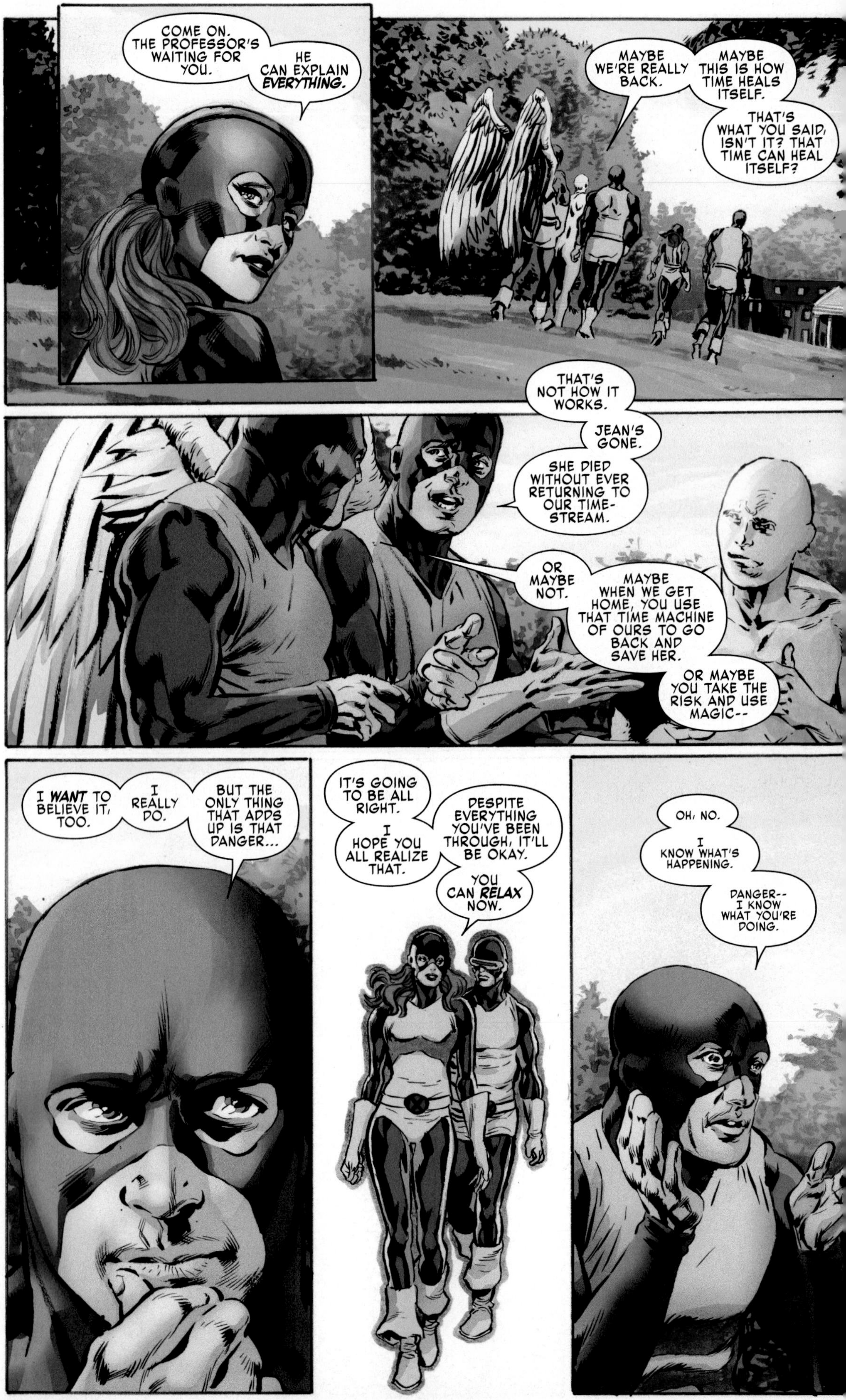
COME ON. THE PROFESSOR'S WAITING FOR YOU.
HE CAN EXPLAIN *EVERYTHING.*
MAYBE WE'RE REALLY BACK.
MAYBE THIS IS HOW TIME HEALS ITSELF.
THAT'S WHAT YOU SAID, ISN'T IT? THAT TIME CAN HEAL ITSELF?
THAT'S NOT HOW IT WORKS.
JEAN'S GONE.
SHE DIED WITHOUT EVER RETURNING TO OUR TIME-STREAM.
OR MAYBE NOT.
MAYBE WHEN WE GET HOME, YOU USE THAT TIME MACHINE OF OURS TO GO BACK AND SAVE HER.
OR MAYBE YOU TAKE THE RISK AND USE MAGIC--
I *WANT* TO BELIEVE IT, TOO.
I REALLY DO.
BUT THE ONLY THING THAT ADDS UP IS THAT DANGER...
IT'S GOING TO BE ALL RIGHT.
I HOPE YOU ALL REALIZE THAT.
DESPITE EVERYTHING YOU'VE BEEN THROUGH, IT'LL BE OKAY.
YOU CAN *RELAX* NOW.
OH, NO.
I KNOW WHAT'S HAPPENING.
DANGER-- I KNOW WHAT YOU'RE DOING.

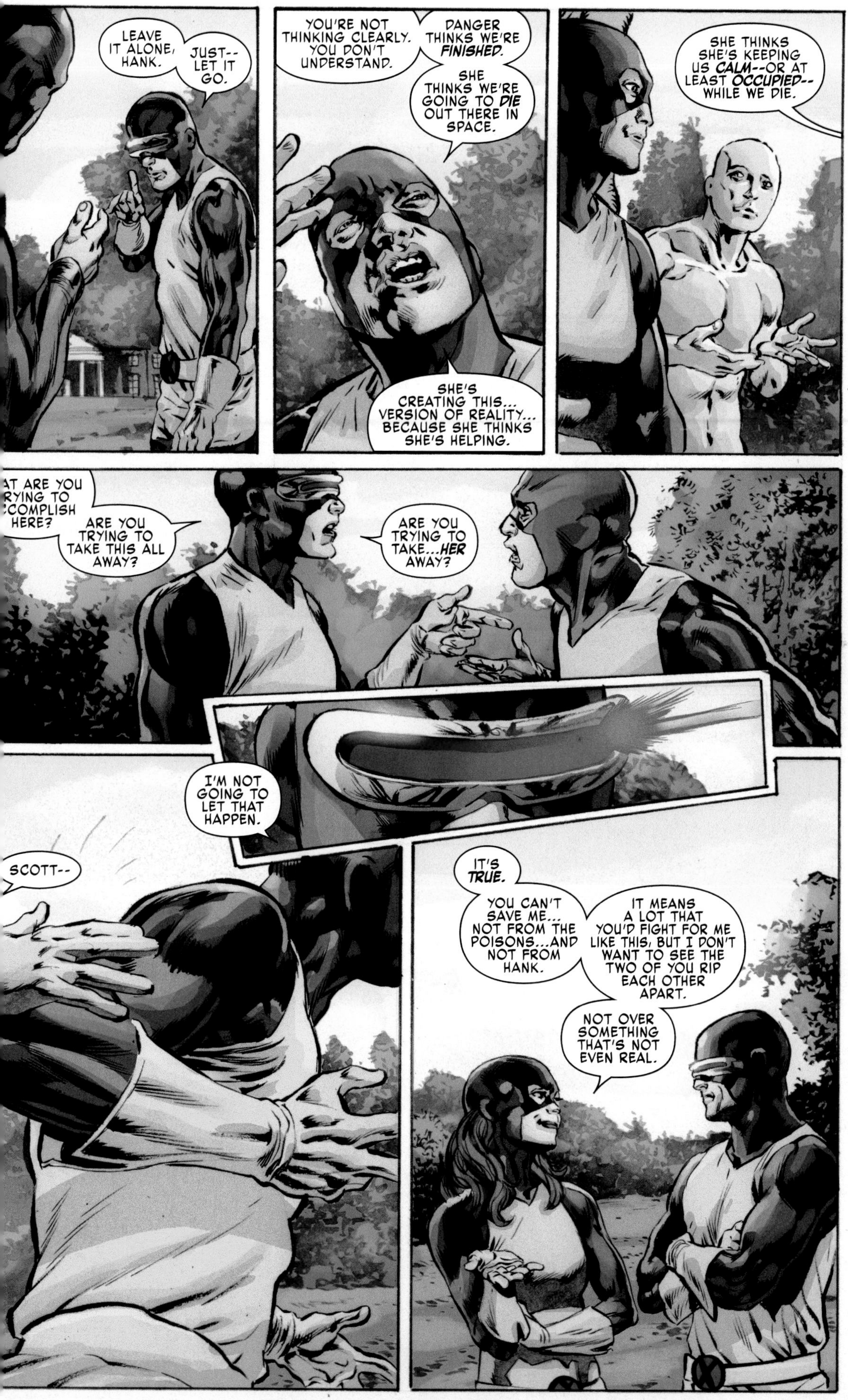
LEAVE IT ALONE, HANK.
JUST--LET IT GO.
YOU'RE NOT THINKING CLEARLY. YOU DON'T UNDERSTAND.
DANGER THINKS WE'RE FINISHED.
SHE THINKS WE'RE GOING TO DIE OUT THERE IN SPACE.
SHE'S CREATING THIS... VERSION OF REALITY... BECAUSE SHE THINKS SHE'S HELPING.
SHE THINKS SHE'S KEEPING US CALM--OR AT LEAST OCCUPIED--WHILE WE DIE.
AT ARE YOU RYING TO CCOMPLISH HERE?
ARE YOU TRYING TO TAKE THIS ALL AWAY?
ARE YOU TRYING TO TAKE...HER AWAY?
I'M NOT GOING TO LET THAT HAPPEN.
SCOTT--
IT'S TRUE.
YOU CAN'T SAVE ME... NOT FROM THE POISONS...AND NOT FROM HANK.
IT MEANS A LOT THAT YOU'D FIGHT FOR ME LIKE THIS, BUT I DON'T WANT TO SEE THE TWO OF YOU RIP EACH OTHER APART.
NOT OVER SOMETHING THAT'S NOT EVEN REAL.

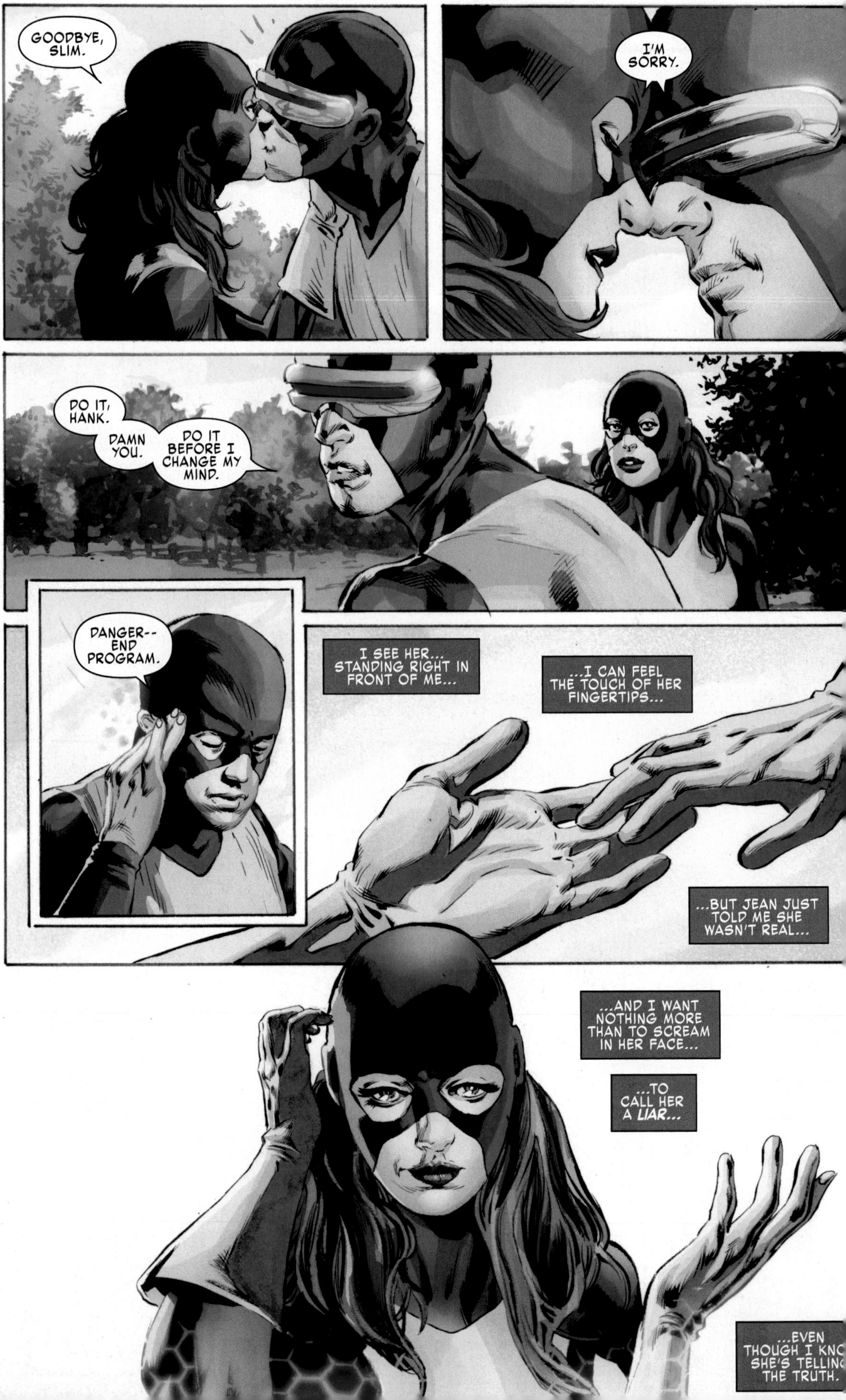
GOODBYE, SLIM.
I'M SORRY.
DO IT, HANK.
DAMN YOU.
DO IT BEFORE I CHANGE MY MIND.
DANGER-- END PROGRAM.
I SEE HER... STANDING RIGHT IN FRONT OF ME...
...I CAN FEEL THE TOUCH OF HER FINGERTIPS...
...BUT JEAN JUST TOLD ME SHE WASN'T REAL...
...AND I WANT NOTHING MORE THAN TO SCREAM IN HER FACE...
...TO CALL HER A LIAR...
...EVEN THOUGH I KNO SHE'S TELLING THE TRUTH.

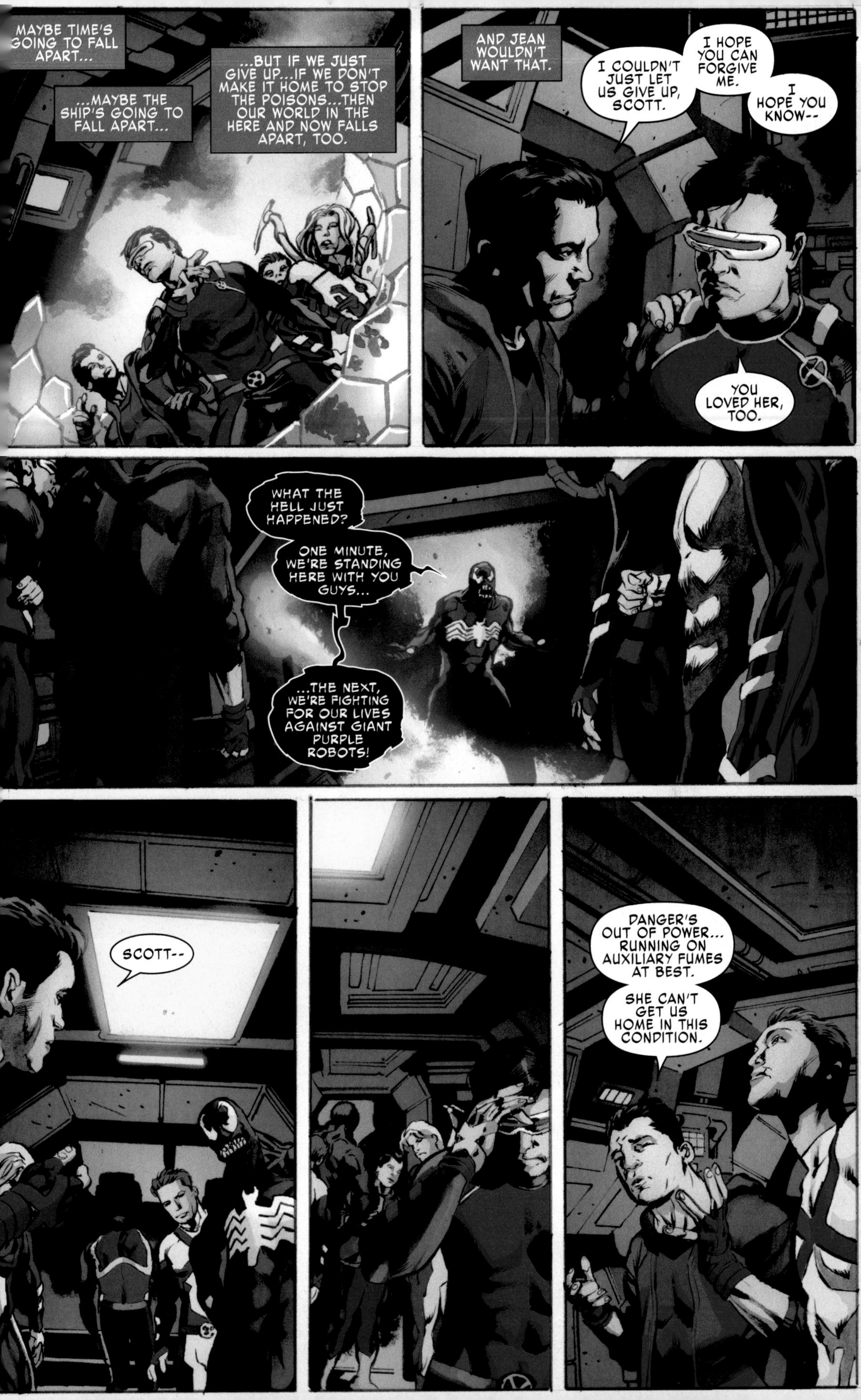
MAYBE TIME'S GOING TO FALL APART...
...MAYBE THE SHIP'S GOING TO FALL APART...
...BUT IF WE JUST GIVE UP...IF WE DON'T MAKE IT HOME TO STOP THE POISONS...THEN OUR WORLD IN THE HERE AND NOW FALLS APART, TOO.
AND JEAN WOULDN'T WANT THAT.
I COULDN'T JUST LET US GIVE UP, SCOTT.
I HOPE YOU CAN FORGIVE ME.
I HOPE YOU KNOW--
YOU LOVED HER, TOO.
WHAT THE HELL JUST HAPPENED?
ONE MINUTE, WE'RE STANDING HERE WITH YOU GUYS...
...THE NEXT, WE'RE FIGHTING FOR OUR LIVES AGAINST GIANT PURPLE ROBOTS!
SCOTT--
DANGER'S OUT OF POWER... RUNNING ON AUXILIARY FUMES AT BEST.
SHE CAN'T GET US HOME IN THIS CONDITION.

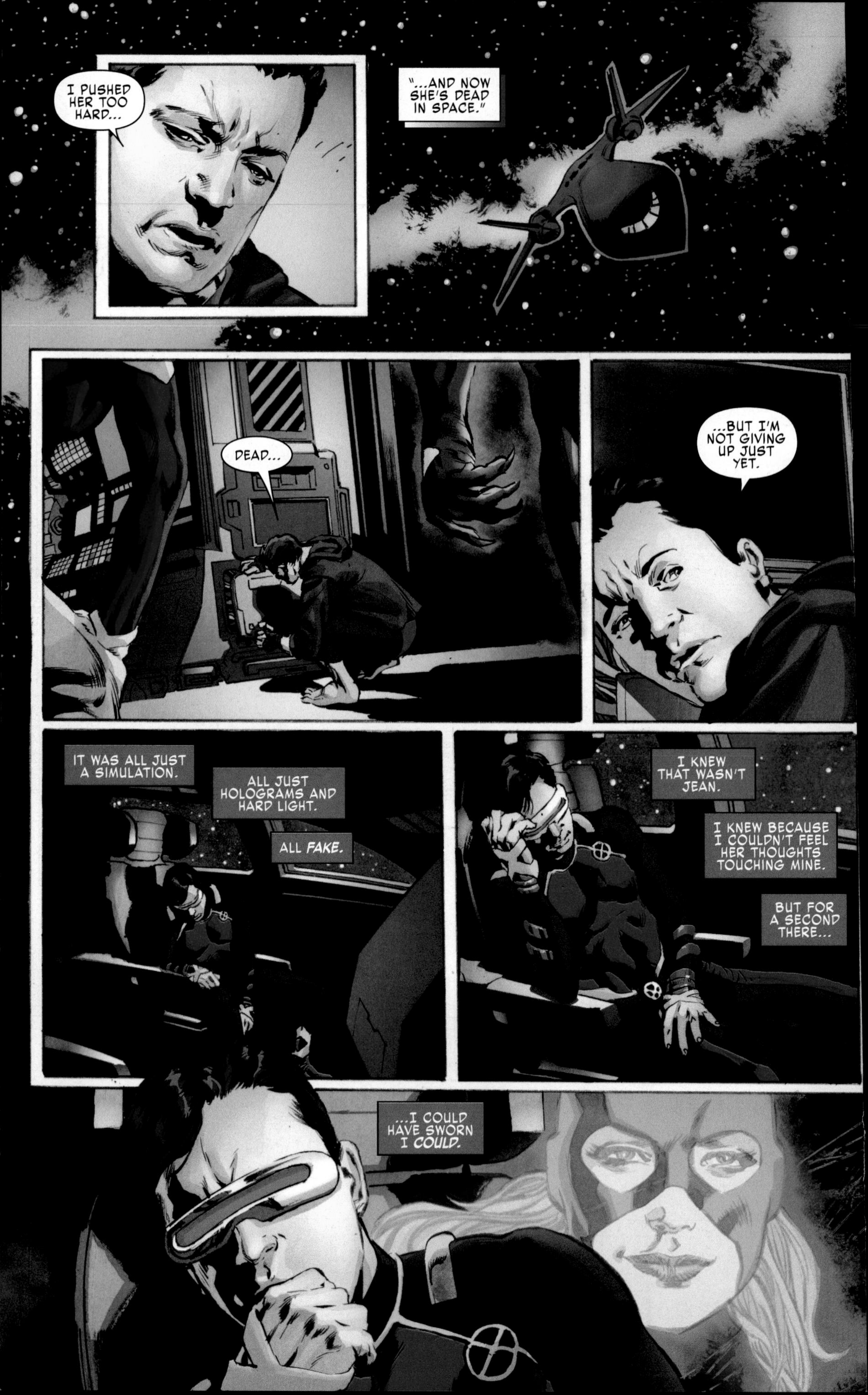

I PUSHED HER TOO HARD...
"...AND NOW SHE'S DEAD IN SPACE."
DEAD...
...BUT I'M NOT GIVING UP JUST YET.
IT WAS ALL JUST A SIMULATION.
ALL JUST HOLOGRAMS AND HARD LIGHT.
ALL FAKE.
I KNEW THAT WASN'T JEAN.
I KNEW BECAUSE I COULDN'T FEEL HER THOUGHTS TOUCHING MINE.
BUT FOR A SECOND THERE...
...I COULD HAVE SWORN I COULD.

26

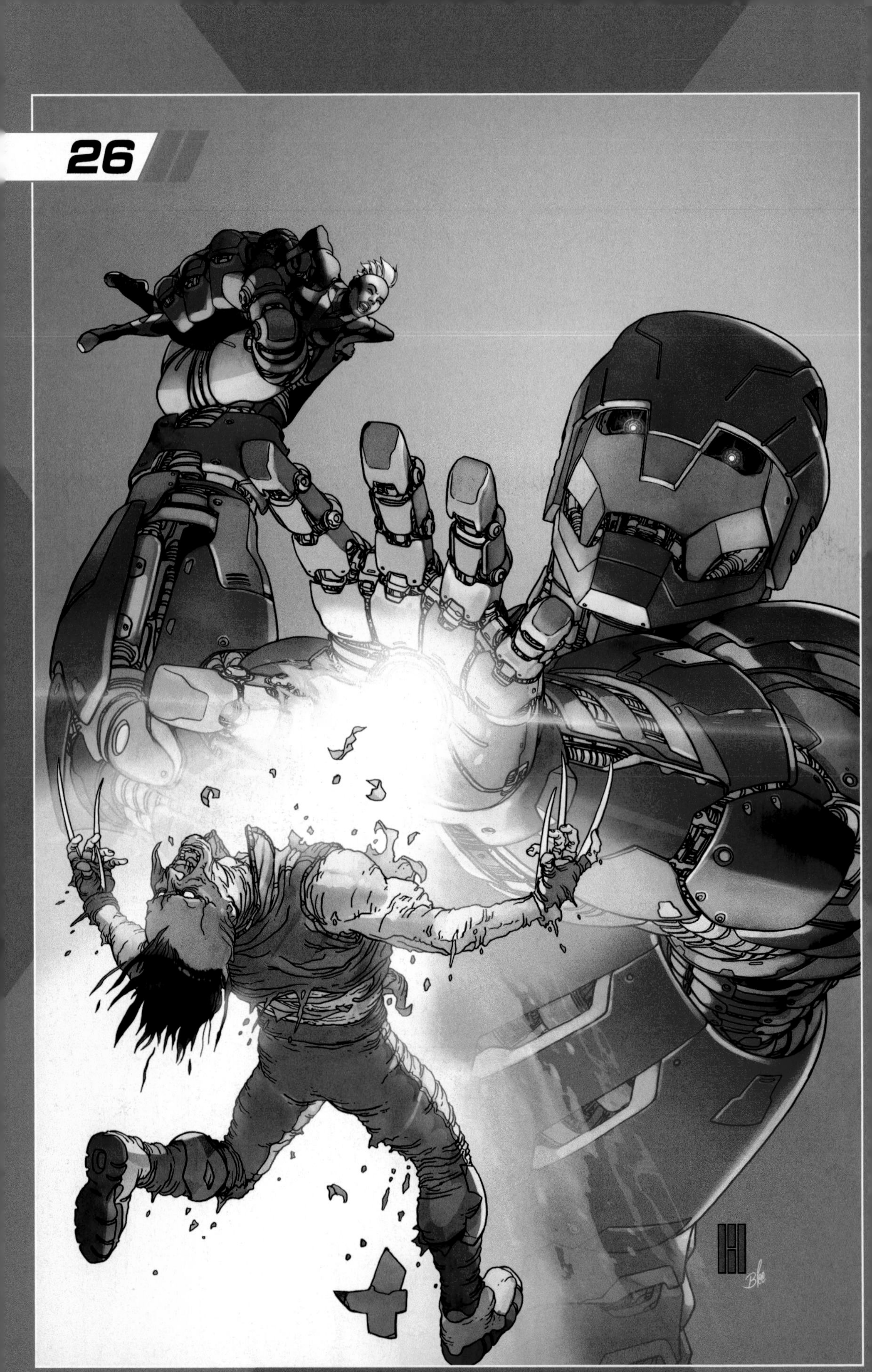

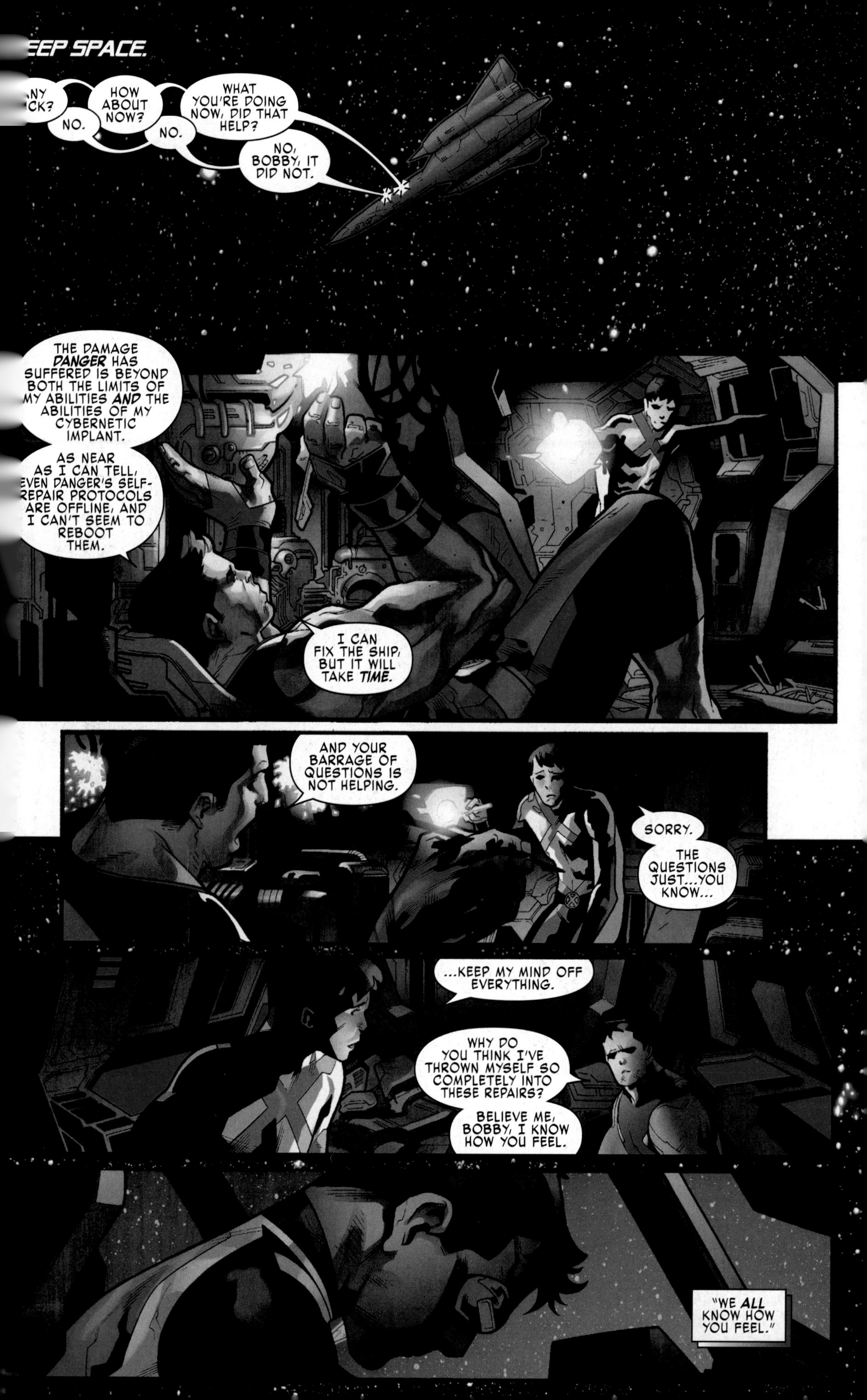

EEP SPACE.
...NY ...CK?
NO.
HOW ABOUT NOW?
NO.
WHAT YOU'RE DOING NOW, DID THAT HELP?
NO, BOBBY, IT DID NOT.
THE DAMAGE DANGER HAS SUFFERED IS BEYOND BOTH THE LIMITS OF MY ABILITIES AND THE ABILITIES OF MY CYBERNETIC IMPLANT.
AS NEAR AS I CAN TELL, EVEN DANGER'S SELF-REPAIR PROTOCOLS ARE OFFLINE, AND I CAN'T SEEM TO REBOOT THEM.
I CAN FIX THE SHIP, BUT IT WILL TAKE TIME.
AND YOUR BARRAGE OF QUESTIONS IS NOT HELPING.
SORRY.
THE QUESTIONS JUST...YOU KNOW...
...KEEP MY MIND OFF EVERYTHING.
WHY DO YOU THINK I'VE THROWN MYSELF SO COMPLETELY INTO THESE REPAIRS?
BELIEVE ME, BOBBY, I KNOW HOW YOU FEEL.
"WE ALL KNOW HOW YOU FEEL."

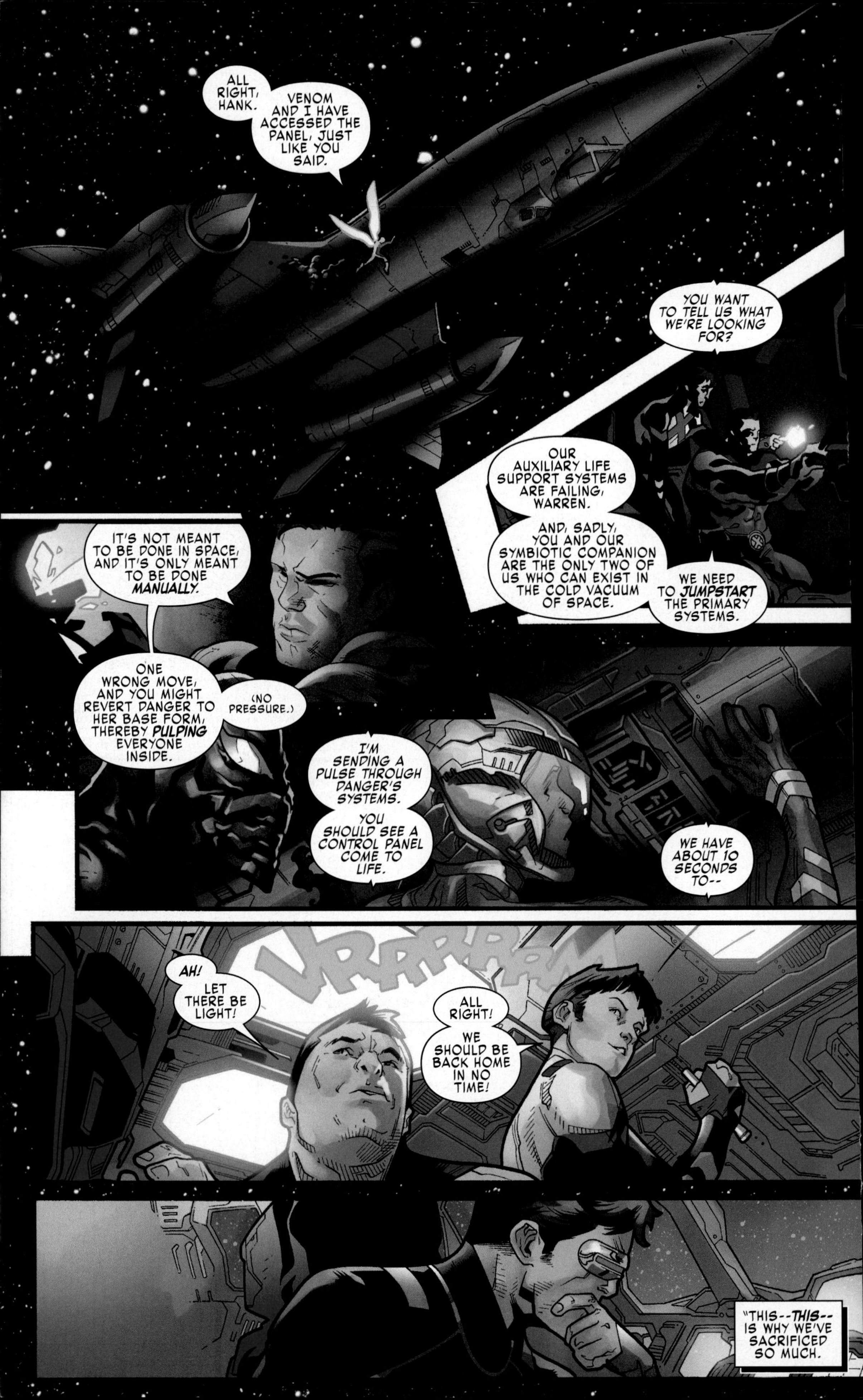
ALL RIGHT, HANK.
VENOM AND I HAVE ACCESSED THE PANEL, JUST LIKE YOU SAID.
YOU WANT TO TELL US WHAT WE'RE LOOKING FOR?
OUR AUXILIARY LIFE SUPPORT SYSTEMS ARE FAILING, WARREN.
AND, SADLY, YOU AND OUR SYMBIOTIC COMPANION ARE THE ONLY TWO OF US WHO CAN EXIST IN THE COLD VACUUM OF SPACE.
WE NEED TO JUMPSTART THE PRIMARY SYSTEMS.
IT'S NOT MEANT TO BE DONE IN SPACE, AND IT'S ONLY MEANT TO BE DONE MANUALLY.
ONE WRONG MOVE, AND YOU MIGHT REVERT DANGER TO HER BASE FORM, THEREBY PULPING EVERYONE INSIDE.
(NO PRESSURE.)
I'M SENDING A PULSE THROUGH DANGER'S SYSTEMS.
YOU SHOULD SEE A CONTROL PANEL COME TO LIFE.
WE HAVE ABOUT 10 SECONDS TO--
VRRRRRM
AH! LET THERE BE LIGHT!
ALL RIGHT!
WE SHOULD BE BACK HOME IN NO TIME!
"THIS--THIS-- IS WHY WE'VE SACRIFICED SO MUCH.

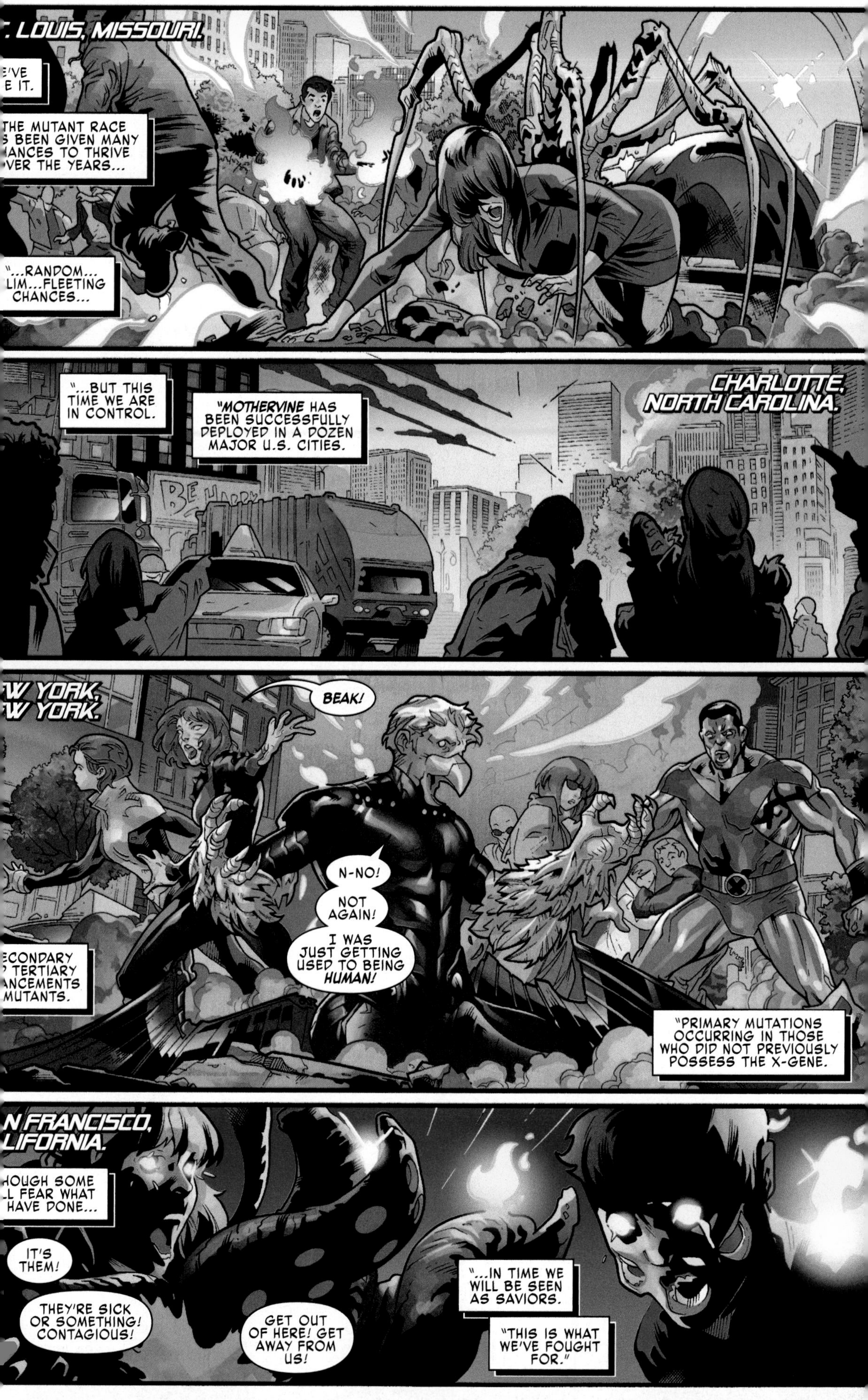

. LOUIS, MISSOURI.
E'VE E IT.
THE MUTANT RACE S BEEN GIVEN MANY IANCES TO THRIVE VER THE YEARS...
"...RANDOM... LIM...FLEETING CHANCES...
"...BUT THIS TIME WE ARE IN CONTROL.
"MOTHERVINE HAS BEEN SUCCESSFULLY DEPLOYED IN A DOZEN MAJOR U.S. CITIES.
CHARLOTTE, NORTH CAROLINA.
W YORK, W YORK.
BEAK!
N-NO!
NOT AGAIN!
I WAS JUST GETTING USED TO BEING HUMAN!
ECONDARY TERTIARY ANCEMENTS MUTANTS.
"PRIMARY MUTATIONS OCCURRING IN THOSE WHO DID NOT PREVIOUSLY POSSESS THE X-GENE.
N FRANCISCO, LIFORNIA.
HOUGH SOME L FEAR WHAT HAVE DONE...
IT'S THEM!
THEY'RE SICK OR SOMETHING! CONTAGIOUS!
GET OUT OF HERE! GET AWAY FROM US!
"...IN TIME WE WILL BE SEEN AS SAVIORS.
"THIS IS WHAT WE'VE FOUGHT FOR."

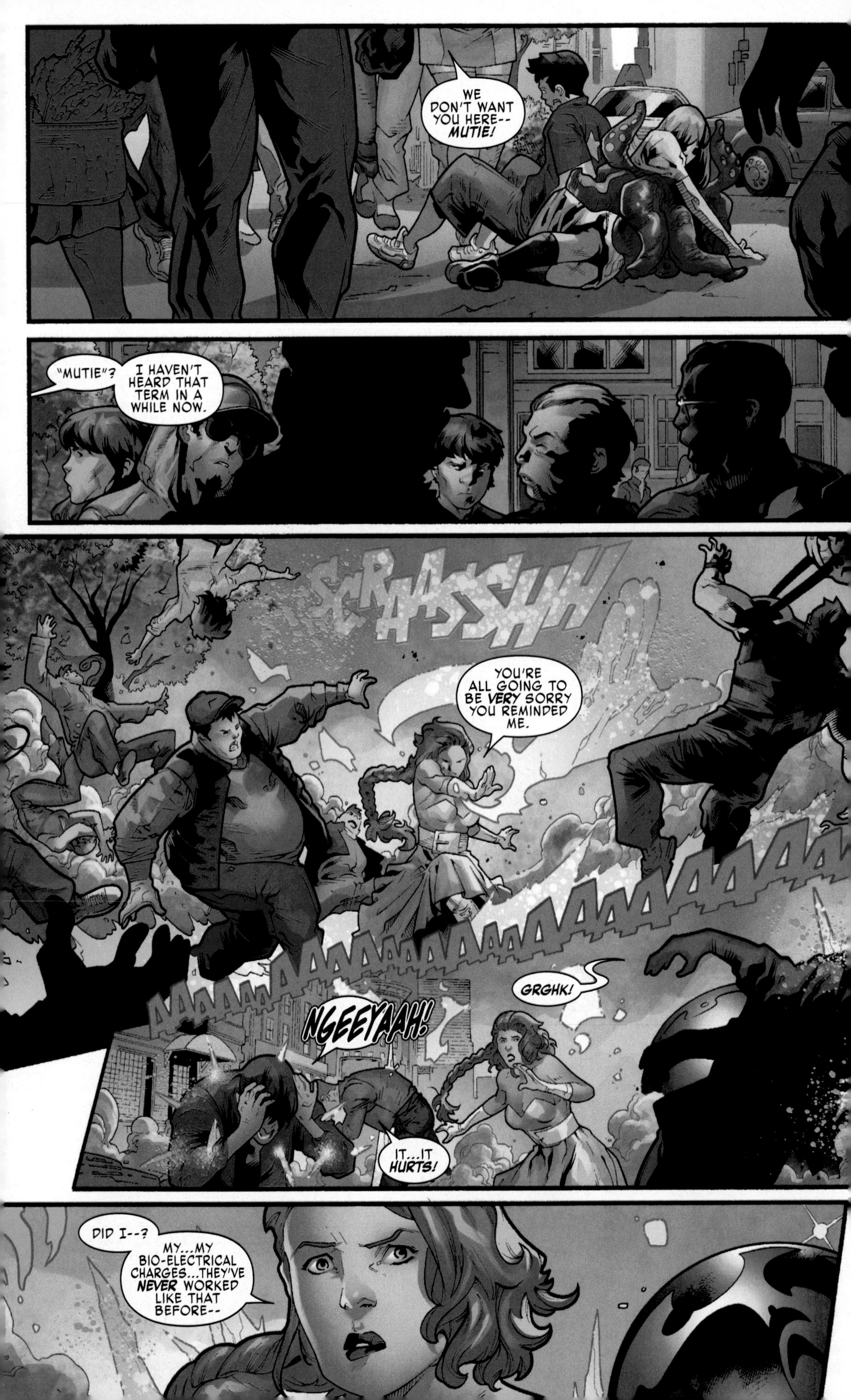

WE DON'T WANT YOU HERE-- MUTIE!
"MUTIE"?
I HAVEN'T HEARD THAT TERM IN A WHILE NOW.
SCRAASHH
YOU'RE ALL GOING TO BE VERY SORRY YOU REMINDED ME.
AAAAAAAAAAAAAAAAAAAAAAAAAAAAAAAAAAAA
NGEEYAAH!
GRGHK!
IT...IT HURTS!
DID I--?
MY...MY BIO-ELECTRICAL CHARGES...THEY'VE NEVER WORKED LIKE THAT BEFORE--

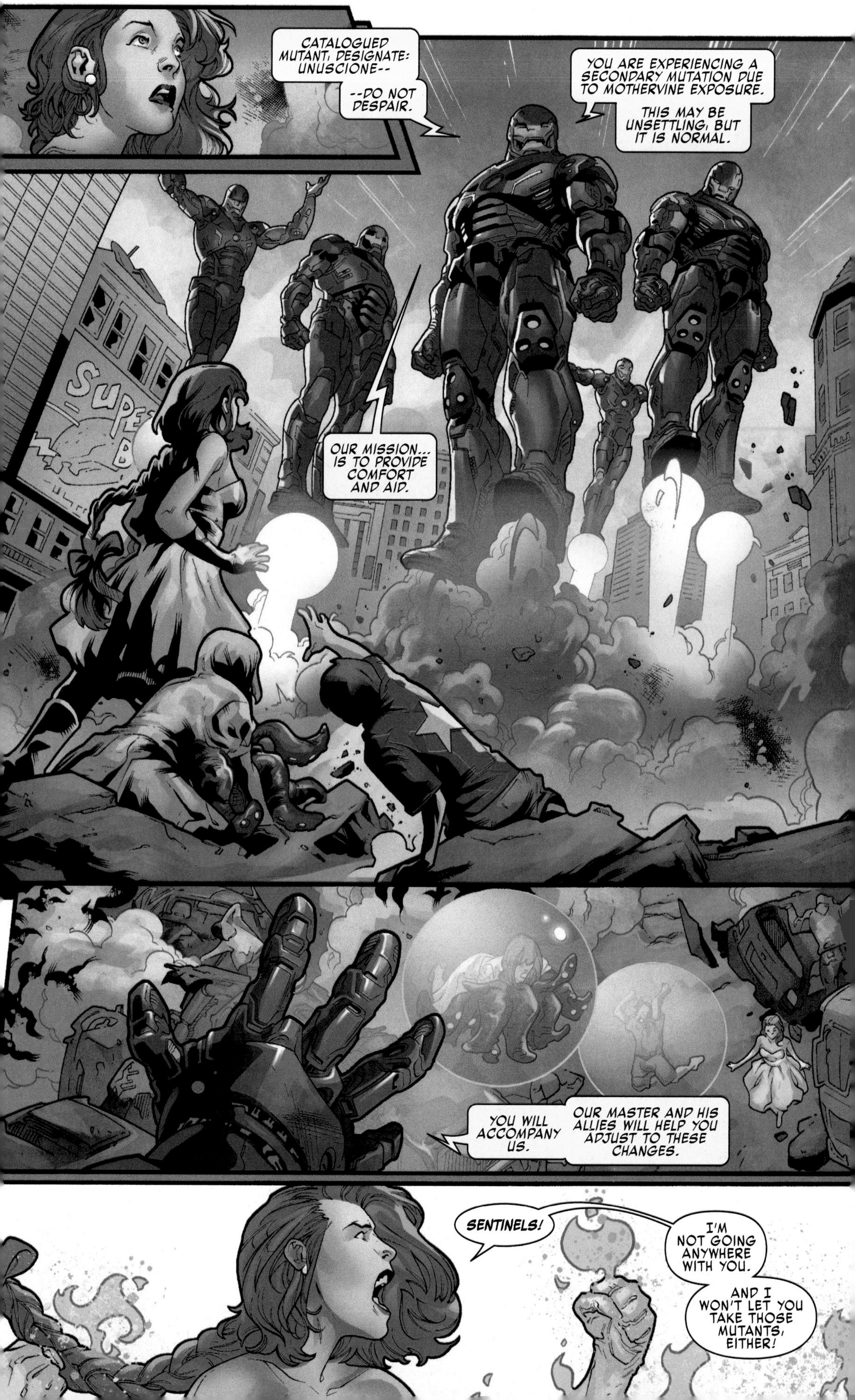

CATALOGUED MUTANT, DESIGNATE: UNUSCIONE--
--DO NOT DESPAIR.
YOU ARE EXPERIENCING A SECONDARY MUTATION DUE TO MOTHERVINE EXPOSURE.
THIS MAY BE UNSETTLING, BUT IT IS NORMAL.
OUR MISSION... IS TO PROVIDE COMFORT AND AID.
YOU WILL ACCOMPANY US.
OUR MASTER AND HIS ALLIES WILL HELP YOU ADJUST TO THESE CHANGES.
SENTINELS!
I'M NOT GOING ANYWHERE WITH YOU.
AND I WON'T LET YOU TAKE THOSE MUTANTS, EITHER!

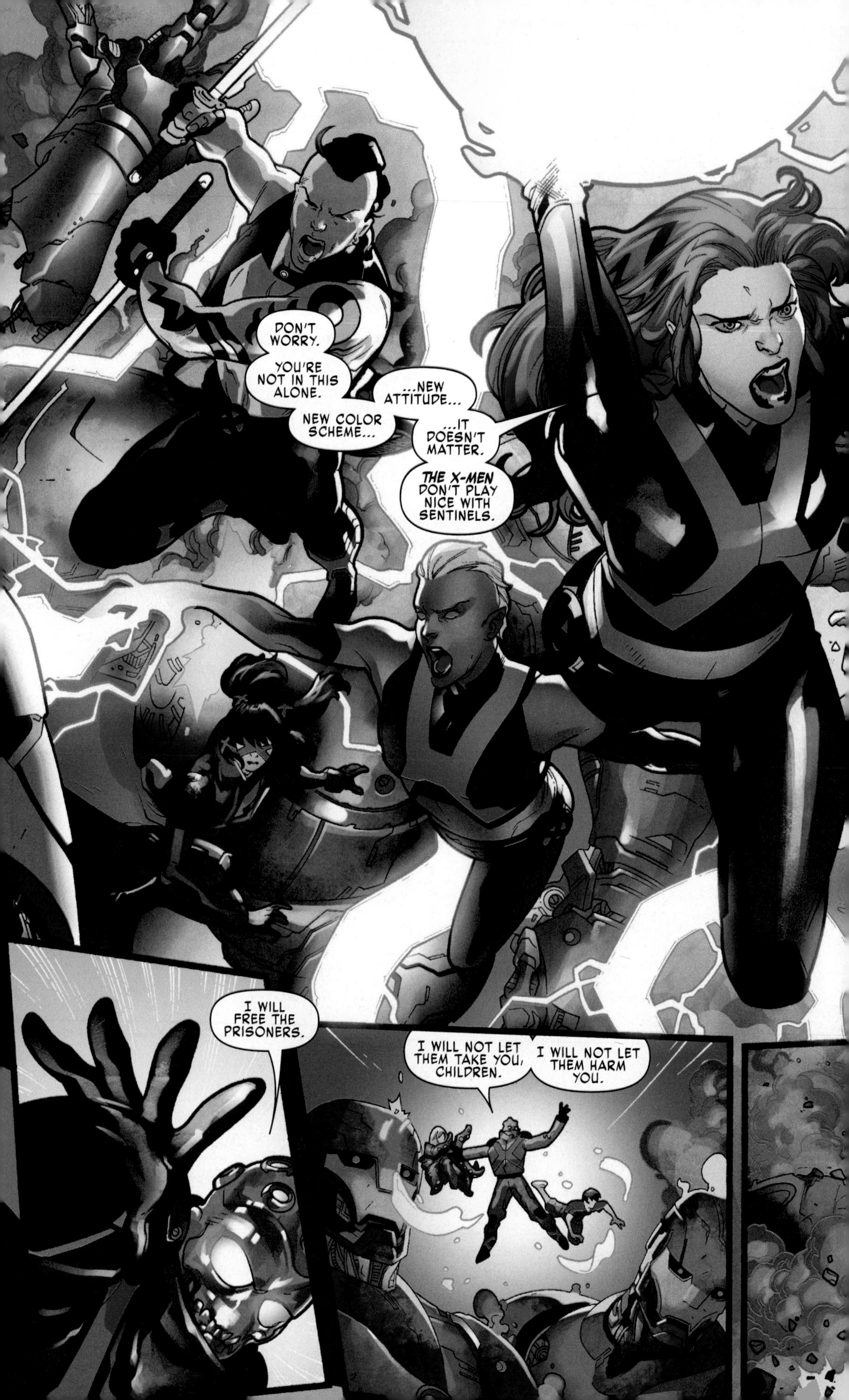
DON'T WORRY.
YOU'RE NOT IN THIS ALONE.
NEW COLOR SCHEME...
...NEW ATTITUDE...
...IT DOESN'T MATTER.
THE X-MEN DON'T PLAY NICE WITH SENTINELS.
I WILL FREE THE PRISONERS.
I WILL NOT LET THEM TAKE YOU, CHILDREN.
I WILL NOT LET THEM HARM YOU.

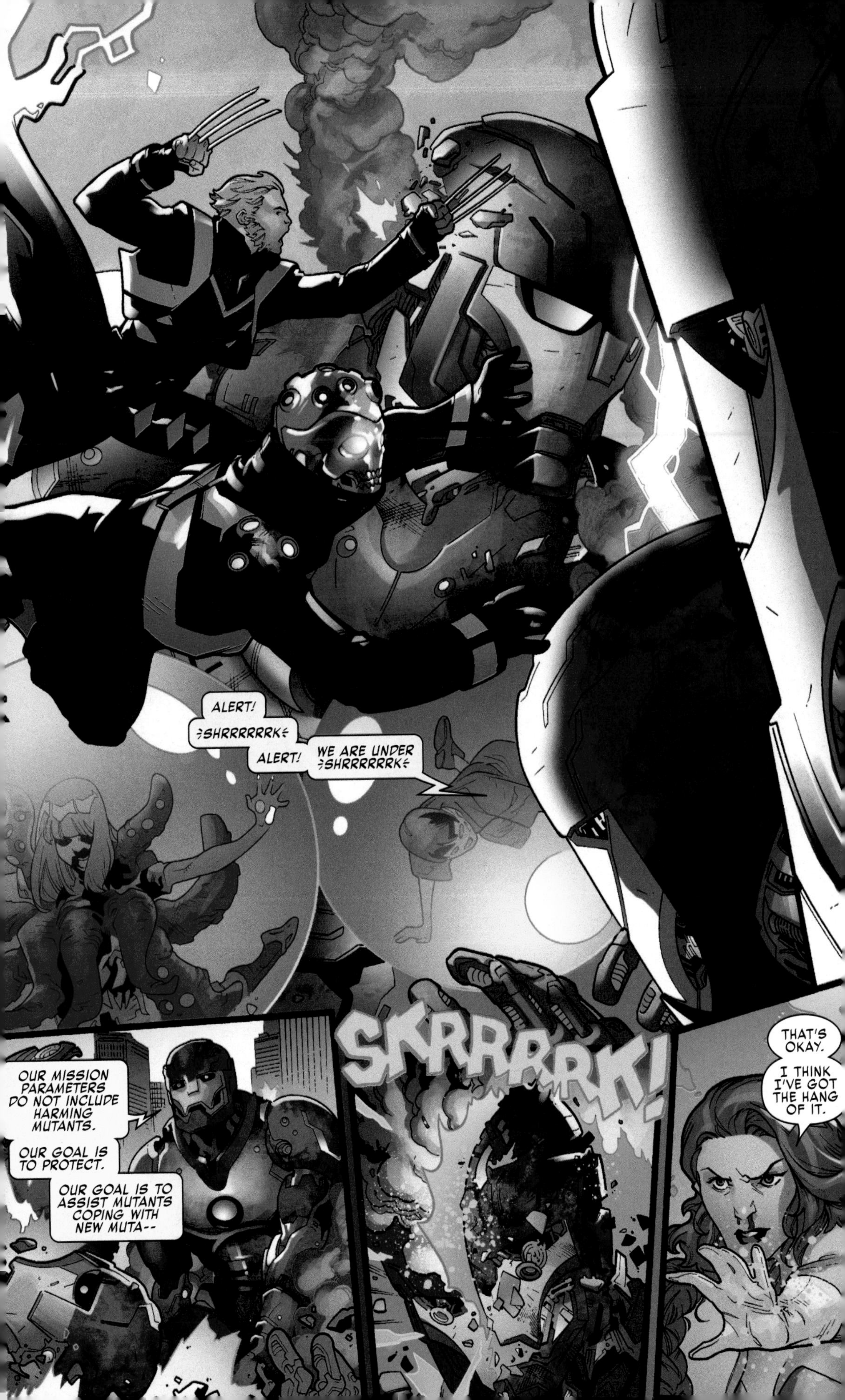

ALERT!
⇒SHRRRRRRK⇐
ALERT!
WE ARE UNDER ⇒SHRRRRRRK⇐
OUR MISSION PARAMETERS DO NOT INCLUDE HARMING MUTANTS.
OUR GOAL IS TO PROTECT.
OUR GOAL IS TO ASSIST MUTANTS COPING WITH NEW MUTA--
SKRRRRK!
THAT'S OKAY.
I THINK I'VE GOT THE HANG OF IT.

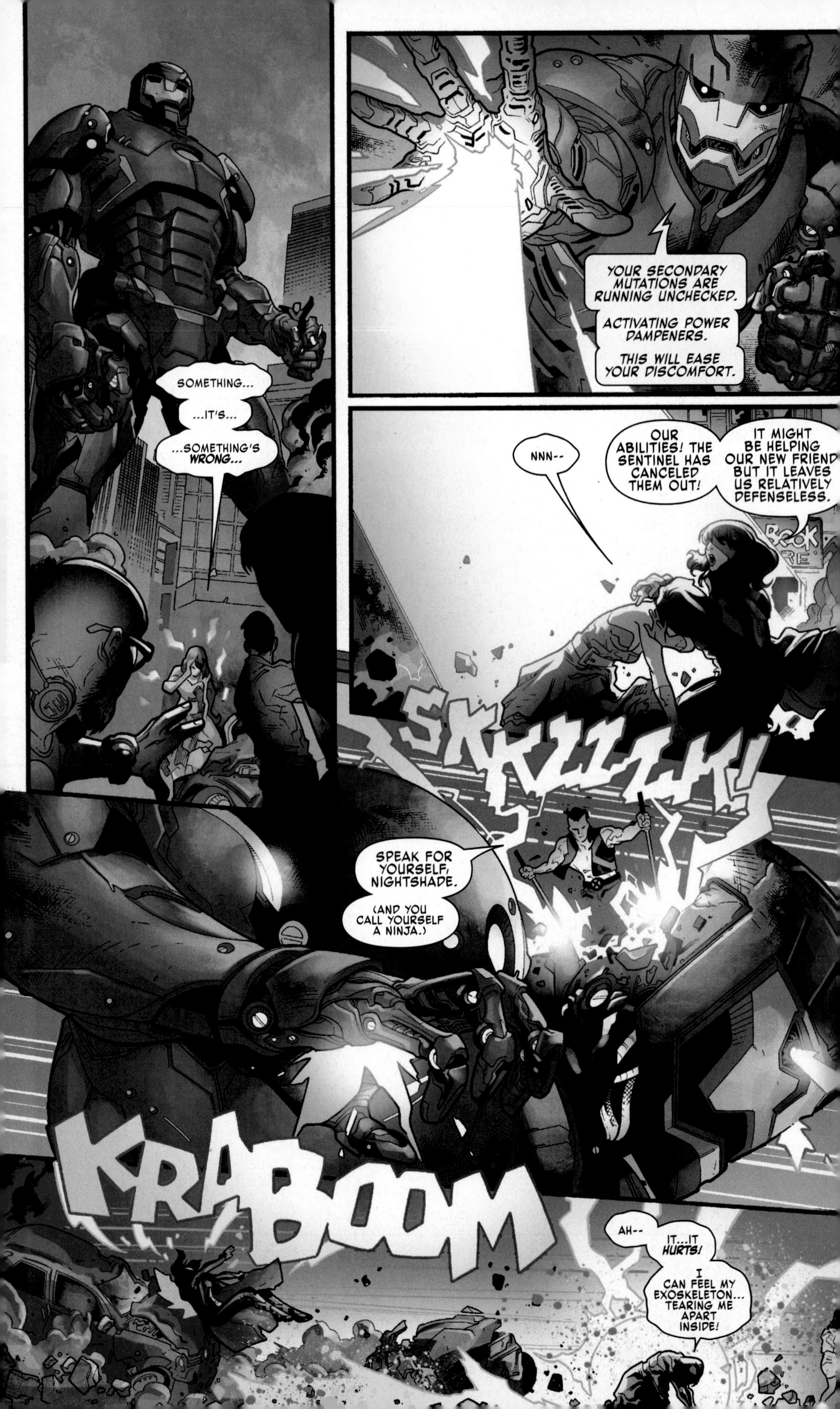
SOMETHING...
...IT'S...
...SOMETHING'S WRONG...
YOUR SECONDARY MUTATIONS ARE RUNNING UNCHECKED.
ACTIVATING POWER DAMPENERS.
THIS WILL EASE YOUR DISCOMFORT.
NNN--
OUR ABILITIES! THE SENTINEL HAS CANCELED THEM OUT!
IT MIGHT BE HELPING OUR NEW FRIEND BUT IT LEAVES US RELATIVELY DEFENSELESS.
SKLLLK!
SPEAK FOR YOURSELF, NIGHTSHADE.
(AND YOU CALL YOURSELF A NINJA.)
KRABOOM
AH--
IT...IT HURTS!
I CAN FEEL MY EXOSKELETON... TEARING ME APART INSIDE!

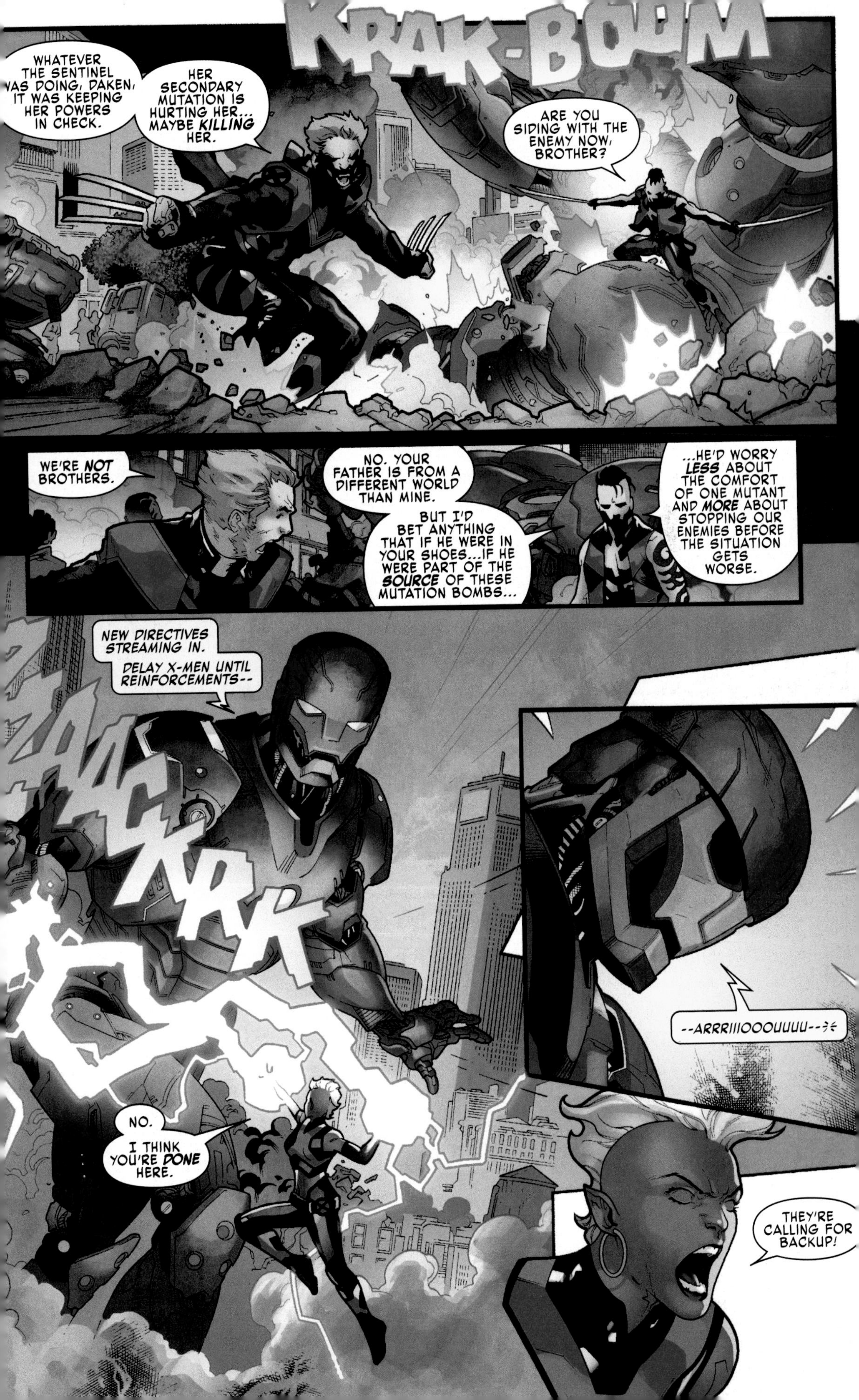
KRAK-BOOM
WHATEVER THE SENTINEL WAS DOING, DAKEN, IT WAS KEEPING HER POWERS IN CHECK.
HER SECONDARY MUTATION IS HURTING HER... MAYBE KILLING HER.
ARE YOU SIDING WITH THE ENEMY NOW, BROTHER?
WE'RE NOT BROTHERS.
NO. YOUR FATHER IS FROM A DIFFERENT WORLD THAN MINE.
BUT I'D BET ANYTHING THAT IF HE WERE IN YOUR SHOES...IF HE WERE PART OF THE SOURCE OF THESE MUTATION BOMBS...
...HE'D WORRY LESS ABOUT THE COMFORT OF ONE MUTANT AND MORE ABOUT STOPPING OUR ENEMIES BEFORE THE SITUATION GETS WORSE.
NEW DIRECTIVES STREAMING IN.
DELAY X-MEN UNTIL REINFORCEMENTS--
ZACKRK
--ARRRIIIOOOUUUU--
NO.
I THINK YOU'RE DONE HERE.
THEY'RE CALLING FOR BACKUP!

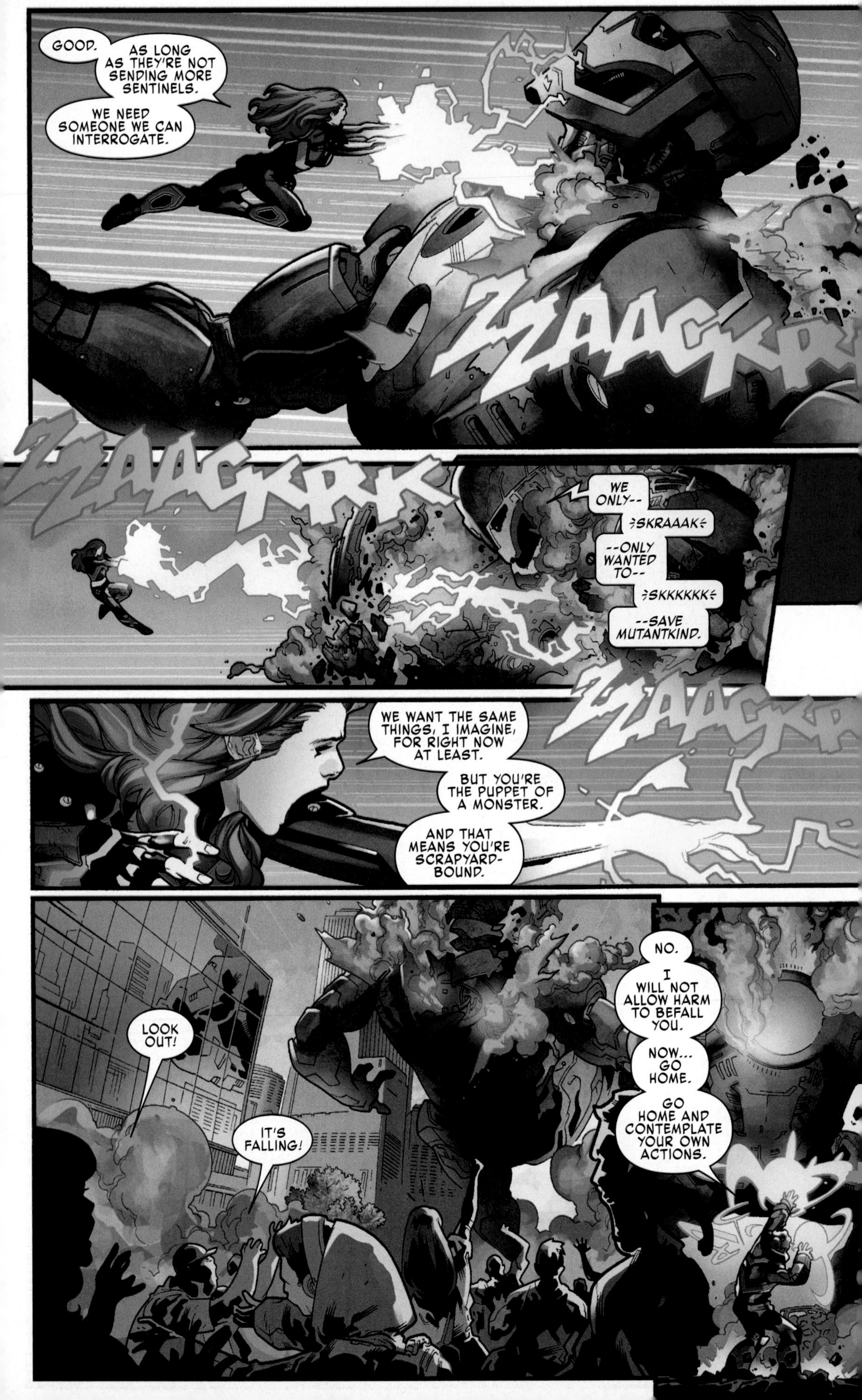
GOOD.
AS LONG AS THEY'RE NOT SENDING MORE SENTINELS.
WE NEED SOMEONE WE CAN INTERROGATE.
ZZAACKR
ZZAACKRK
WE ONLY--
SKRAAAK
--ONLY WANTED TO--
SKKKKKK
--SAVE MUTANTKIND.
ZZAACKR
WE WANT THE SAME THINGS, I IMAGINE, FOR RIGHT NOW AT LEAST.
BUT YOU'RE THE PUPPET OF A MONSTER.
AND THAT MEANS YOU'RE SCRAPYARD-BOUND.
LOOK OUT!
IT'S FALLING!
NO.
I WILL NOT ALLOW HARM TO BEFALL YOU.
NOW... GO HOME.
GO HOME AND CONTEMPLATE YOUR OWN ACTIONS.

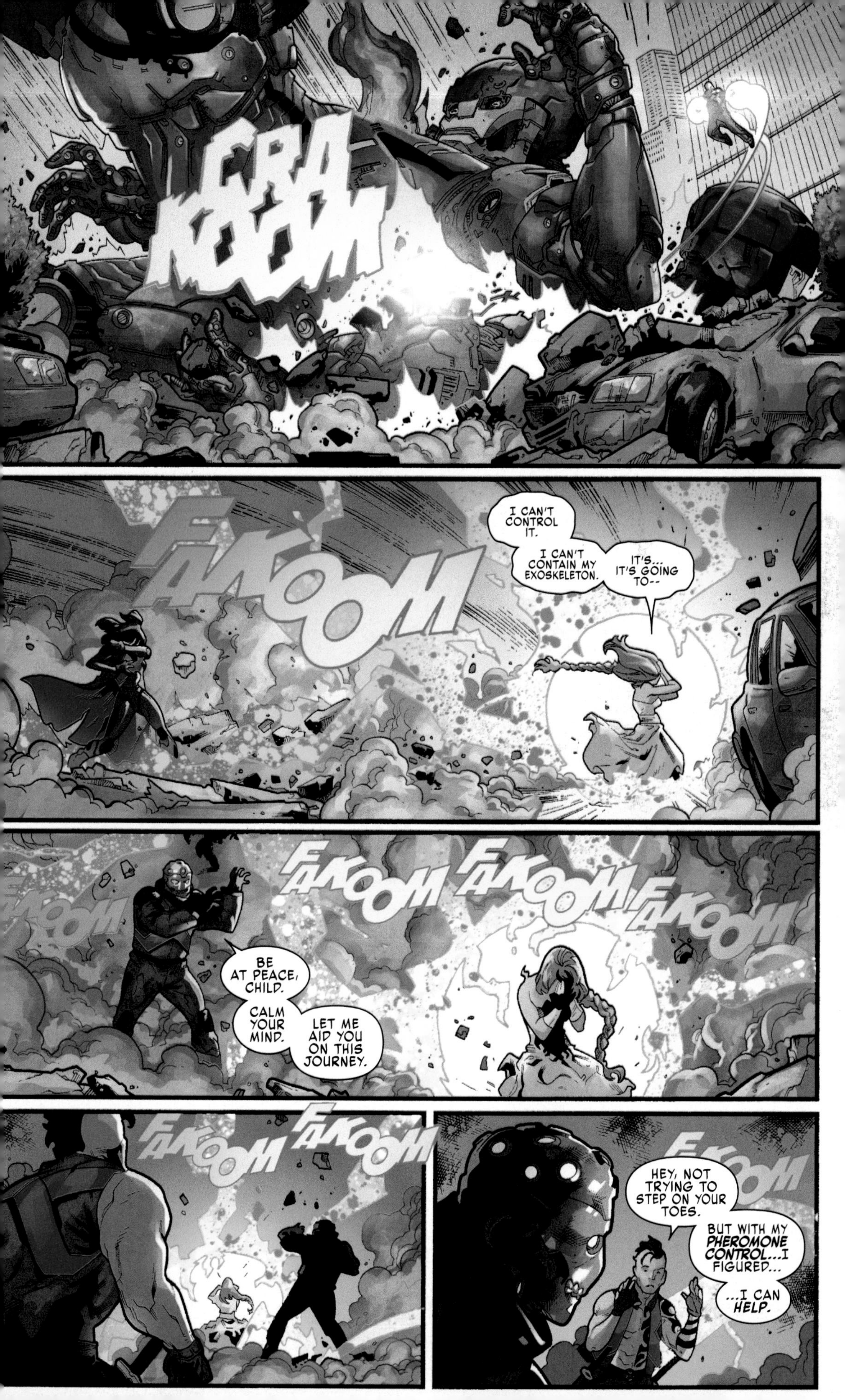
CRA KOOM
FAKOOM
I CAN'T CONTROL IT.
I CAN'T CONTAIN MY EXOSKELETON.
IT'S... IT'S GOING TO--
FAKOOM FAKOOM FAKOOM
BE AT PEACE, CHILD.
CALM YOUR MIND.
LET ME AID YOU ON THIS JOURNEY.
FAKOOM FAKOOM
HEY, NOT TRYING TO STEP ON YOUR TOES.
BUT WITH MY *PHEROMONE CONTROL*...I FIGURED...
...I CAN *HELP.*

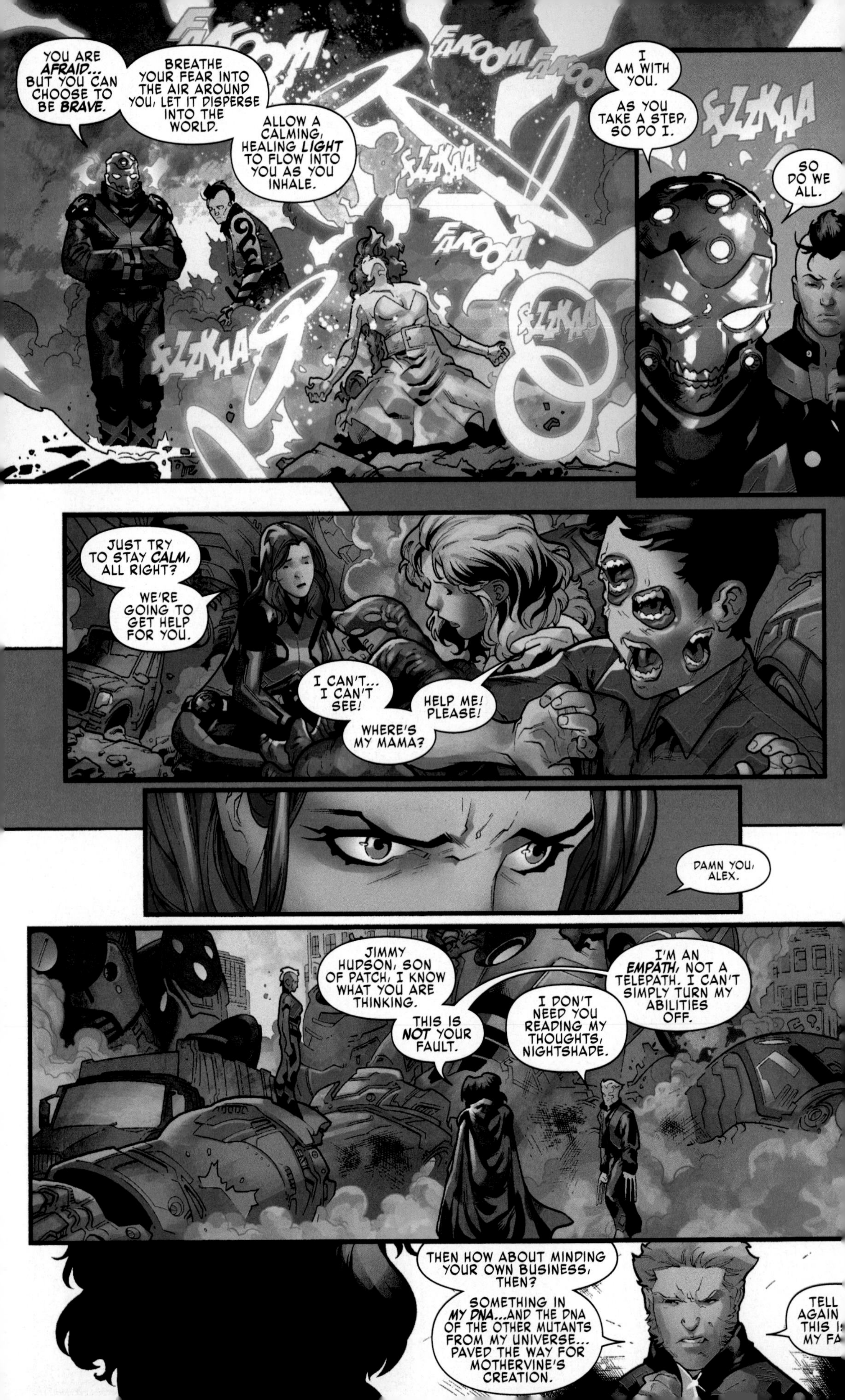

FAKOOM
YOU ARE AFRAID... BUT YOU CAN CHOOSE TO BE BRAVE.
BREATHE YOUR FEAR INTO THE AIR AROUND YOU, LET IT DISPERSE INTO THE WORLD.
FAKOOM FAKOOM
ALLOW A CALMING, HEALING LIGHT TO FLOW INTO YOU AS YOU INHALE.
SZZKAA
FAKOOM
SZZKAA
SZZKAA
I AM WITH YOU.
AS YOU TAKE A STEP, SO DO I.
SZZKAA
SO DO WE ALL.
JUST TRY TO STAY CALM, ALL RIGHT?
WE'RE GOING TO GET HELP FOR YOU.
I CAN'T... I CAN'T SEE!
HELP ME! PLEASE!
WHERE'S MY MAMA?
DAMN YOU, ALEX.
JIMMY HUDSON, SON OF PATCH, I KNOW WHAT YOU ARE THINKING.
THIS IS NOT YOUR FAULT.
I DON'T NEED YOU READING MY THOUGHTS, NIGHTSHADE.
I'M AN EMPATH, NOT A TELEPATH. I CAN'T SIMPLY TURN MY ABILITIES OFF.
THEN HOW ABOUT MINDING YOUR OWN BUSINESS, THEN?
SOMETHING IN MY DNA...AND THE DNA OF THE OTHER MUTANTS FROM MY UNIVERSE... PAVED THE WAY FOR MOTHERVINE'S CREATION.

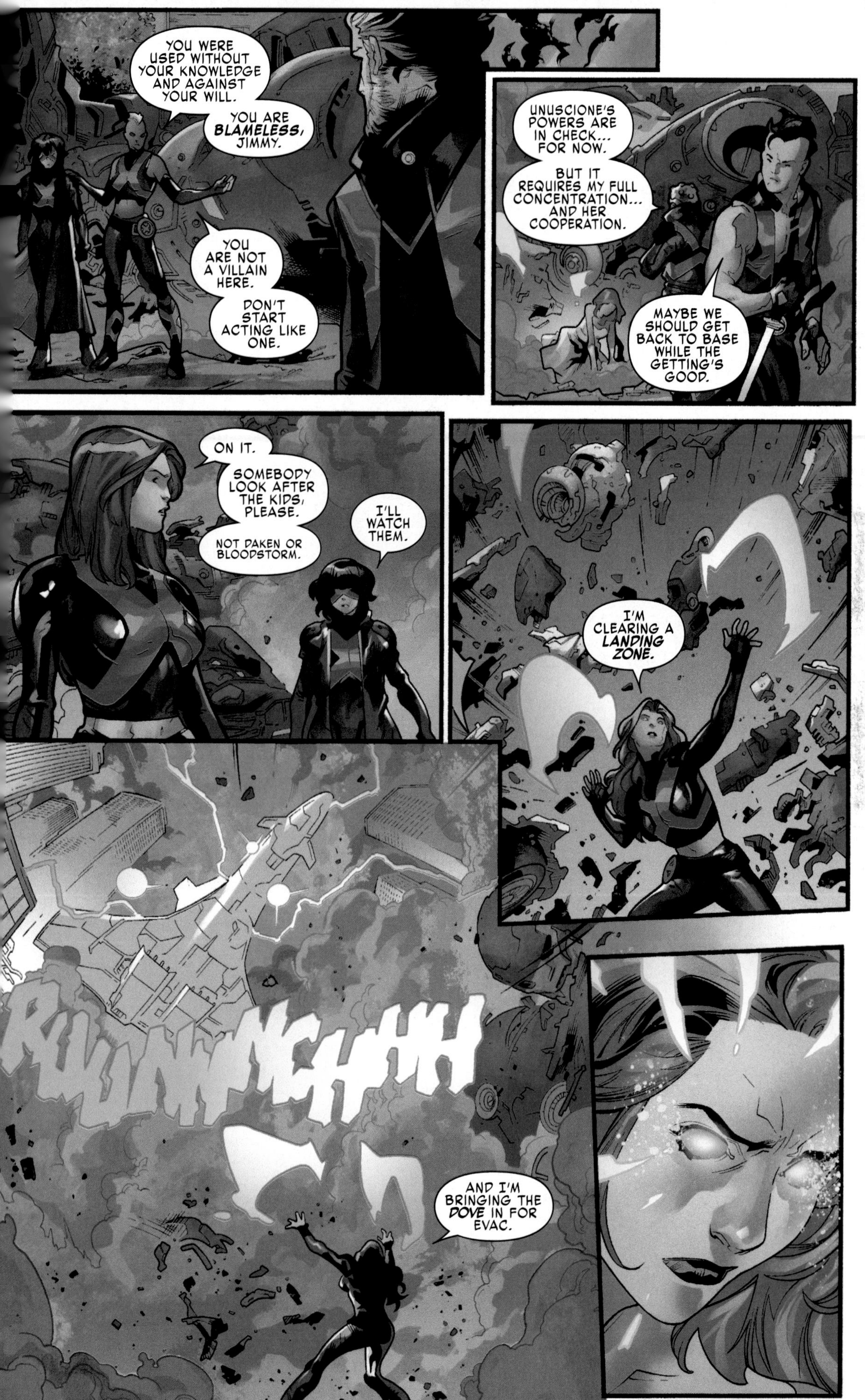
YOU WERE USED WITHOUT YOUR KNOWLEDGE AND AGAINST YOUR WILL.
YOU ARE BLAMELESS, JIMMY.
YOU ARE NOT A VILLAIN HERE.
DON'T START ACTING LIKE ONE.
UNUSCIONE'S POWERS ARE IN CHECK... FOR NOW.
BUT IT REQUIRES MY FULL CONCENTRATION... AND HER COOPERATION.
MAYBE WE SHOULD GET BACK TO BASE WHILE THE GETTING'S GOOD.
ON IT.
SOMEBODY LOOK AFTER THE KIDS, PLEASE.
NOT DAKEN OR BLOODSTORM.
I'LL WATCH THEM.
I'M CLEARING A LANDING ZONE.
RUUMMCHHH
AND I'M BRINGING THE DOVE IN FOR EVAC.

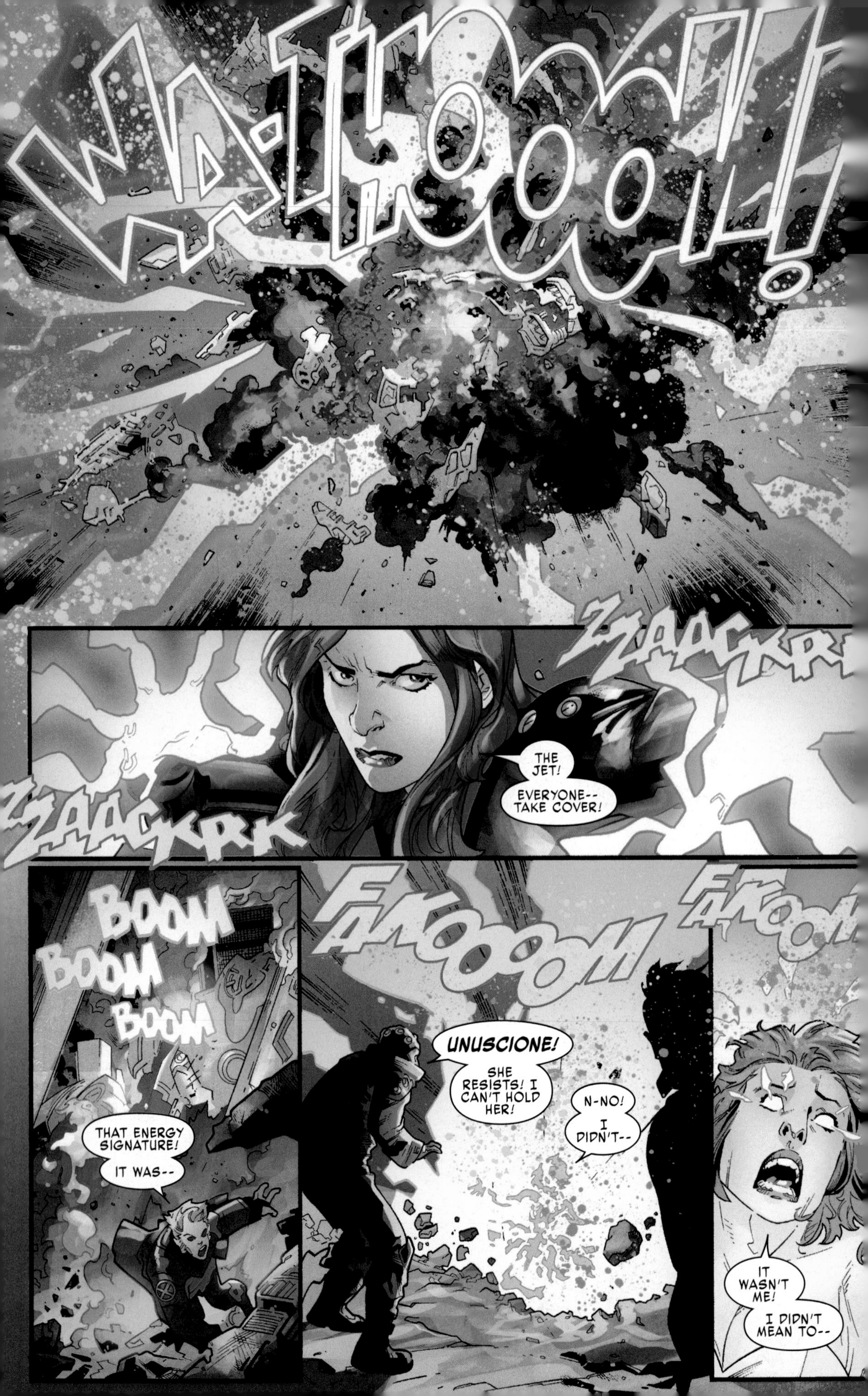

THE JET!
EVERYONE-- TAKE COVER!
BOOM BOOM BOOM
THAT ENERGY SIGNATURE!
IT WAS--
UNUSCIONE!
SHE RESISTS! I CAN'T HOLD HER!
N-NO! I DIDN'T--
IT WASN'T ME!
I DIDN'T MEAN TO--

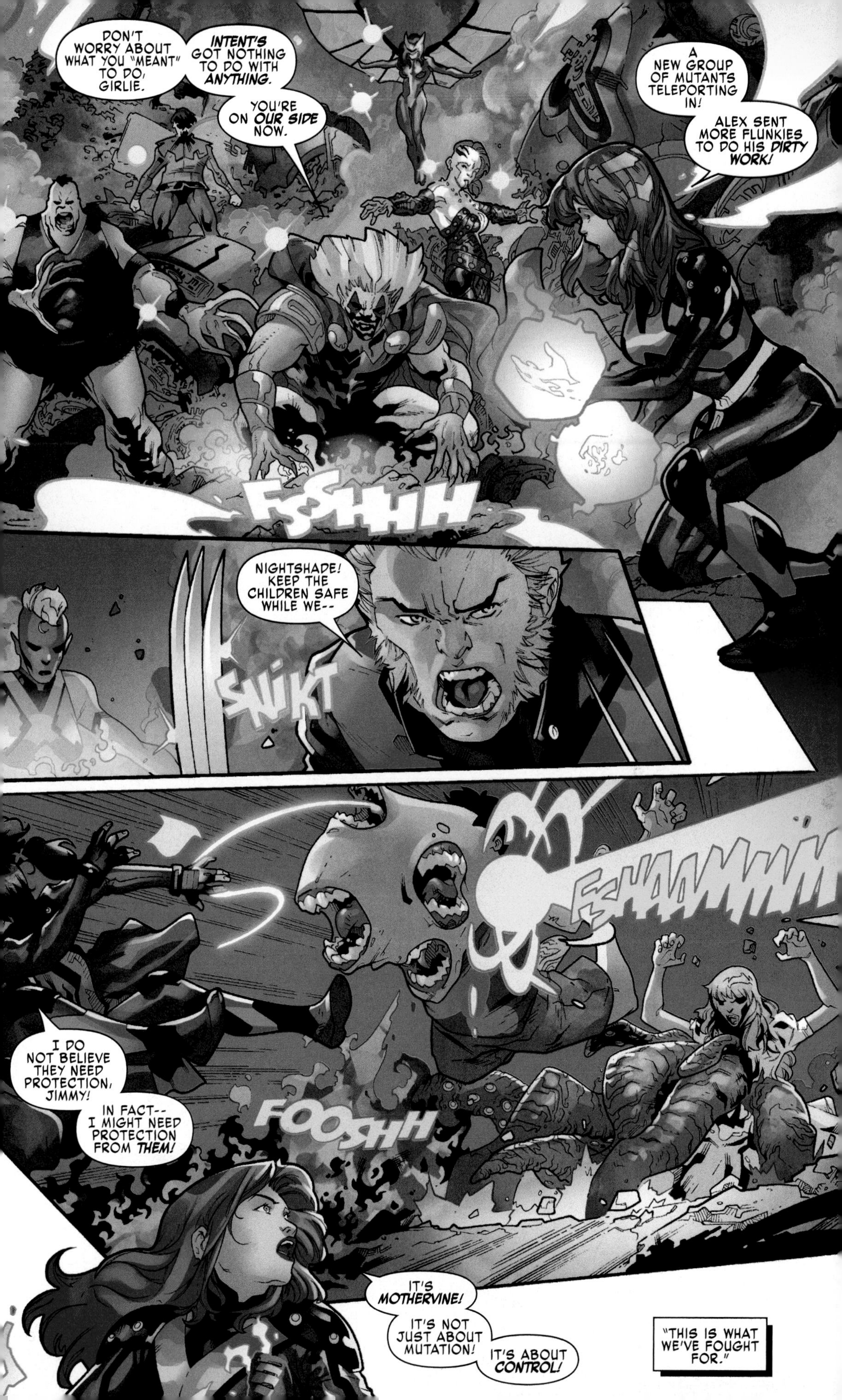

DON'T WORRY ABOUT WHAT YOU "MEANT" TO DO, GIRLIE.
INTENT'S GOT NOTHING TO DO WITH ANYTHING.
YOU'RE ON OUR SIDE NOW.
A NEW GROUP OF MUTANTS TELEPORTING IN!
ALEX SENT MORE FLUNKIES TO DO HIS DIRTY WORK!
FSSHHH
NIGHTSHADE! KEEP THE CHILDREN SAFE WHILE WE--
SNIKT
FSHAAAMMM
I DO NOT BELIEVE THEY NEED PROTECTION, JIMMY!
IN FACT-- I MIGHT NEED PROTECTION FROM THEM!
FOOSHH
IT'S MOTHERVINE!
IT'S NOT JUST ABOUT MUTATION!
IT'S ABOUT CONTROL!
"THIS IS WHAT WE'VE FOUGHT FOR."

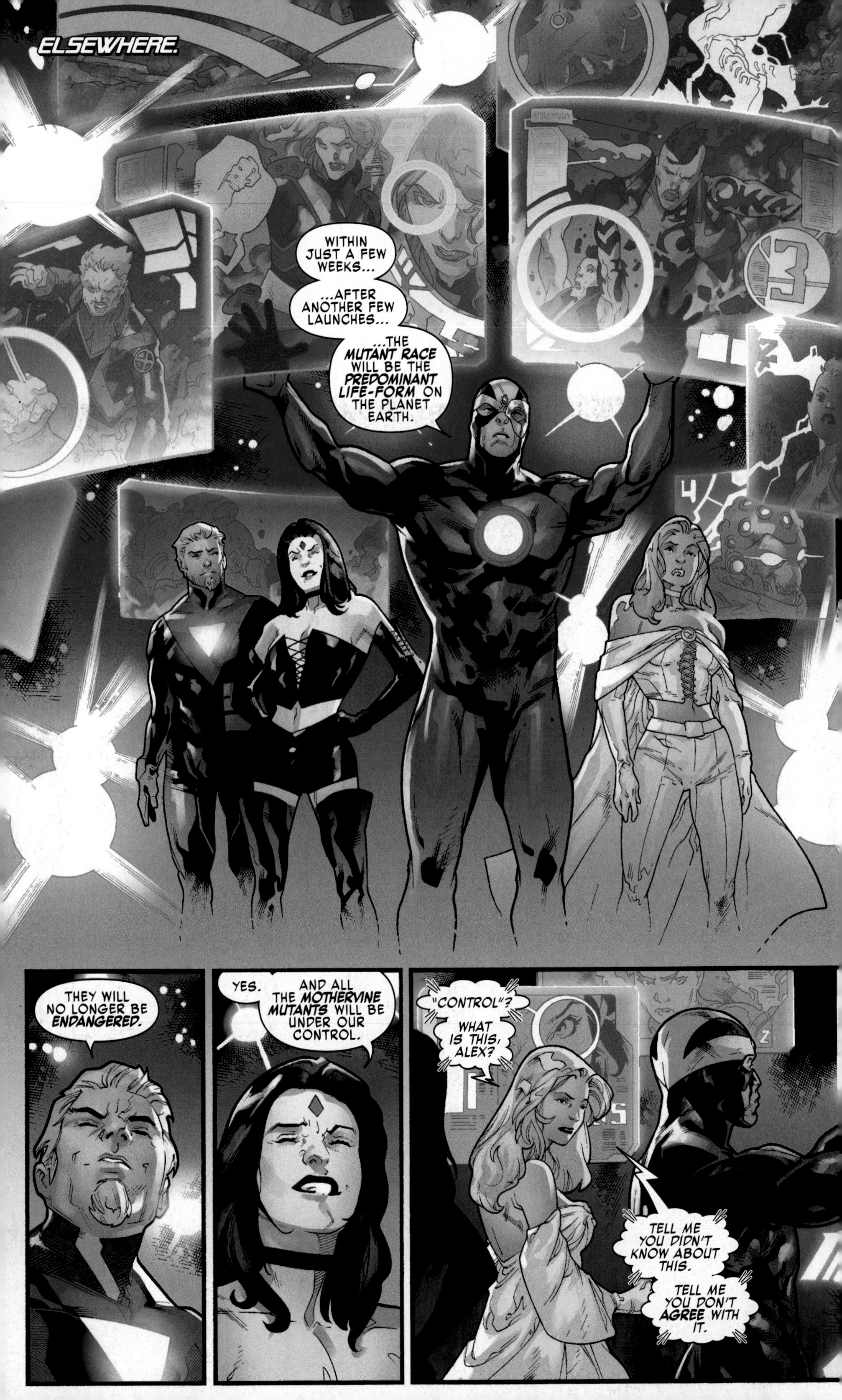

ELSEWHERE.
WITHIN JUST A FEW WEEKS...
...AFTER ANOTHER FEW LAUNCHES...
...THE MUTANT RACE WILL BE THE PREDOMINANT LIFE-FORM ON THE PLANET EARTH.
THEY WILL NO LONGER BE ENDANGERED.
YES.
AND ALL THE MOTHERVINE MUTANTS WILL BE UNDER OUR CONTROL.
"CONTROL"?
WHAT IS THIS, ALEX?
TELL ME YOU DIDN'T KNOW ABOUT THIS.
TELL ME YOU DON'T AGREE WITH IT.

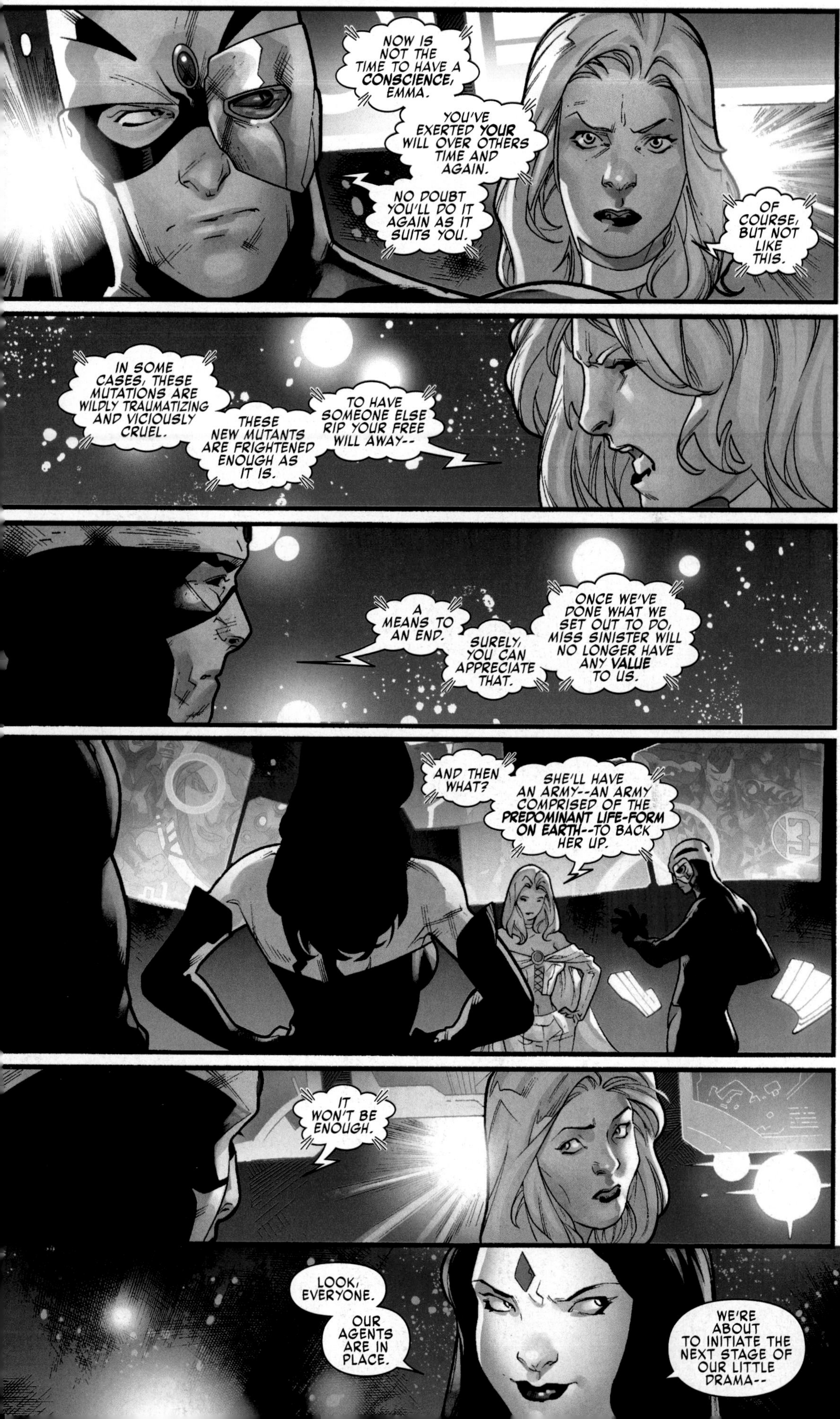
NOW IS NOT THE TIME TO HAVE A CONSCIENCE, EMMA.
YOU'VE EXERTED YOUR WILL OVER OTHERS TIME AND AGAIN.
NO DOUBT YOU'LL DO IT AGAIN AS IT SUITS YOU.
OF COURSE, BUT NOT LIKE THIS.
IN SOME CASES, THESE MUTATIONS ARE WILDLY TRAUMATIZING AND VICIOUSLY CRUEL.
THESE NEW MUTANTS ARE FRIGHTENED ENOUGH AS IT IS.
TO HAVE SOMEONE ELSE RIP YOUR FREE WILL AWAY--
A MEANS TO AN END.
SURELY, YOU CAN APPRECIATE THAT.
ONCE WE'VE DONE WHAT WE SET OUT TO DO, MISS SINISTER WILL NO LONGER HAVE ANY VALUE TO US.
AND THEN WHAT?
SHE'LL HAVE AN ARMY--AN ARMY COMPRISED OF THE PREDOMINANT LIFE-FORM ON EARTH--TO BACK HER UP.
IT WON'T BE ENOUGH.
LOOK, EVERYONE.
OUR AGENTS ARE IN PLACE.
WE'RE ABOUT TO INITIATE THE NEXT STAGE OF OUR LITTLE DRAMA--

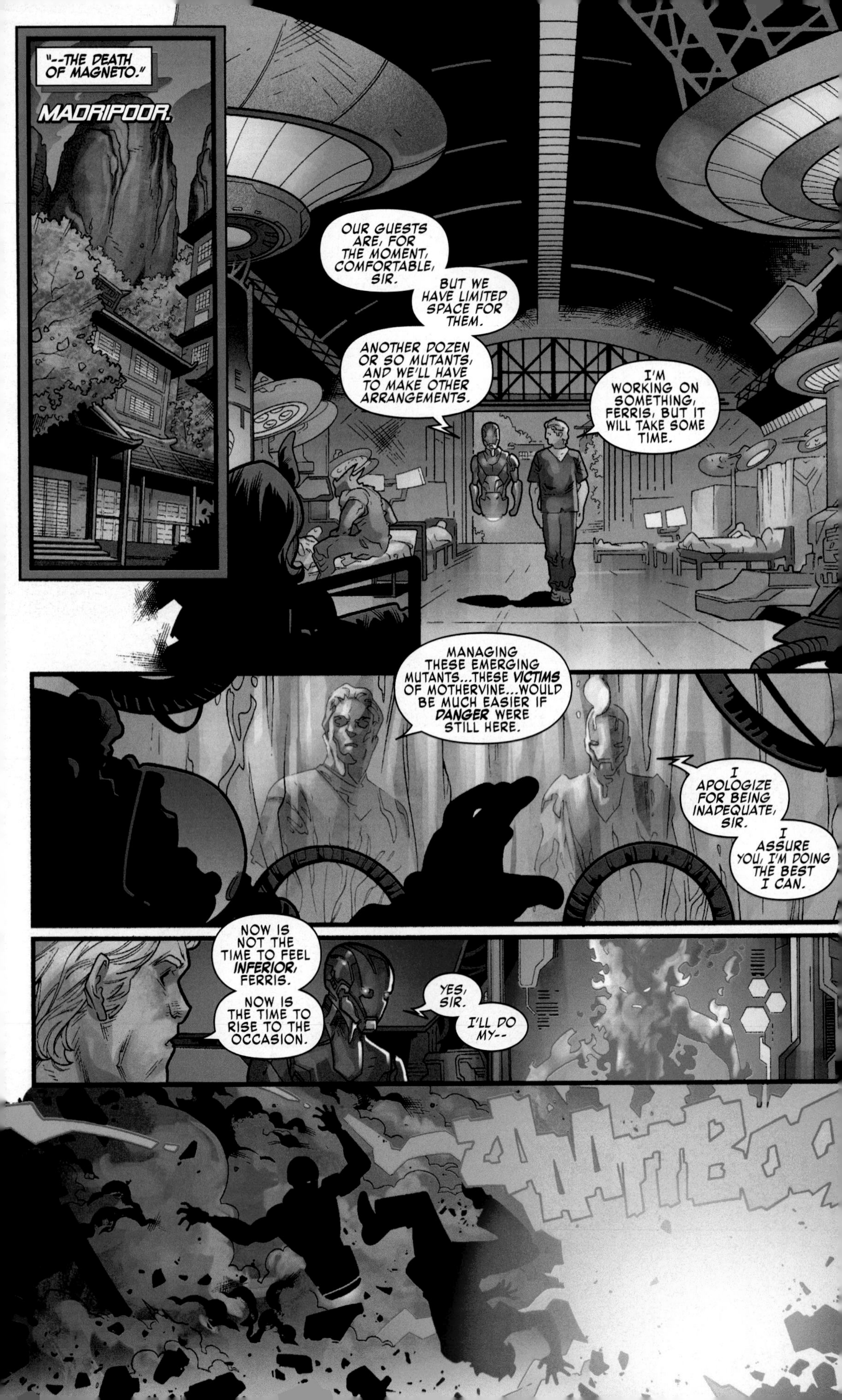

"--THE DEATH OF MAGNETO."
MADRIPOOR.
OUR GUESTS ARE, FOR THE MOMENT, COMFORTABLE, SIR.
BUT WE HAVE LIMITED SPACE FOR THEM.
ANOTHER DOZEN OR SO MUTANTS, AND WE'LL HAVE TO MAKE OTHER ARRANGEMENTS.
I'M WORKING ON SOMETHING, FERRIS, BUT IT WILL TAKE SOME TIME.
MANAGING THESE EMERGING MUTANTS...THESE VICTIMS OF MOTHERVINE...WOULD BE MUCH EASIER IF DANGER WERE STILL HERE.
I APOLOGIZE FOR BEING INADEQUATE, SIR.
I ASSURE YOU, I'M DOING THE BEST I CAN.
NOW IS NOT THE TIME TO FEEL INFERIOR, FERRIS.
NOW IS THE TIME TO RISE TO THE OCCASION.
YES, SIR.
I'LL DO MY--

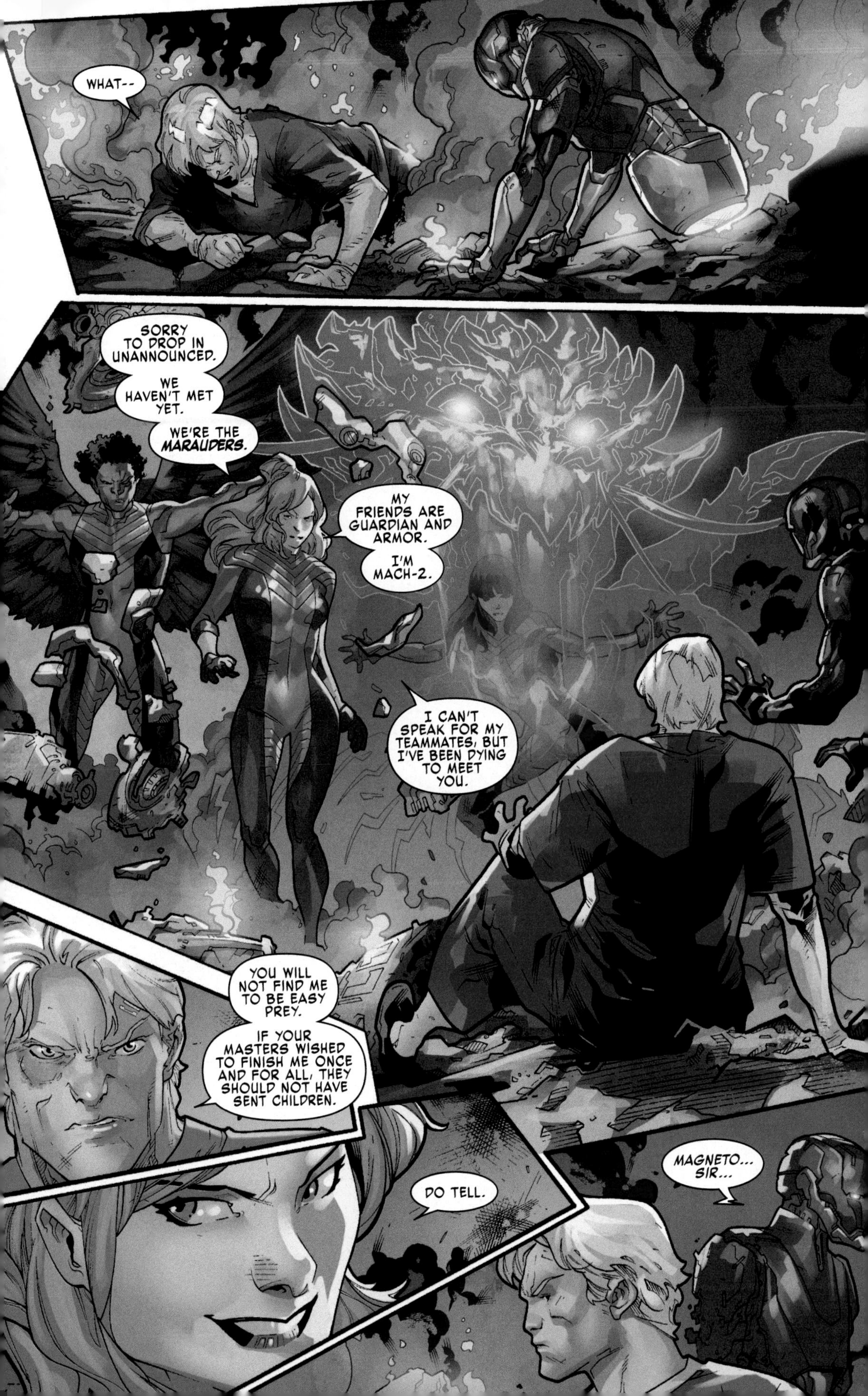
WHAT--
SORRY TO DROP IN UNANNOUNCED.
WE HAVEN'T MET YET.
WE'RE THE *MARAUDERS.*
MY FRIENDS ARE GUARDIAN AND ARMOR.
I'M MACH-2.
I CAN'T SPEAK FOR MY TEAMMATES, BUT I'VE BEEN DYING TO MEET YOU.
YOU WILL NOT FIND ME TO BE EASY PREY.
IF YOUR MASTERS WISHED TO FINISH ME ONCE AND FOR ALL, THEY SHOULD NOT HAVE SENT CHILDREN.
DO TELL.
MAGNETO... SIR...

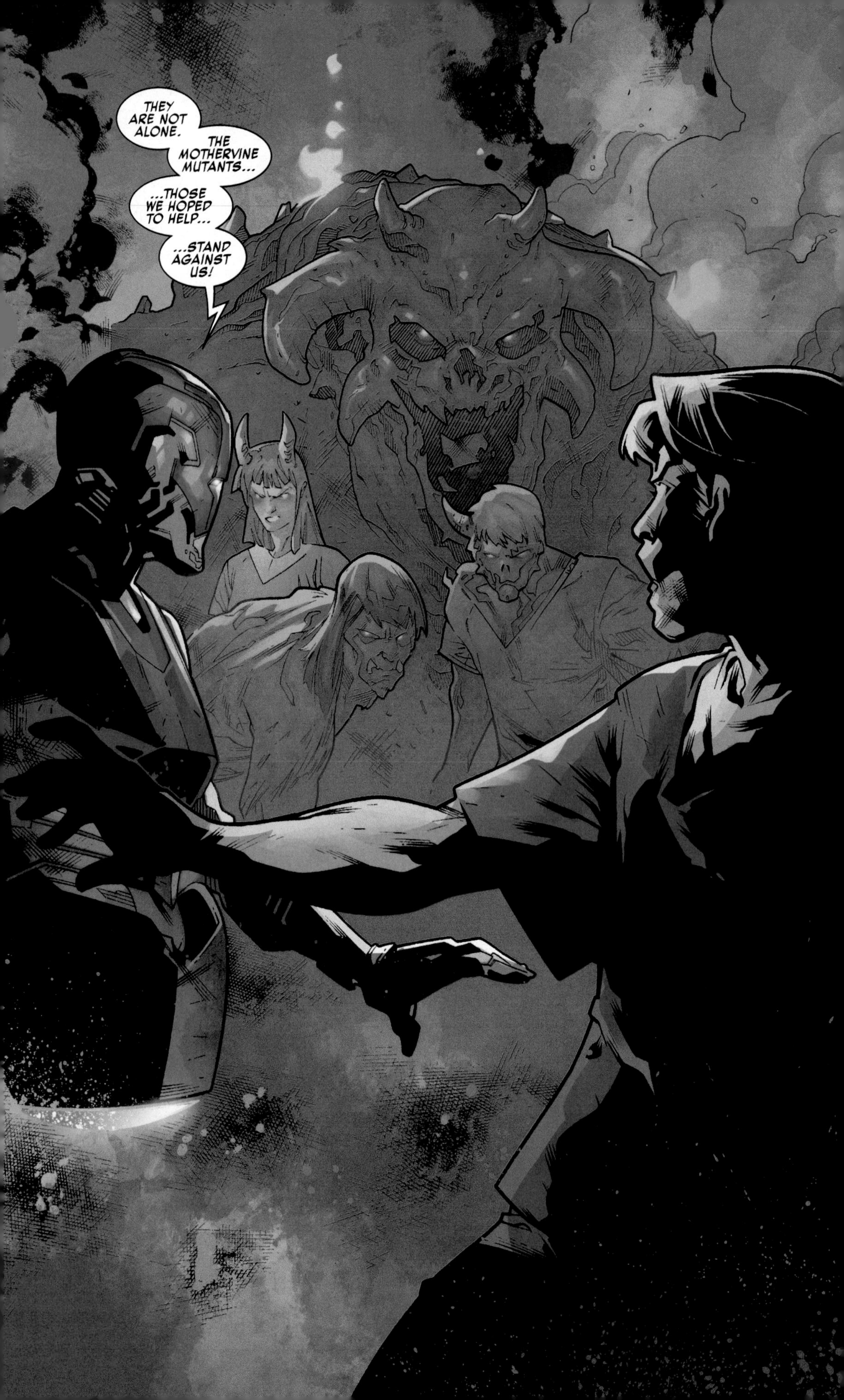
THEY ARE NOT ALONE.
THE MOTHERVINE MUTANTS...
...THOSE WE HOPED TO HELP...
...STAND AGAINST US!

27

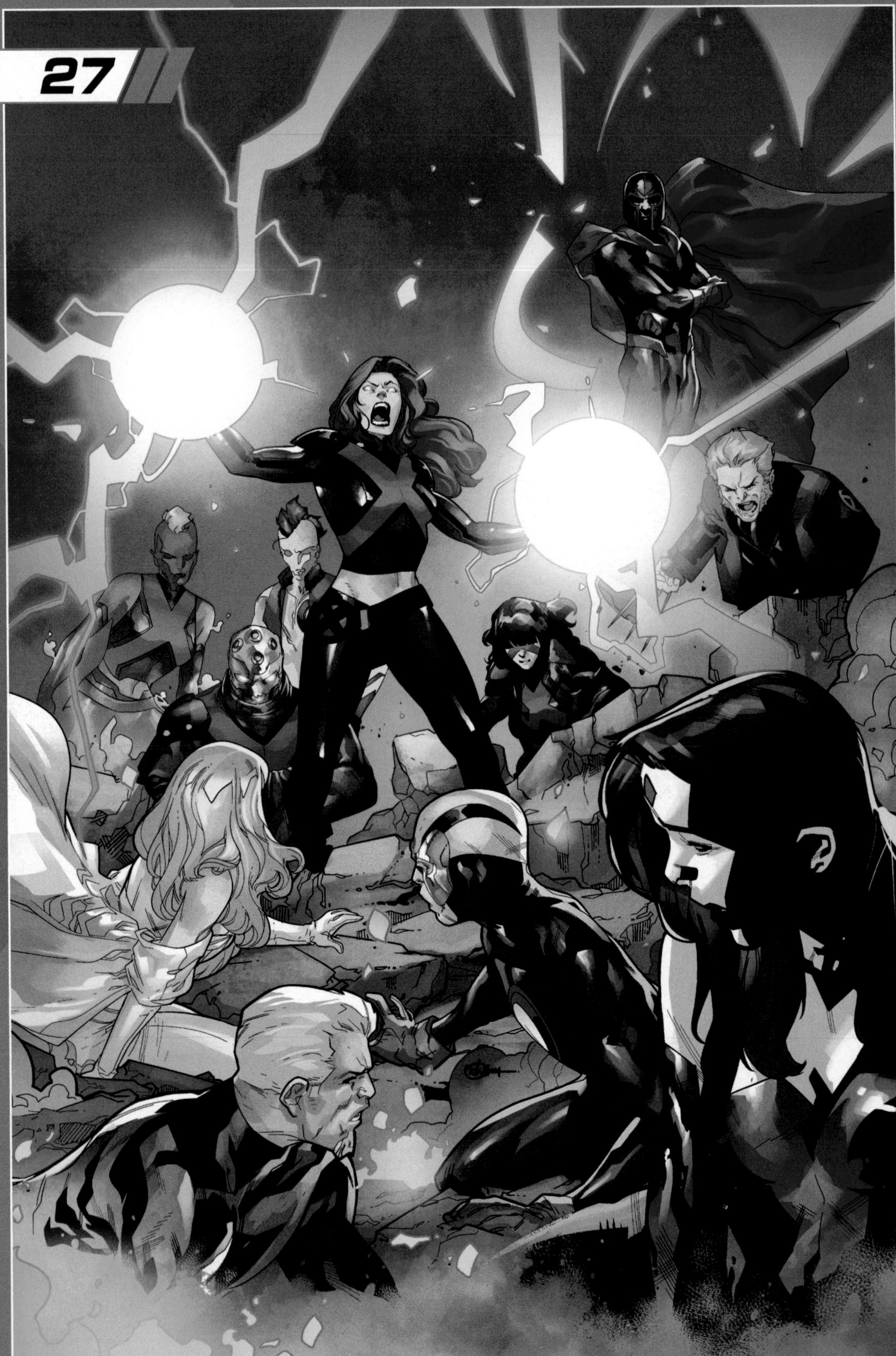

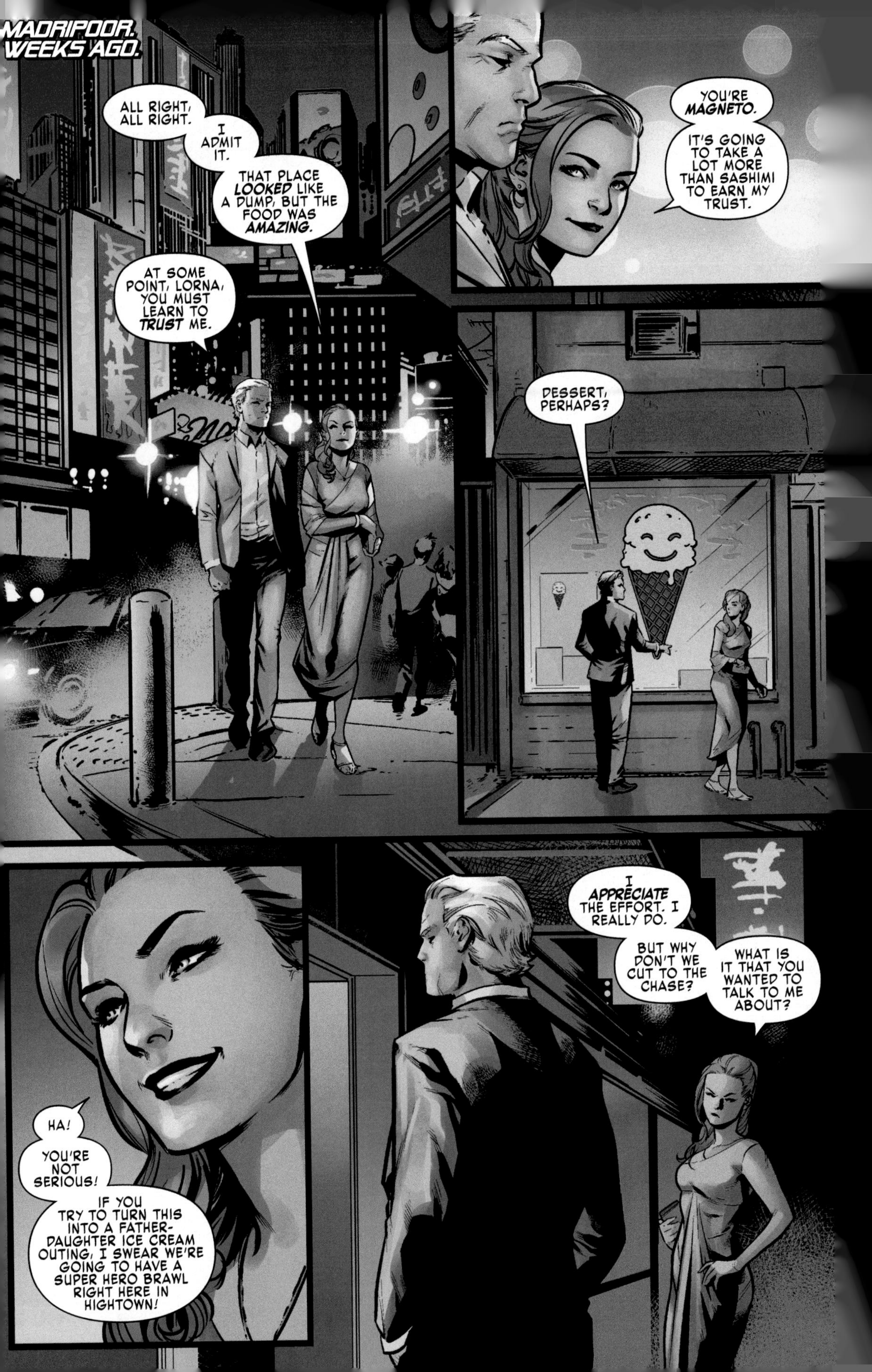
MADRIPOOR. WEEKS AGO.
ALL RIGHT, ALL RIGHT.
I ADMIT IT.
THAT PLACE LOOKED LIKE A DUMP, BUT THE FOOD WAS AMAZING.
AT SOME POINT, LORNA, YOU MUST LEARN TO TRUST ME.
YOU'RE MAGNETO.
IT'S GOING TO TAKE A LOT MORE THAN SASHIMI TO EARN MY TRUST.
DESSERT, PERHAPS?
HA!
YOU'RE NOT SERIOUS!
IF YOU TRY TO TURN THIS INTO A FATHER-DAUGHTER ICE CREAM OUTING, I SWEAR WE'RE GOING TO HAVE A SUPER HERO BRAWL RIGHT HERE IN HIGHTOWN!
I APPRECIATE THE EFFORT. I REALLY DO.
BUT WHY DON'T WE CUT TO THE CHASE?
WHAT IS IT THAT YOU WANTED TO TALK TO ME ABOUT?

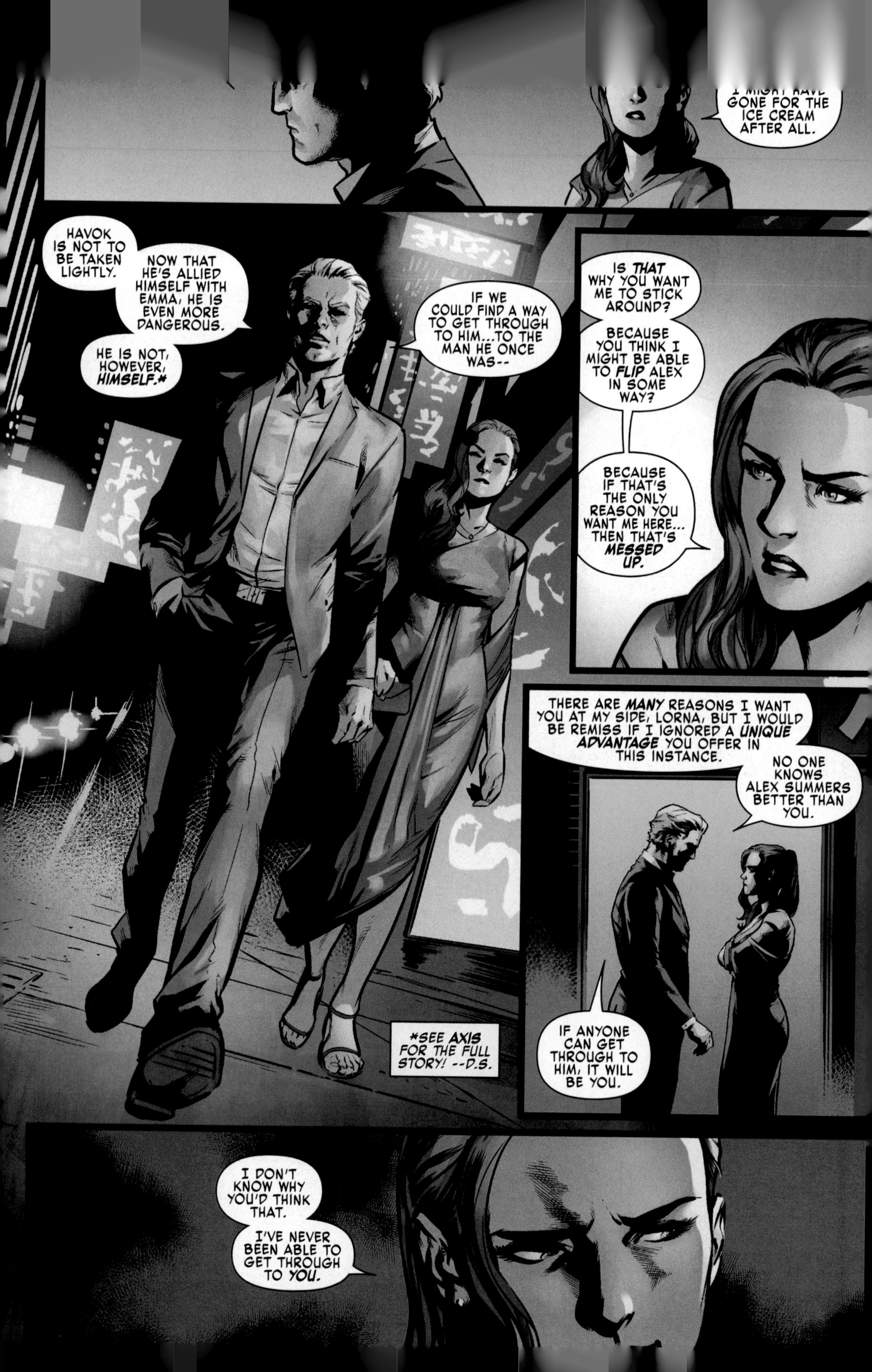
I MIGHT HAVE GONE FOR THE ICE CREAM AFTER ALL.
HAVOK IS NOT TO BE TAKEN LIGHTLY.
NOW THAT HE'S ALLIED HIMSELF WITH EMMA, HE IS EVEN MORE DANGEROUS.
HE IS NOT, HOWEVER, HIMSELF.*
IF WE COULD FIND A WAY TO GET THROUGH TO HIM...TO THE MAN HE ONCE WAS--
*SEE AXIS FOR THE FULL STORY! --D.S.
IS THAT WHY YOU WANT ME TO STICK AROUND?
BECAUSE YOU THINK I MIGHT BE ABLE TO FLIP ALEX IN SOME WAY?
BECAUSE IF THAT'S THE ONLY REASON YOU WANT ME HERE... THEN THAT'S MESSED UP.
THERE ARE MANY REASONS I WANT YOU AT MY SIDE, LORNA, BUT I WOULD BE REMISS IF I IGNORED A UNIQUE ADVANTAGE YOU OFFER IN THIS INSTANCE.
NO ONE KNOWS ALEX SUMMERS BETTER THAN YOU.
IF ANYONE CAN GET THROUGH TO HIM, IT WILL BE YOU.
I DON'T KNOW WHY YOU'D THINK THAT.
I'VE NEVER BEEN ABLE TO GET THROUGH TO YOU.

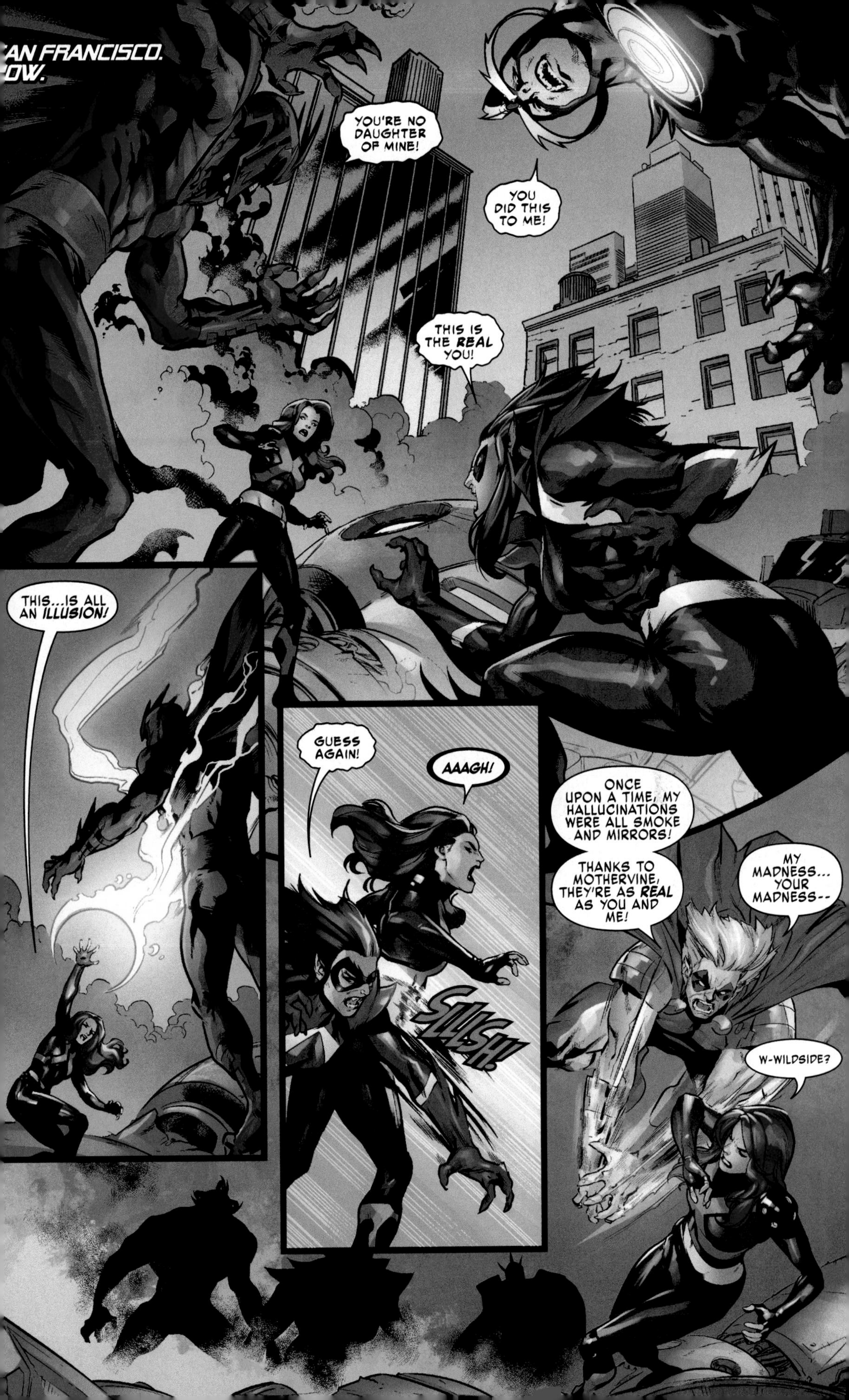
AN FRANCISCO.
OW.
YOU'RE NO DAUGHTER OF MINE!
YOU DID THIS TO ME!
THIS IS THE REAL YOU!
THIS...IS ALL AN ILLUSION!
GUESS AGAIN!
AAAGH!
SLLISH!
ONCE UPON A TIME, MY HALLUCINATIONS WERE ALL SMOKE AND MIRRORS!
THANKS TO MOTHERVINE, THEY'RE AS REAL AS YOU AND ME!
MY MADNESS... YOUR MADNESS--
W-WILDSIDE?

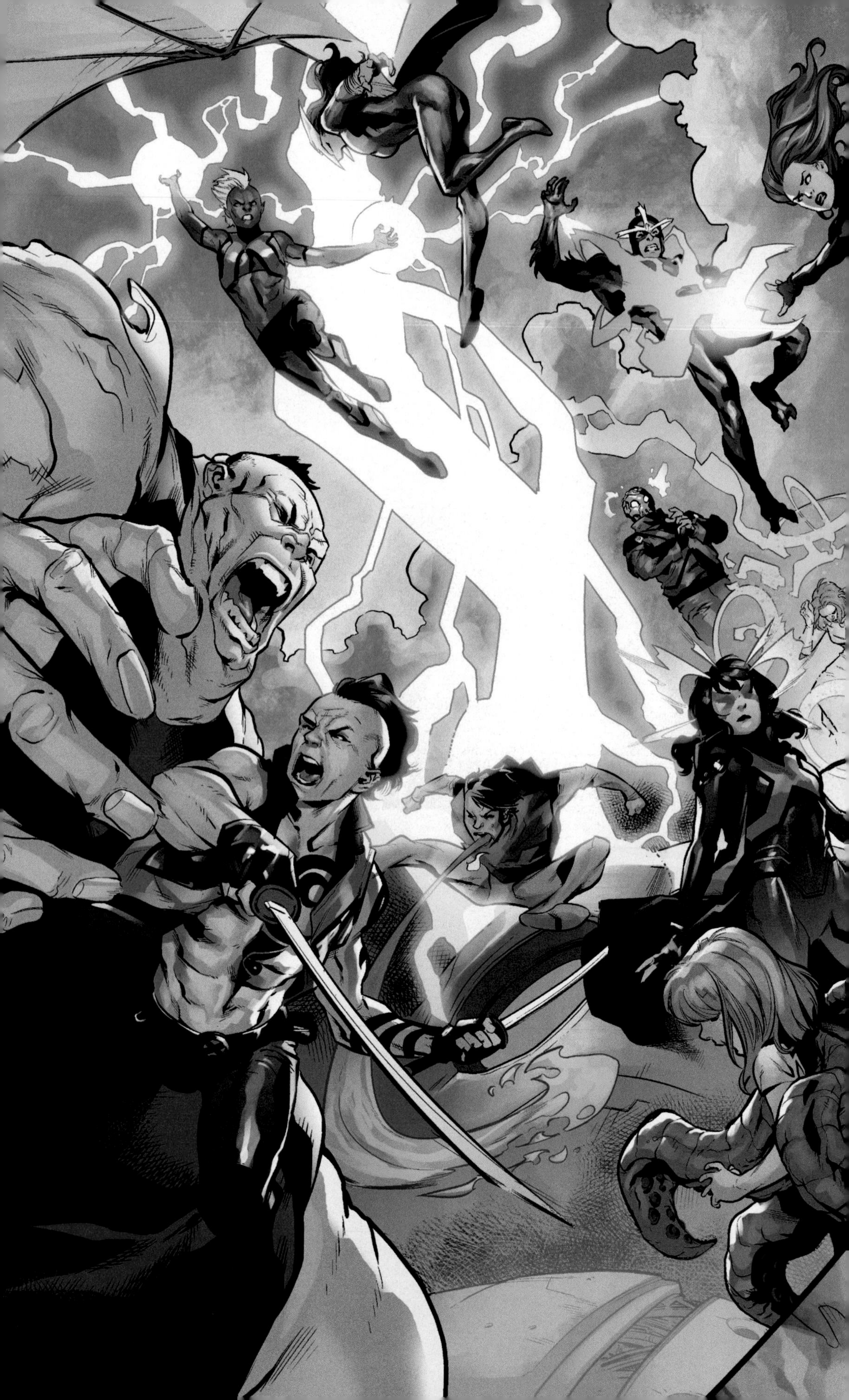

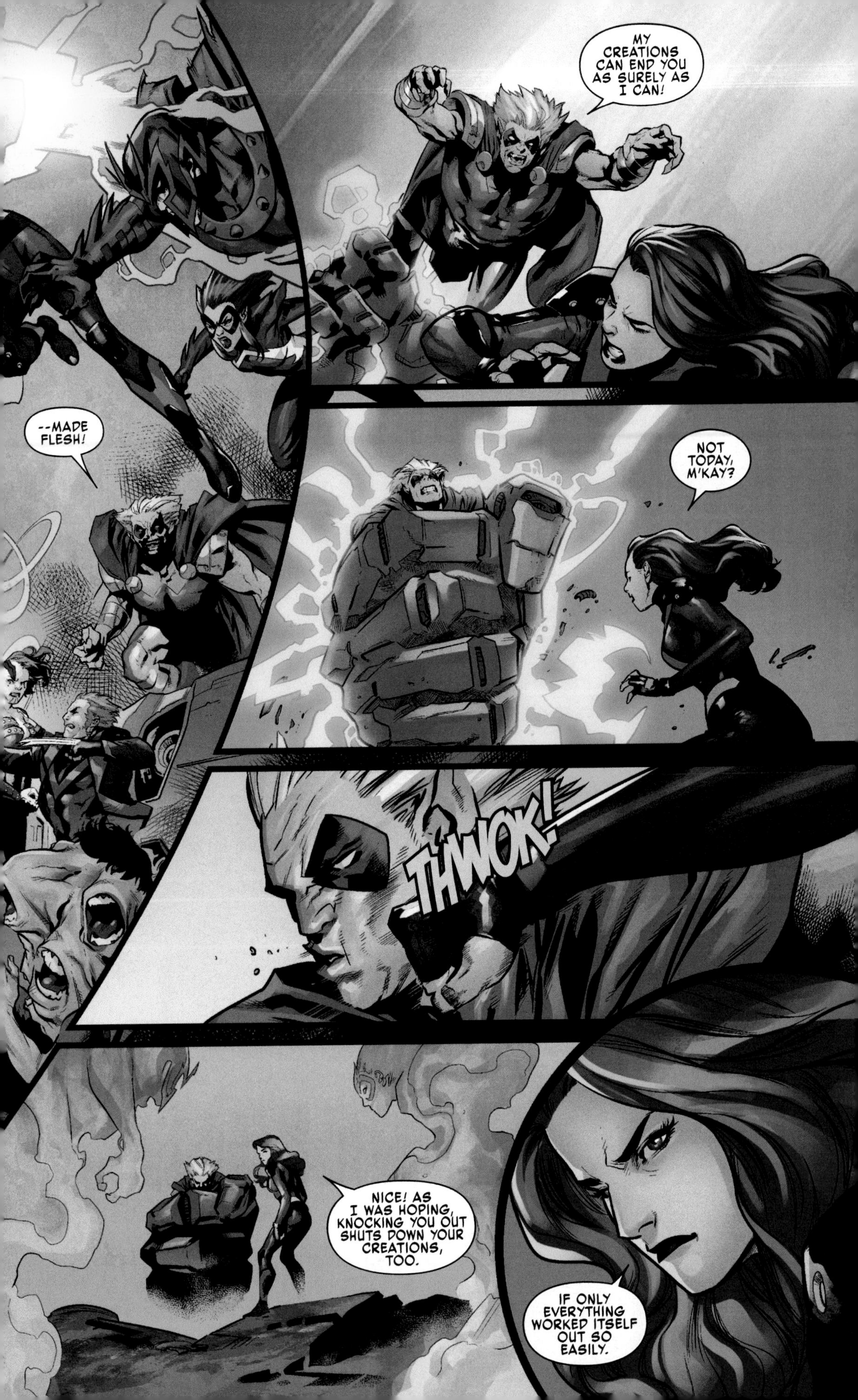

MY CREATIONS CAN END YOU AS SURELY AS I CAN!
--MADE FLESH!
NOT TODAY, M'KAY?
THWOK!
NICE! AS I WAS HOPING, KNOCKING YOU OUT SHUTS DOWN YOUR CREATIONS, TOO.
IF ONLY EVERYTHING WORKED ITSELF OUT SO EASILY.

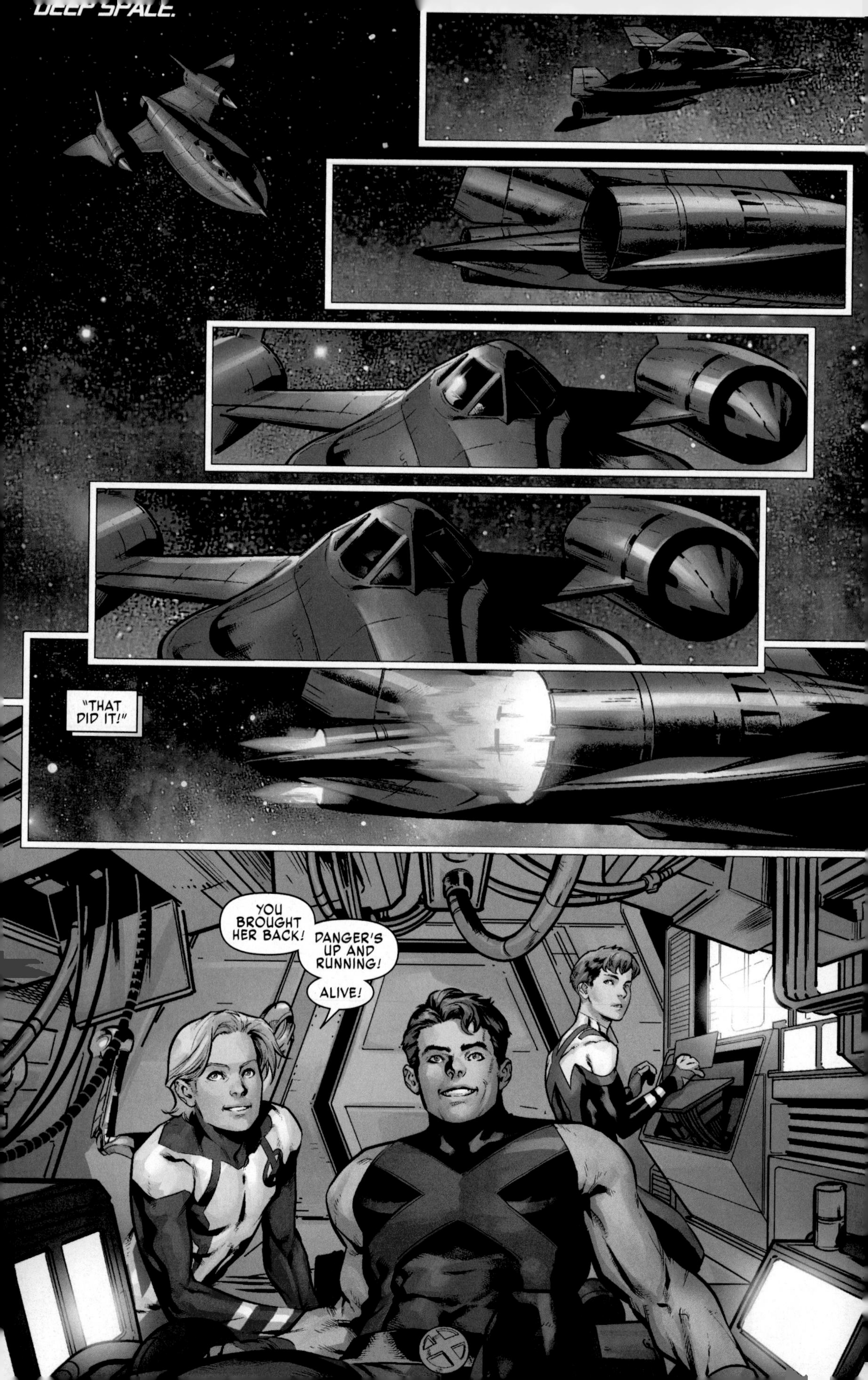
DEEP SPACE.
"THAT DID IT!"
YOU BROUGHT HER BACK!
DANGER'S UP AND RUNNING!
ALIVE!

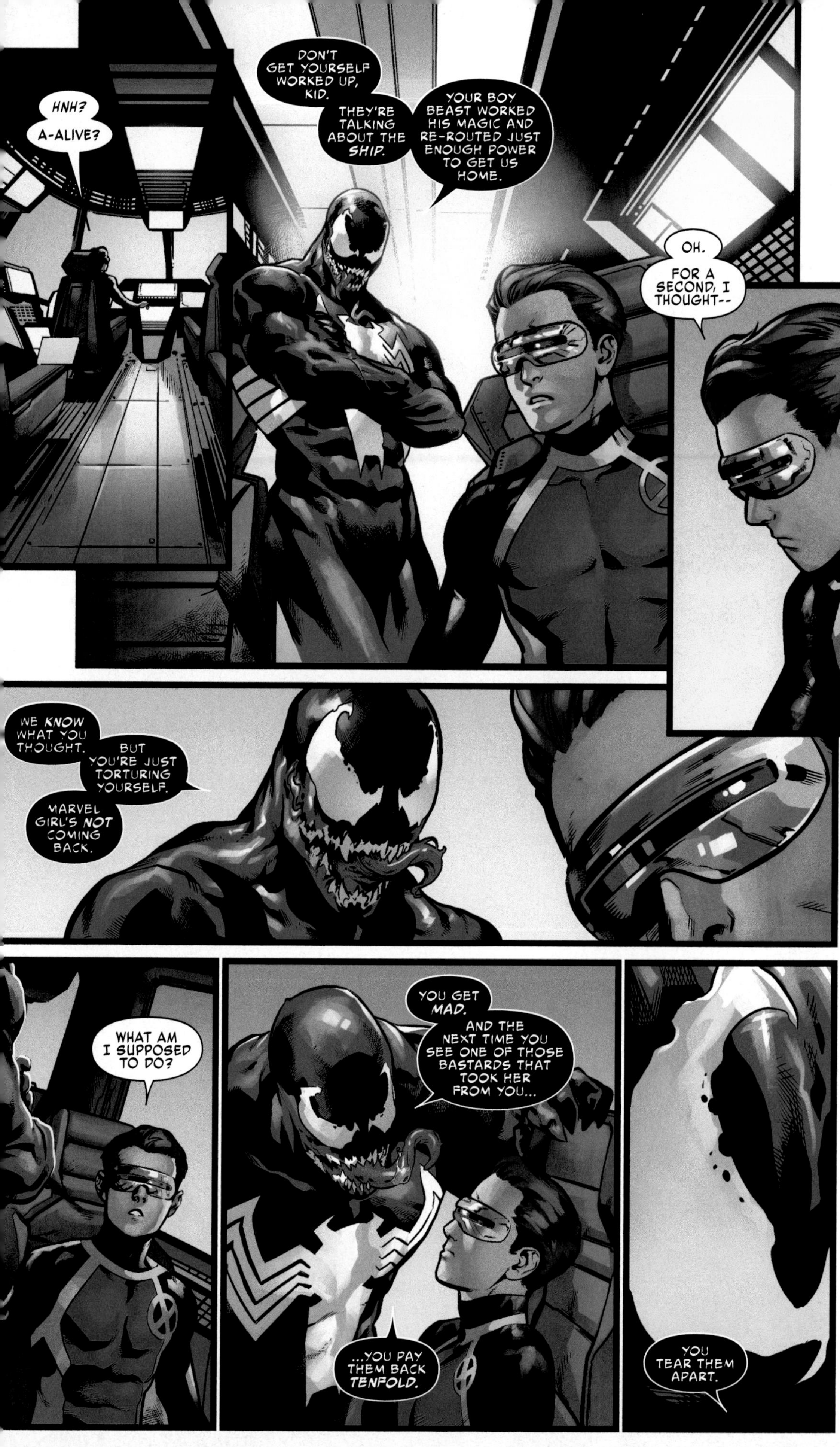
HNH?
A-ALIVE?
DON'T GET YOURSELF WORKED UP, KID.
THEY'RE TALKING ABOUT THE SHIP.
YOUR BOY BEAST WORKED HIS MAGIC AND RE-ROUTED JUST ENOUGH POWER TO GET US HOME.
OH.
FOR A SECOND, I THOUGHT--
WE KNOW WHAT YOU THOUGHT.
BUT YOU'RE JUST TORTURING YOURSELF.
MARVEL GIRL'S NOT COMING BACK.
WHAT AM I SUPPOSED TO DO?
YOU GET MAD.
AND THE NEXT TIME YOU SEE ONE OF THOSE BASTARDS THAT TOOK HER FROM YOU...
...YOU PAY THEM BACK TENFOLD.
YOU TEAR THEM APART.

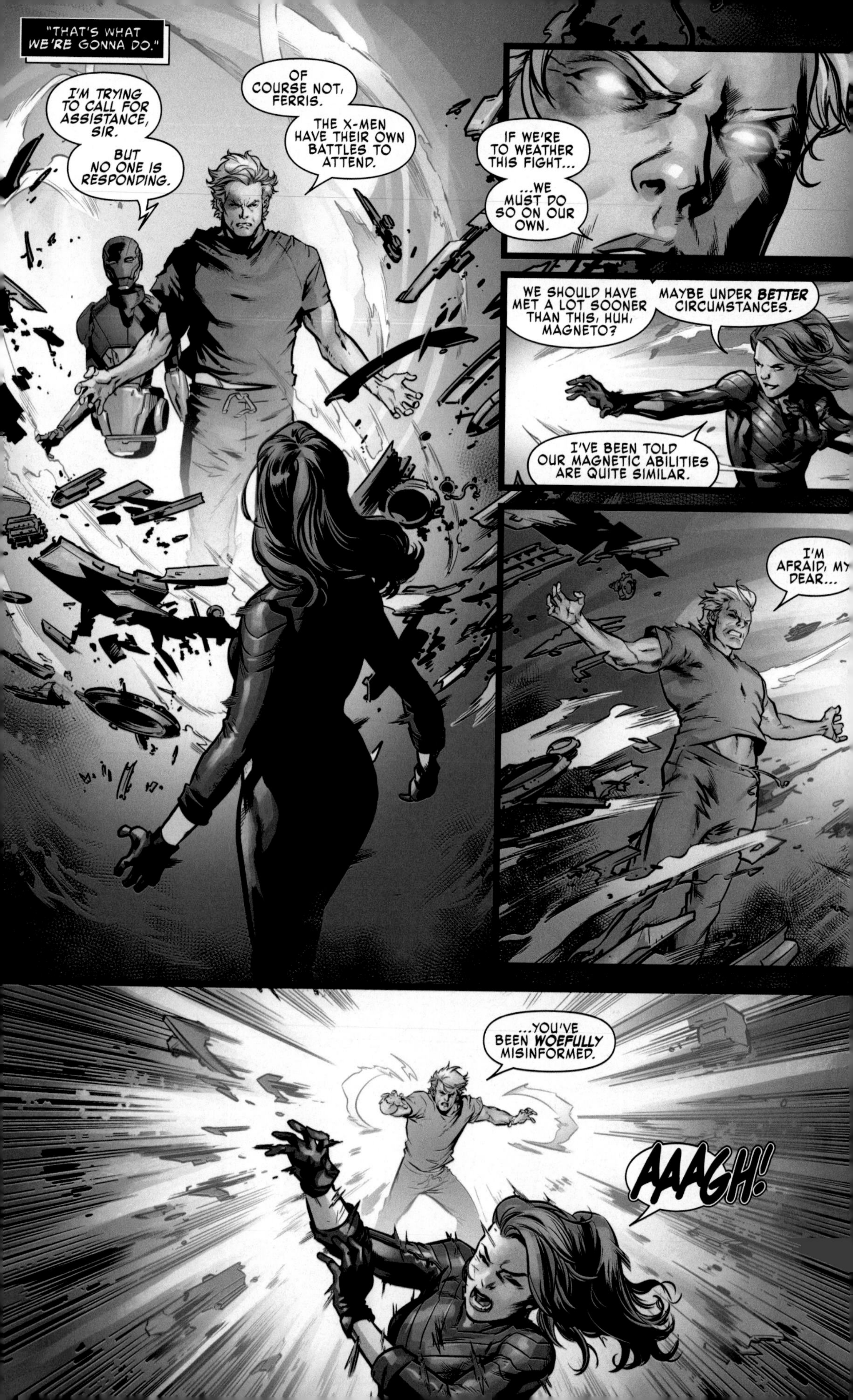
"THAT'S WHAT WE'RE GONNA DO."
I'M TRYING TO CALL FOR ASSISTANCE, SIR.
BUT NO ONE IS RESPONDING.
OF COURSE NOT, FERRIS.
THE X-MEN HAVE THEIR OWN BATTLES TO ATTEND.
IF WE'RE TO WEATHER THIS FIGHT...
...WE MUST DO SO ON OUR OWN.
WE SHOULD HAVE MET A LOT SOONER THAN THIS, HUH, MAGNETO?
MAYBE UNDER BETTER CIRCUMSTANCES.
I'VE BEEN TOLD OUR MAGNETIC ABILITIES ARE QUITE SIMILAR.
I'M AFRAID, MY DEAR...
...YOU'VE BEEN WOEFULLY MISINFORMED.
AAAGH!

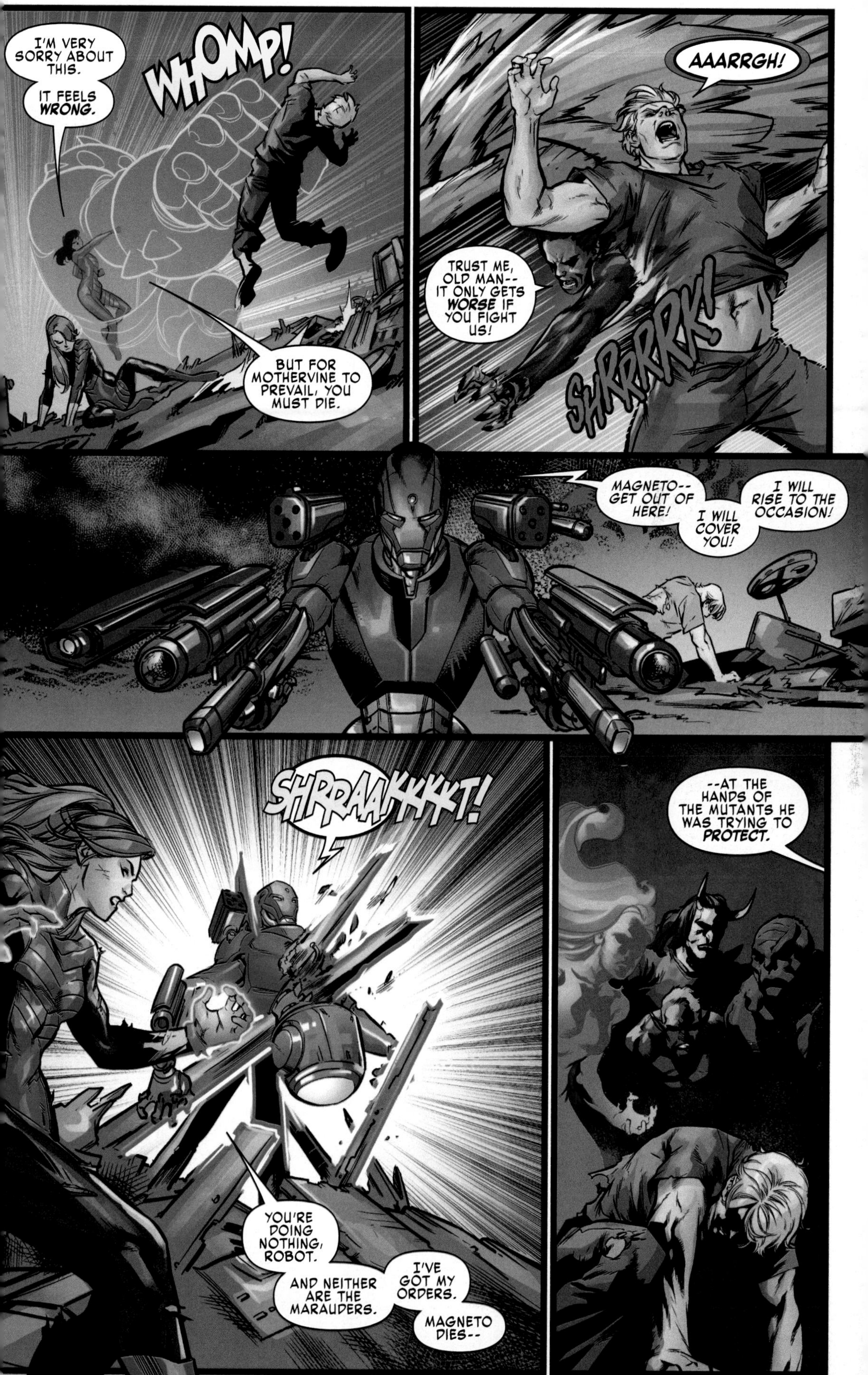
I'M VERY SORRY ABOUT THIS.
IT FEELS WRONG.
WHOMP!
BUT FOR MOTHERVINE TO PREVAIL, YOU MUST DIE.
AAARRGH!
TRUST ME, OLD MAN-- IT ONLY GETS WORSE IF YOU FIGHT US!
SHRRRRK!
MAGNETO-- GET OUT OF HERE!
I WILL COVER YOU!
I WILL RISE TO THE OCCASION!
SHRRAAKKKKT!
YOU'RE DOING NOTHING, ROBOT.
AND NEITHER ARE THE MARAUDERS.
I'VE GOT MY ORDERS.
MAGNETO DIES--
--AT THE HANDS OF THE MUTANTS HE WAS TRYING TO PROTECT.

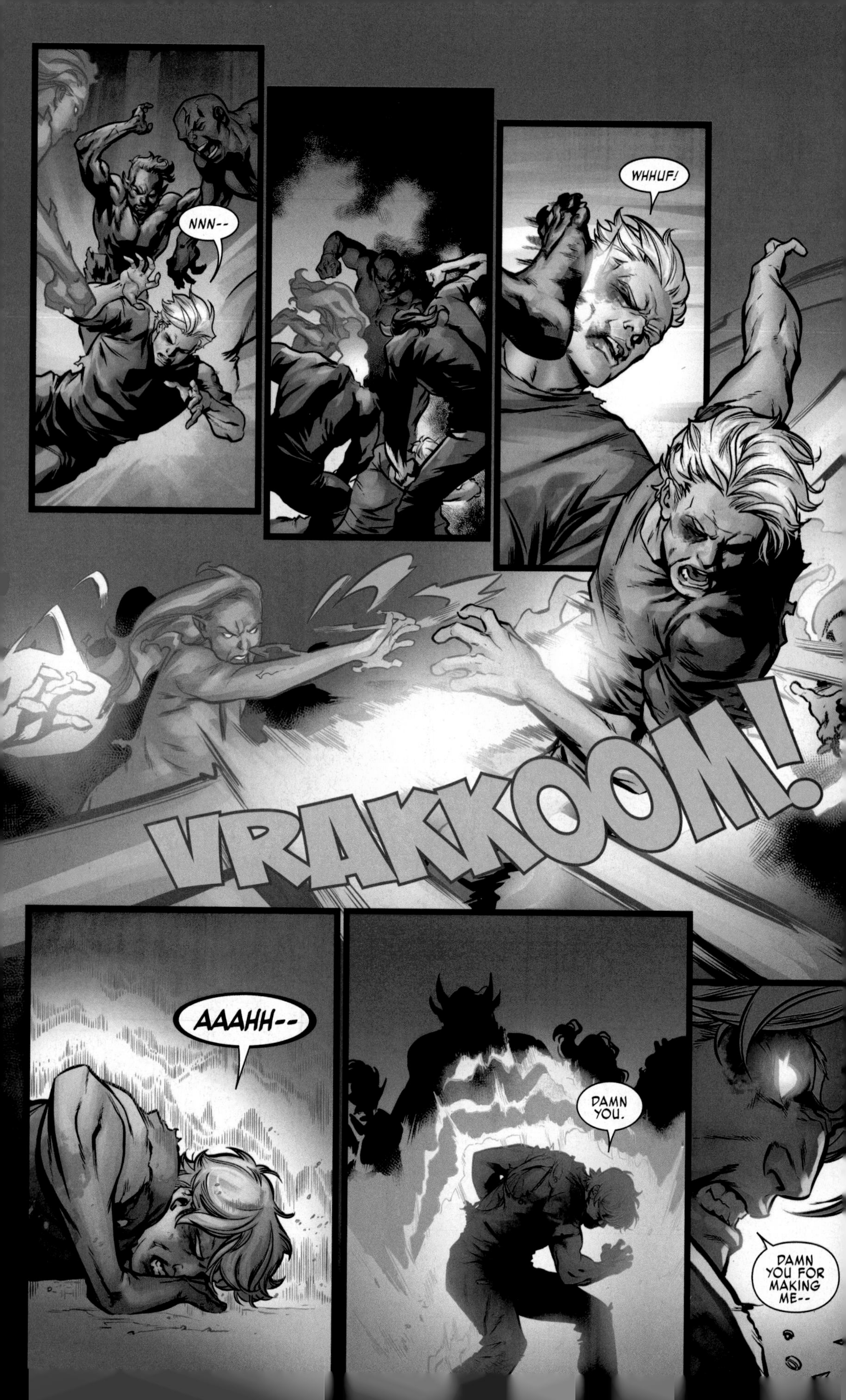
NNN--
WHHUF!
VRAKKOOM!
AAAHH--
DAMN YOU.
DAMN YOU FOR MAKING ME--

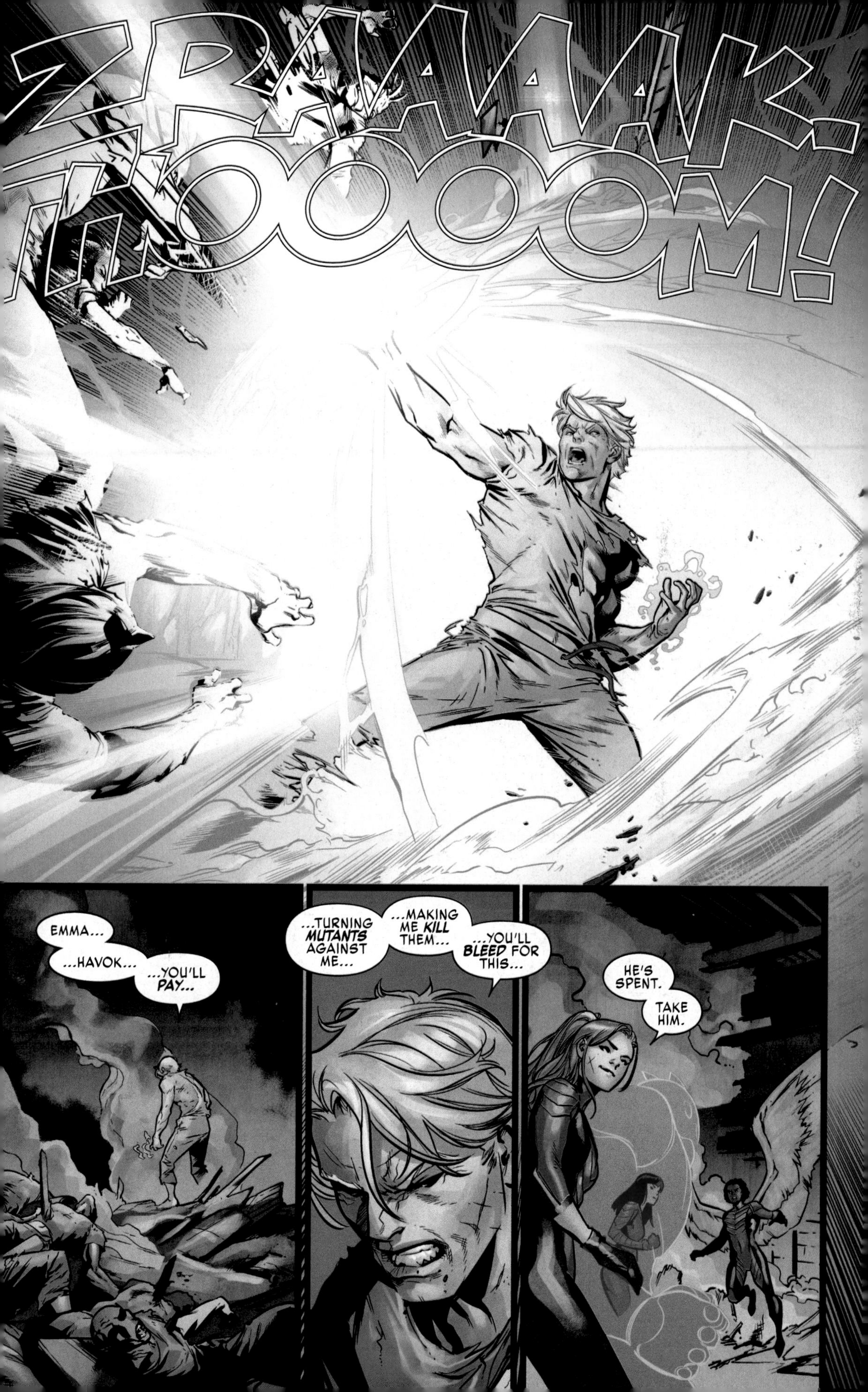
ZRAAAK-THOOOOM!
EMMA...
...HAVOK...
...YOU'LL PAY...
...TURNING MUTANTS AGAINST ME...
...MAKING ME KILL THEM...
...YOU'LL BLEED FOR THIS...
HE'S SPENT.
TAKE HIM.

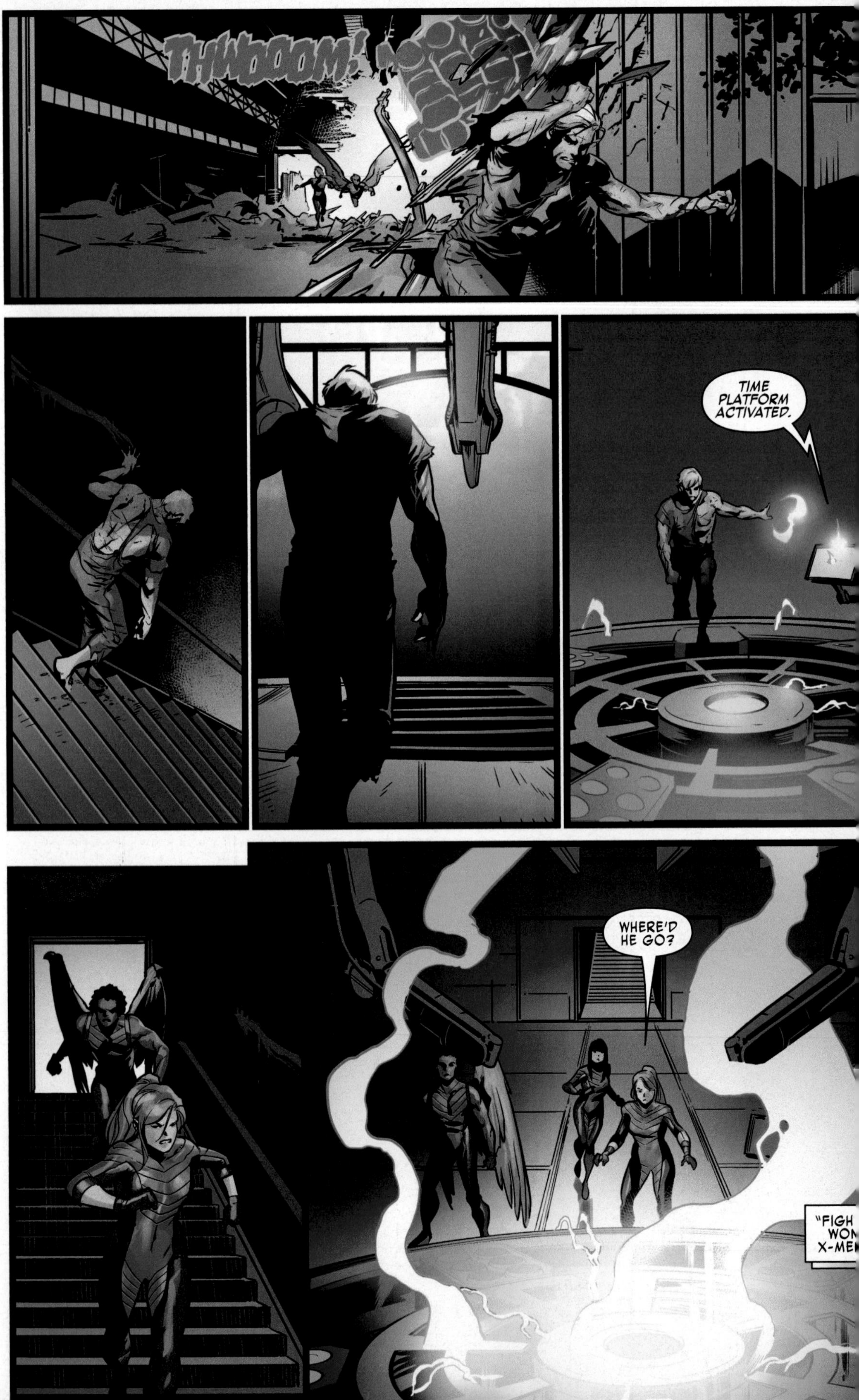
THWOOOM!
TIME PLATFORM ACTIVATED.
WHERE'D HE GO?
"FIGH
WON
X-ME

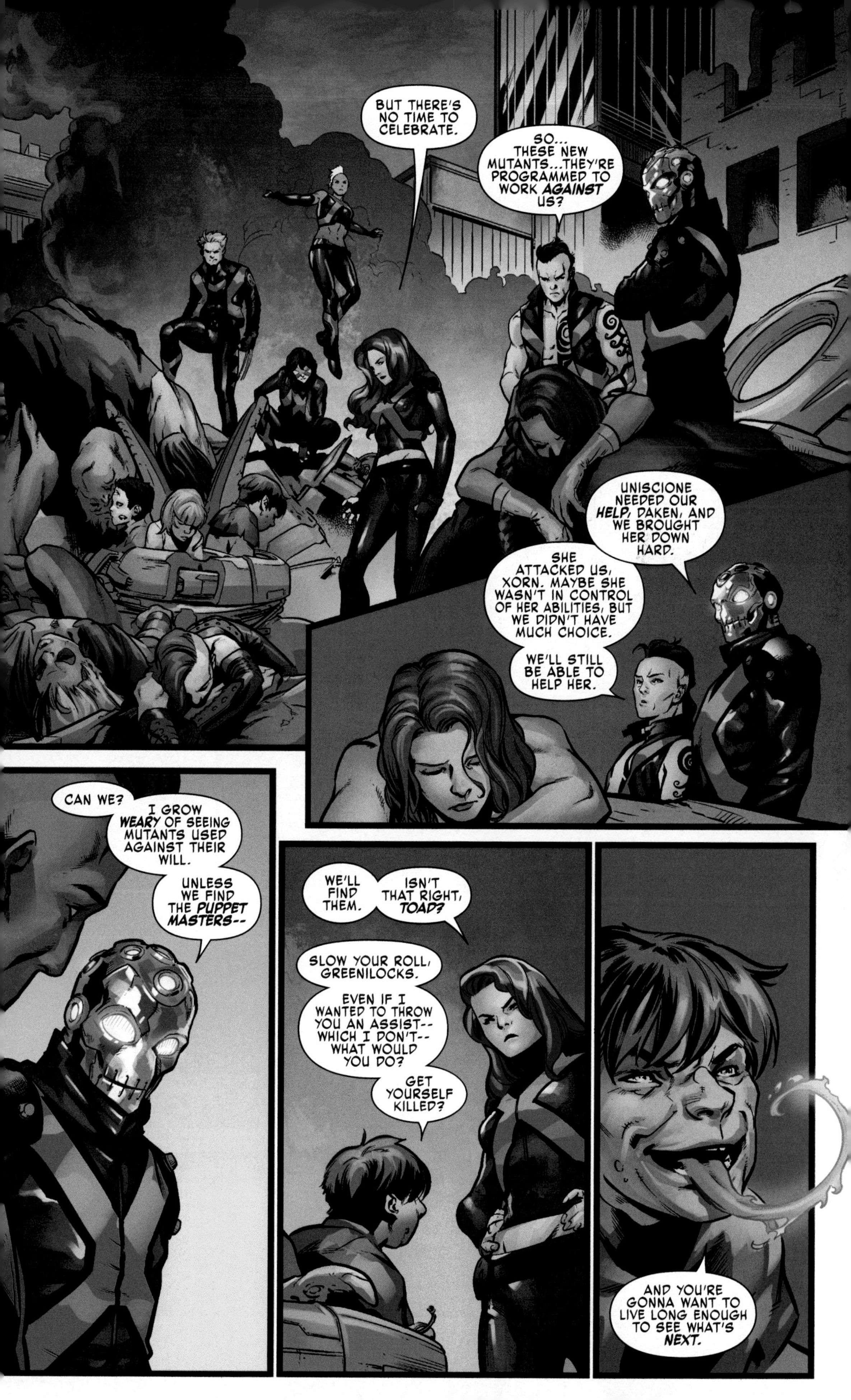
BUT THERE'S NO TIME TO CELEBRATE.
SO... THESE NEW MUTANTS...THEY'RE PROGRAMMED TO WORK AGAINST US?
UNISCIONE NEEDED OUR HELP, DAKEN, AND WE BROUGHT HER DOWN HARD.
SHE ATTACKED US, XORN. MAYBE SHE WASN'T IN CONTROL OF HER ABILITIES, BUT WE DIDN'T HAVE MUCH CHOICE.
WE'LL STILL BE ABLE TO HELP HER.
CAN WE?
I GROW WEARY OF SEEING MUTANTS USED AGAINST THEIR WILL.
UNLESS WE FIND THE PUPPET MASTERS--
WE'LL FIND THEM.
ISN'T THAT RIGHT, TOAD?
SLOW YOUR ROLL, GREENILOCKS.
EVEN IF I WANTED TO THROW YOU AN ASSIST-- WHICH I DON'T-- WHAT WOULD YOU DO?
GET YOURSELF KILLED?
AND YOU'RE GONNA WANT TO LIVE LONG ENOUGH TO SEE WHAT'S NEXT.

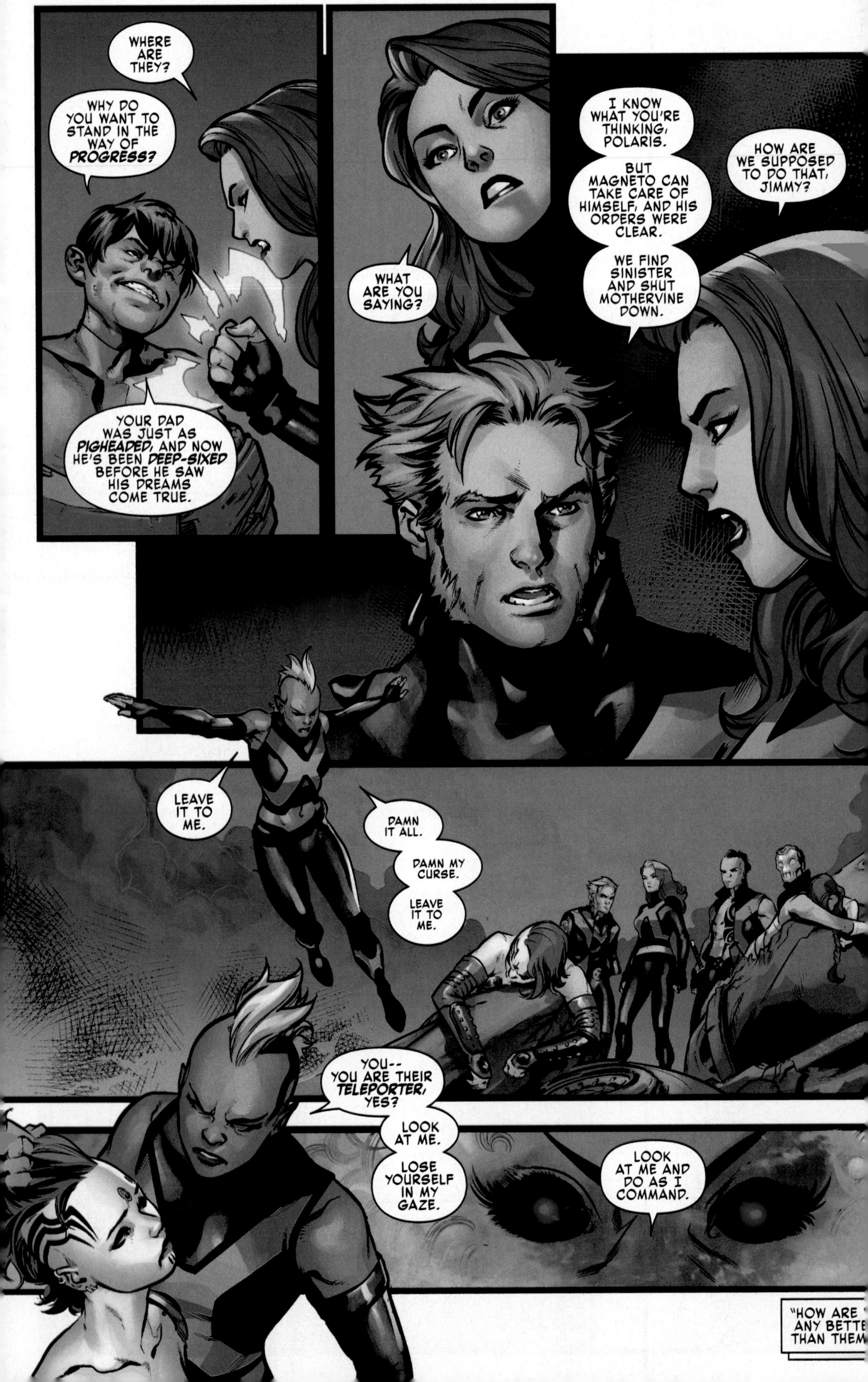
WHERE ARE THEY?
WHY DO YOU WANT TO STAND IN THE WAY OF PROGRESS?
YOUR DAD WAS JUST AS PIGHEADED, AND NOW HE'S BEEN DEEP-SIXED BEFORE HE SAW HIS DREAMS COME TRUE.
WHAT ARE YOU SAYING?
I KNOW WHAT YOU'RE THINKING, POLARIS.
BUT MAGNETO CAN TAKE CARE OF HIMSELF, AND HIS ORDERS WERE CLEAR.
WE FIND SINISTER AND SHUT MOTHERVINE DOWN.
HOW ARE WE SUPPOSED TO DO THAT, JIMMY?
LEAVE IT TO ME.
DAMN IT ALL.
DAMN MY CURSE.
LEAVE IT TO ME.
YOU--YOU ARE THEIR TELEPORTER, YES?
LOOK AT ME.
LOSE YOURSELF IN MY GAZE.
LOOK AT ME AND DO AS I COMMAND.
"HOW ARE ANY BETTE THAN THEM

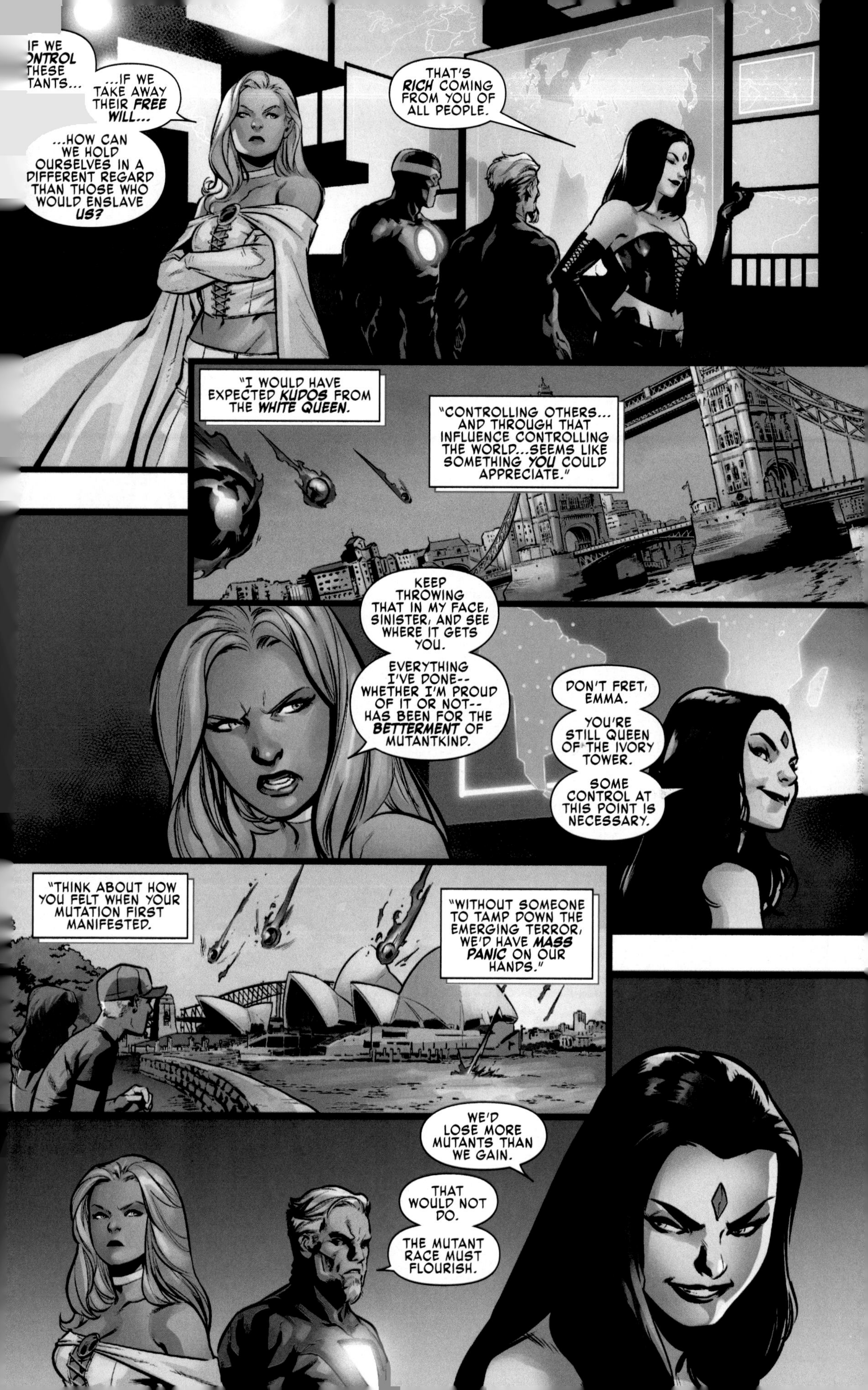

IF WE CONTROL THESE MUTANTS...
...IF WE TAKE AWAY THEIR FREE WILL...
...HOW CAN WE HOLD OURSELVES IN A DIFFERENT REGARD THAN THOSE WHO WOULD ENSLAVE US?
THAT'S RICH COMING FROM YOU OF ALL PEOPLE.
"I WOULD HAVE EXPECTED KUDOS FROM THE WHITE QUEEN.
"CONTROLLING OTHERS... AND THROUGH THAT INFLUENCE CONTROLLING THE WORLD...SEEMS LIKE SOMETHING YOU COULD APPRECIATE."
KEEP THROWING THAT IN MY FACE, SINISTER, AND SEE WHERE IT GETS YOU.
EVERYTHING I'VE DONE--WHETHER I'M PROUD OF IT OR NOT--HAS BEEN FOR THE BETTERMENT OF MUTANTKIND.
DON'T FRET, EMMA.
YOU'RE STILL QUEEN OF THE IVORY TOWER.
SOME CONTROL AT THIS POINT IS NECESSARY.
"THINK ABOUT HOW YOU FELT WHEN YOUR MUTATION FIRST MANIFESTED.
"WITHOUT SOMEONE TO TAMP DOWN THE EMERGING TERROR, WE'D HAVE MASS PANIC ON OUR HANDS."
WE'D LOSE MORE MUTANTS THAN WE GAIN.
THAT WOULD NOT DO.
THE MUTANT RACE MUST FLOURISH.

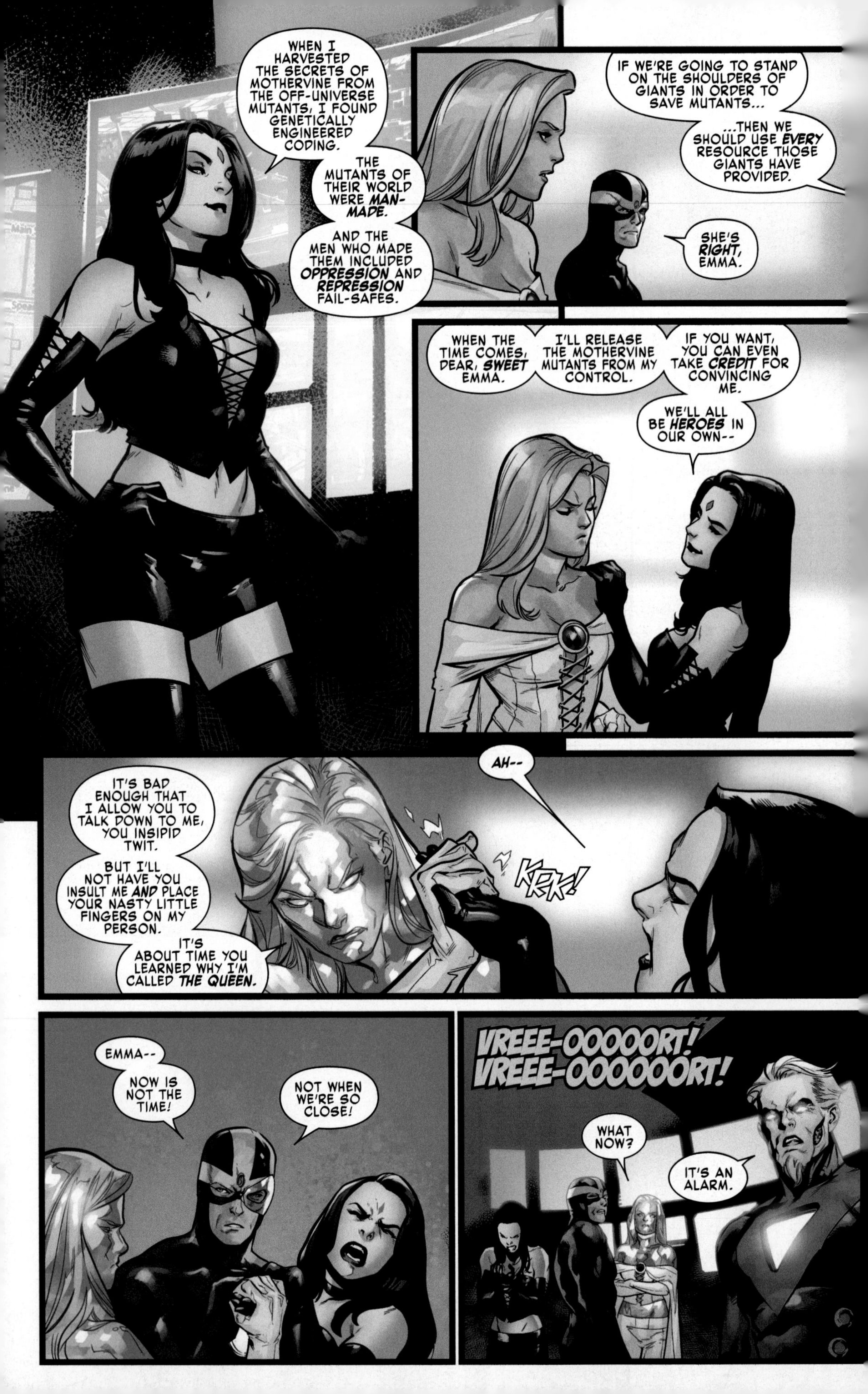
WHEN I HARVESTED THE SECRETS OF MOTHERVINE FROM THE OFF-UNIVERSE MUTANTS, I FOUND GENETICALLY ENGINEERED CODING.
THE MUTANTS OF THEIR WORLD WERE MAN-MADE.
AND THE MEN WHO MADE THEM INCLUDED OPPRESSION AND REPRESSION FAIL-SAFES.
IF WE'RE GOING TO STAND ON THE SHOULDERS OF GIANTS IN ORDER TO SAVE MUTANTS...
...THEN WE SHOULD USE EVERY RESOURCE THOSE GIANTS HAVE PROVIDED.
SHE'S RIGHT, EMMA.
WHEN THE TIME COMES, DEAR, SWEET EMMA.
I'LL RELEASE THE MOTHERVINE MUTANTS FROM MY CONTROL.
IF YOU WANT, YOU CAN EVEN TAKE CREDIT FOR CONVINCING ME.
WE'LL ALL BE HEROES IN OUR OWN--
IT'S BAD ENOUGH THAT I ALLOW YOU TO TALK DOWN TO ME, YOU INSIPID TWIT.
BUT I'LL NOT HAVE YOU INSULT ME AND PLACE YOUR NASTY LITTLE FINGERS ON MY PERSON.
IT'S ABOUT TIME YOU LEARNED WHY I'M CALLED THE QUEEN.
AH--
KRK!
EMMA--
NOW IS NOT THE TIME!
NOT WHEN WE'RE SO CLOSE!
VREEE-OOOOORT! VREEE-OOOOOORT!
WHAT NOW?
IT'S AN ALARM.

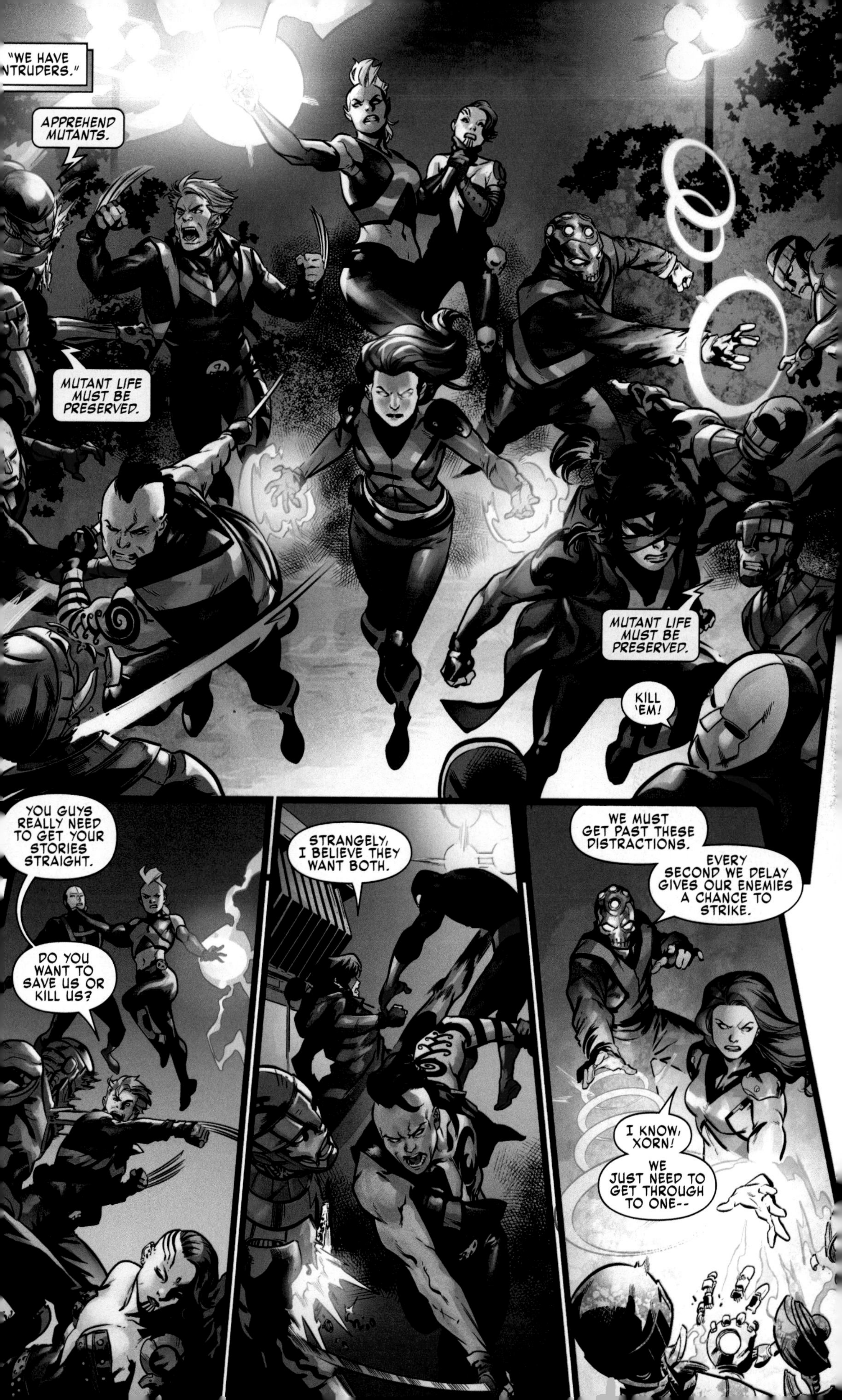
"WE HAVE
NTRUDERS."
APPREHEND MUTANTS.
MUTANT LIFE MUST BE PRESERVED.
MUTANT LIFE MUST BE PRESERVED.
KILL 'EM!
YOU GUYS REALLY NEED TO GET YOUR STORIES STRAIGHT.
DO YOU WANT TO SAVE US OR KILL US?
STRANGELY, I BELIEVE THEY WANT BOTH.
WE MUST GET PAST THESE DISTRACTIONS.
EVERY SECOND WE DELAY GIVES OUR ENEMIES A CHANCE TO STRIKE.
I KNOW, XORN!
WE JUST NEED TO GET THROUGH TO ONE--

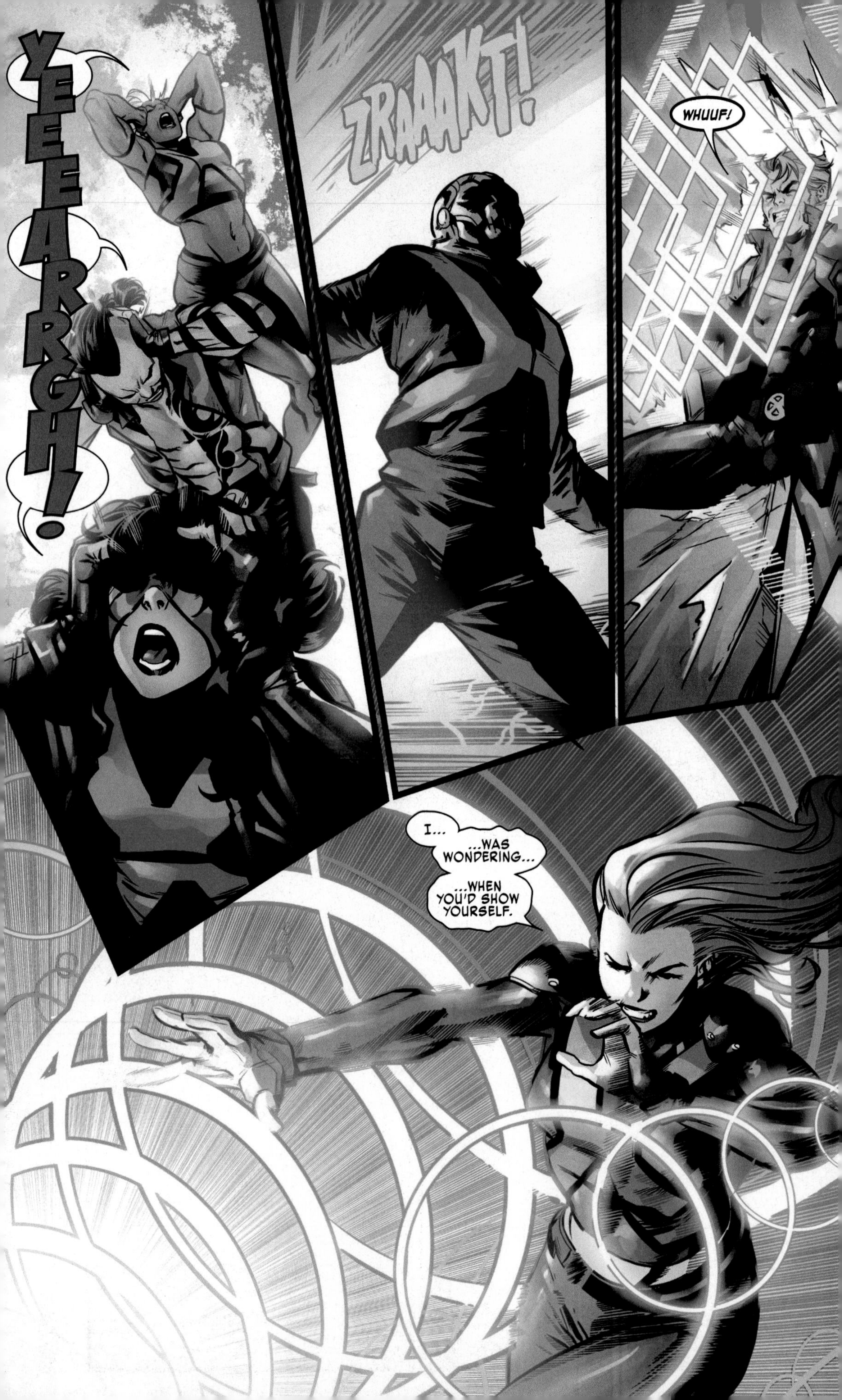
YEEEARRGH!
ZRAAAKT!
WHUUF!
I...
...WAS WONDERING...
...WHEN YOU'D SHOW YOURSELF.

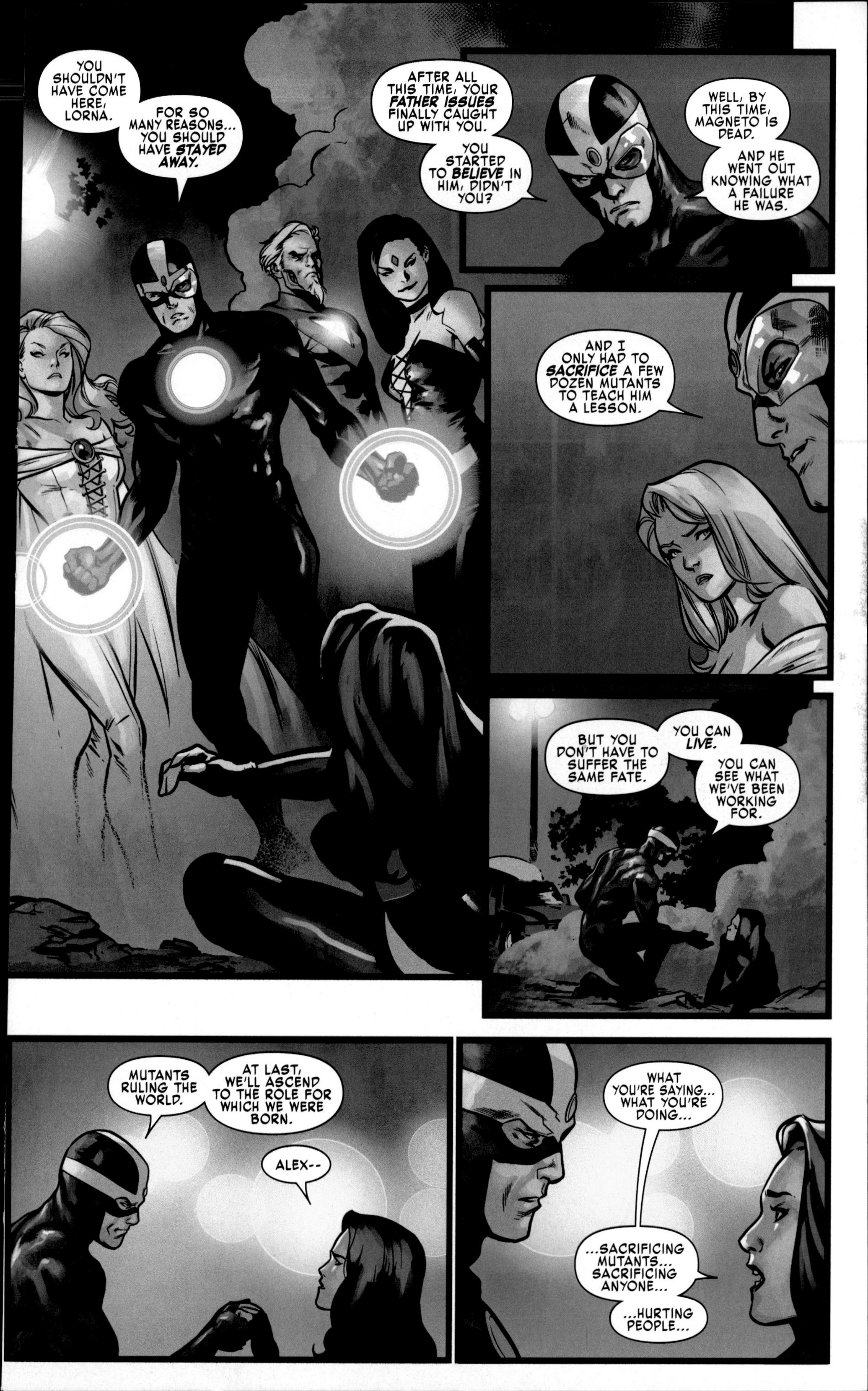
YOU SHOULDN'T HAVE COME HERE, LORNA.
FOR SO MANY REASONS... YOU SHOULD HAVE STAYED AWAY.
AFTER ALL THIS TIME, YOUR FATHER ISSUES FINALLY CAUGHT UP WITH YOU.
YOU STARTED TO BELIEVE IN HIM, DIDN'T YOU?
WELL, BY THIS TIME, MAGNETO IS DEAD.
AND HE WENT OUT KNOWING WHAT A FAILURE HE WAS.
AND I ONLY HAD TO SACRIFICE A FEW DOZEN MUTANTS TO TEACH HIM A LESSON.
BUT YOU DON'T HAVE TO SUFFER THE SAME FATE.
YOU CAN LIVE.
YOU CAN SEE WHAT WE'VE BEEN WORKING FOR.
MUTANTS RULING THE WORLD.
AT LAST, WE'LL ASCEND TO THE ROLE FOR WHICH WE WERE BORN.
ALEX--
WHAT YOU'RE SAYING... WHAT YOU'RE DOING...
...SACRIFICING MUTANTS... SACRIFICING ANYONE...
...HURTING PEOPLE...

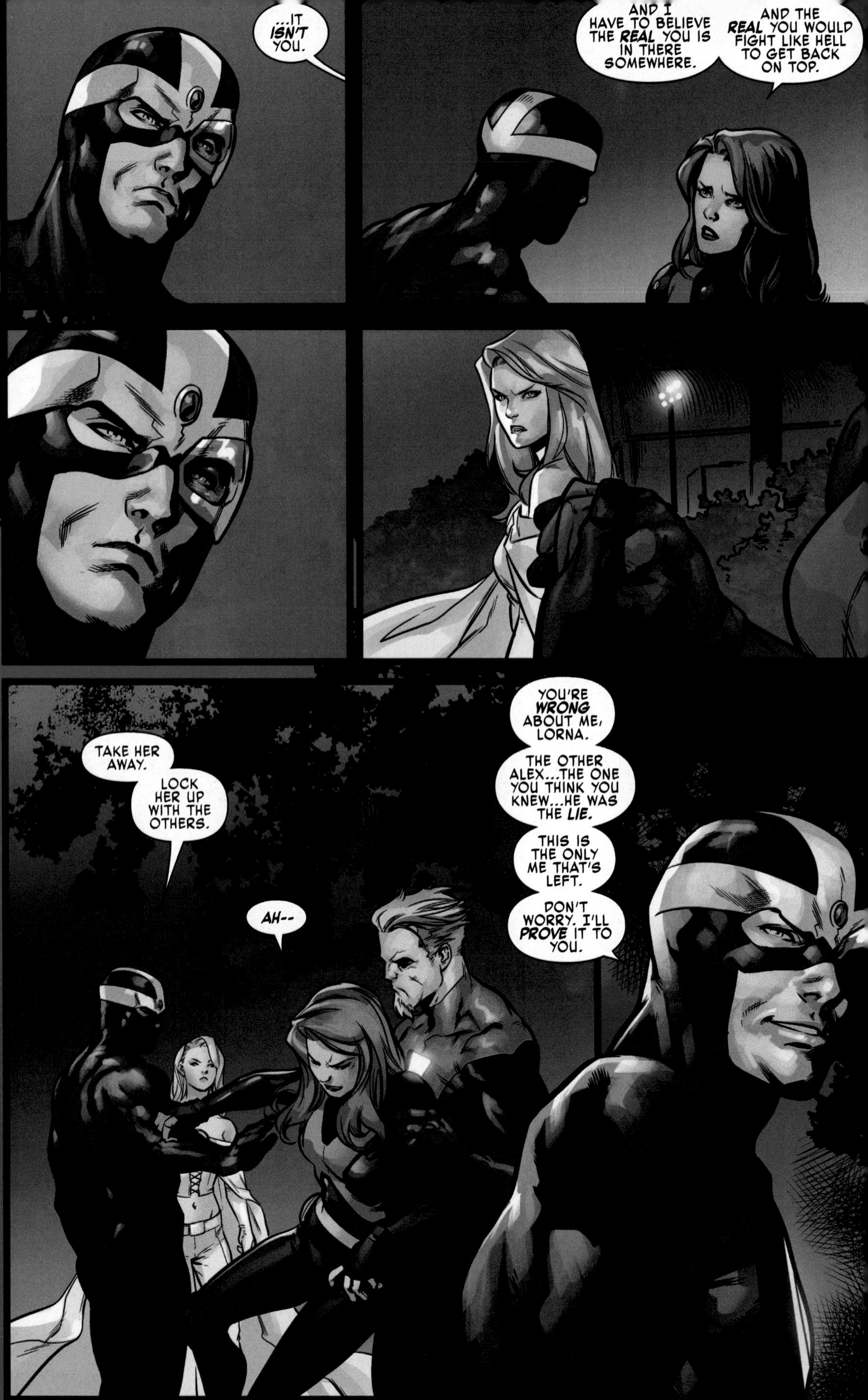
...IT ISN'T YOU.
AND I HAVE TO BELIEVE THE REAL YOU IS IN THERE SOMEWHERE.
AND THE REAL YOU WOULD FIGHT LIKE HELL TO GET BACK ON TOP.
TAKE HER AWAY.
LOCK HER UP WITH THE OTHERS.
AH--
YOU'RE WRONG ABOUT ME, LORNA.
THE OTHER ALEX...THE ONE YOU THINK YOU KNEW...HE WAS THE LIE.
THIS IS THE ONLY ME THAT'S LEFT.
DON'T WORRY. I'LL PROVE IT TO YOU.

28

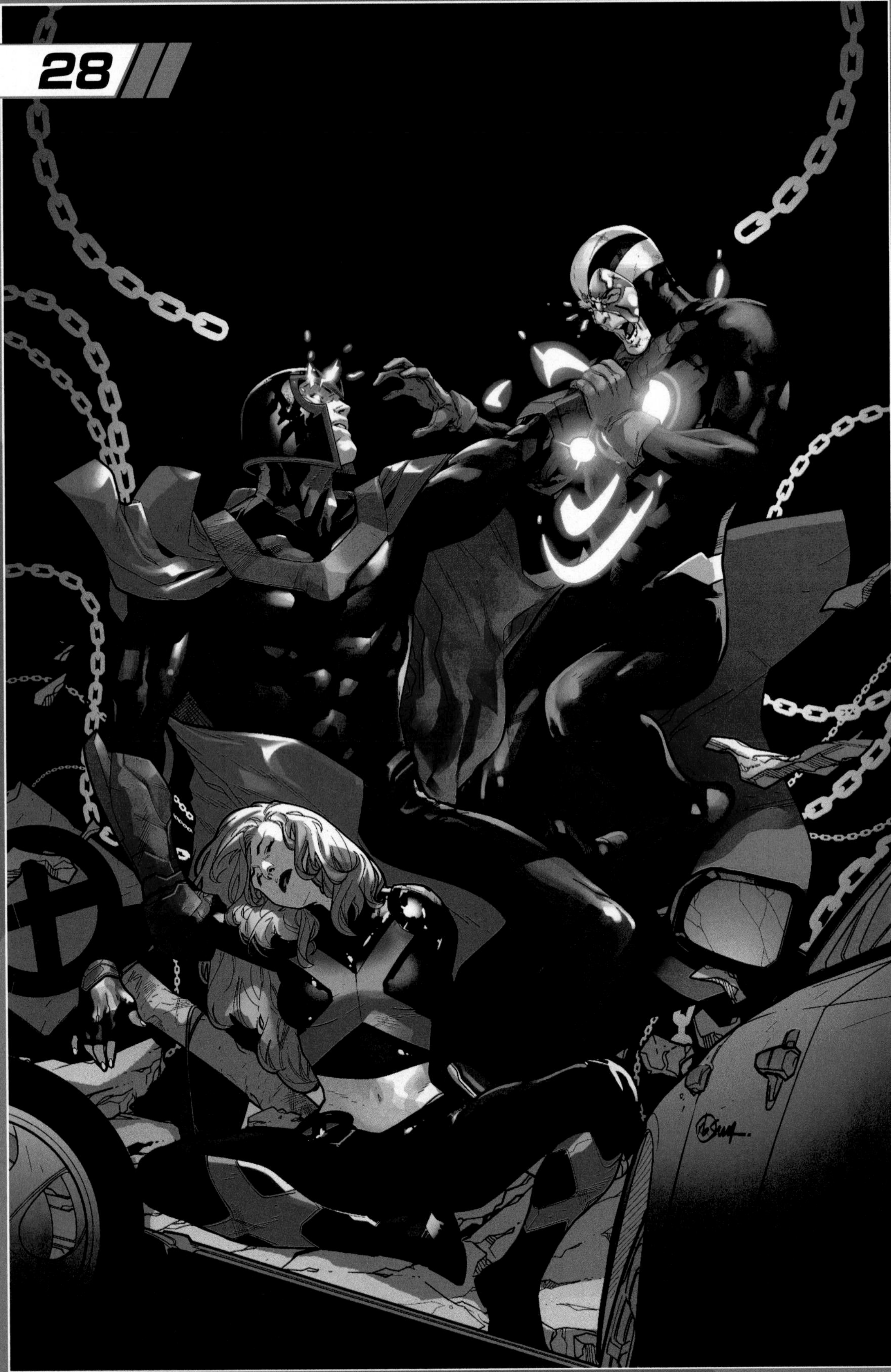

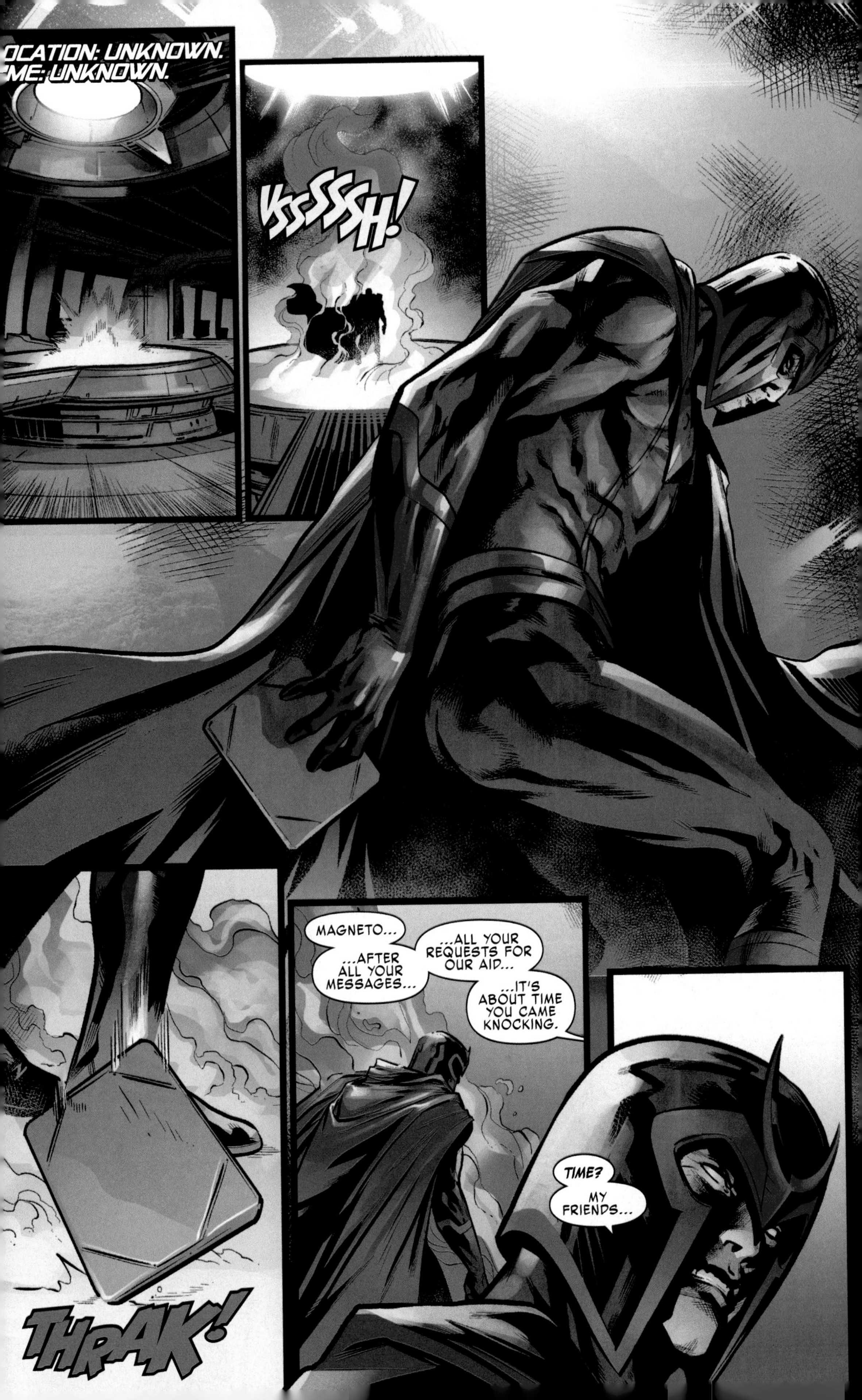

OCATION: UNKNOWN.
ME: UNKNOWN.
KSSSSSH!
THRAK!
MAGNETO...
...AFTER ALL YOUR MESSAGES...
...ALL YOUR REQUESTS FOR OUR AID...
...IT'S ABOUT TIME YOU CAME KNOCKING.
TIME?
MY FRIENDS...

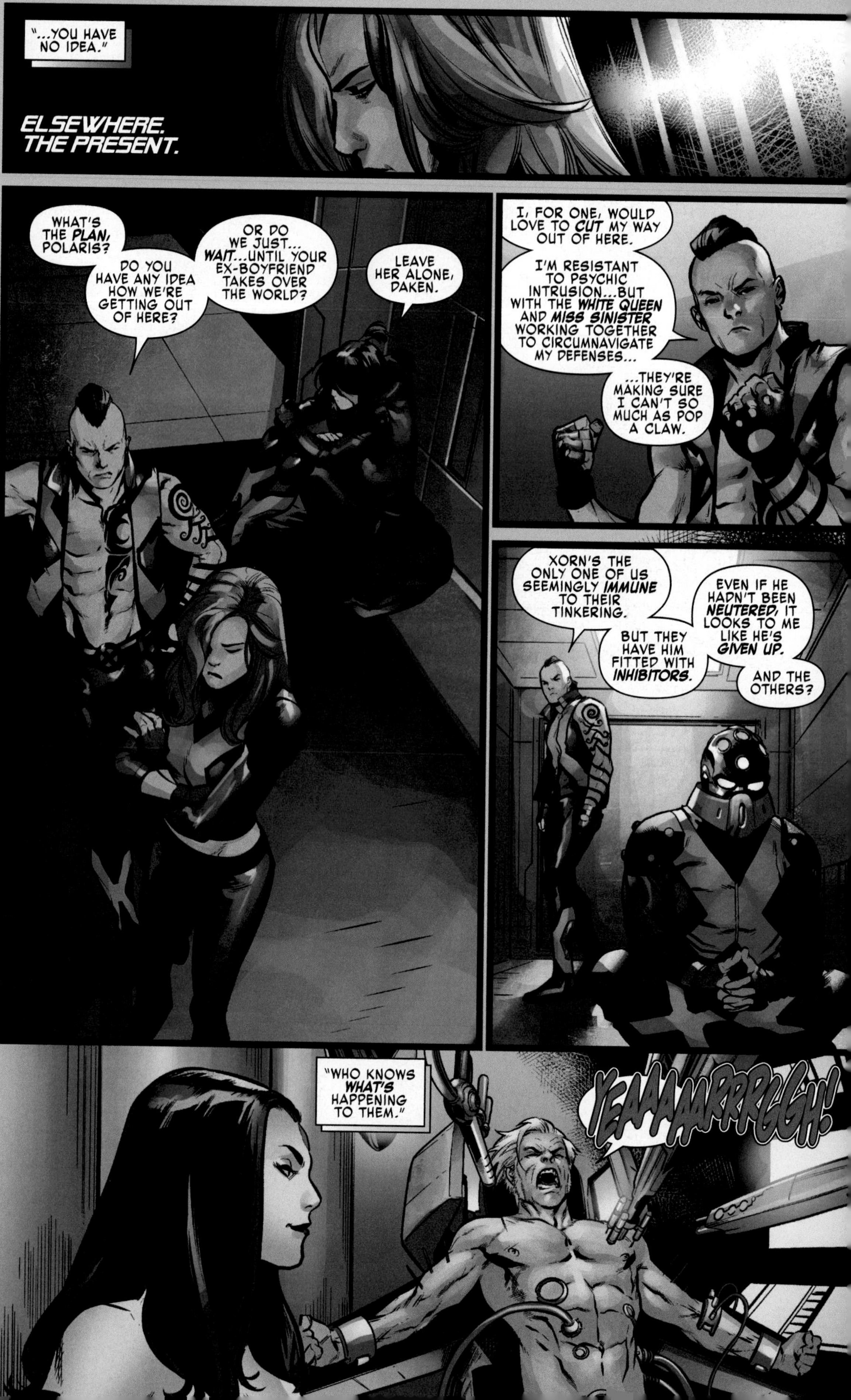
"...YOU HAVE NO IDEA."
ELSEWHERE. THE PRESENT.
WHAT'S THE PLAN, POLARIS?
DO YOU HAVE ANY IDEA HOW WE'RE GETTING OUT OF HERE?
OR DO WE JUST... WAIT...UNTIL YOUR EX-BOYFRIEND TAKES OVER THE WORLD?
LEAVE HER ALONE, DAKEN.
I, FOR ONE, WOULD LOVE TO CUT MY WAY OUT OF HERE.
I'M RESISTANT TO PSYCHIC INTRUSION...BUT WITH THE WHITE QUEEN AND MISS SINISTER WORKING TOGETHER TO CIRCUMNAVIGATE MY DEFENSES...
...THEY'RE MAKING SURE I CAN'T SO MUCH AS POP A CLAW.
XORN'S THE ONLY ONE OF US SEEMINGLY IMMUNE TO THEIR TINKERING.
BUT THEY HAVE HIM FITTED WITH INHIBITORS.
EVEN IF HE HADN'T BEEN NEUTERED, IT LOOKS TO ME LIKE HE'S GIVEN UP.
AND THE OTHERS?
"WHO KNOWS WHAT'S HAPPENING TO THEM."
YEAAAAARRRGGH!

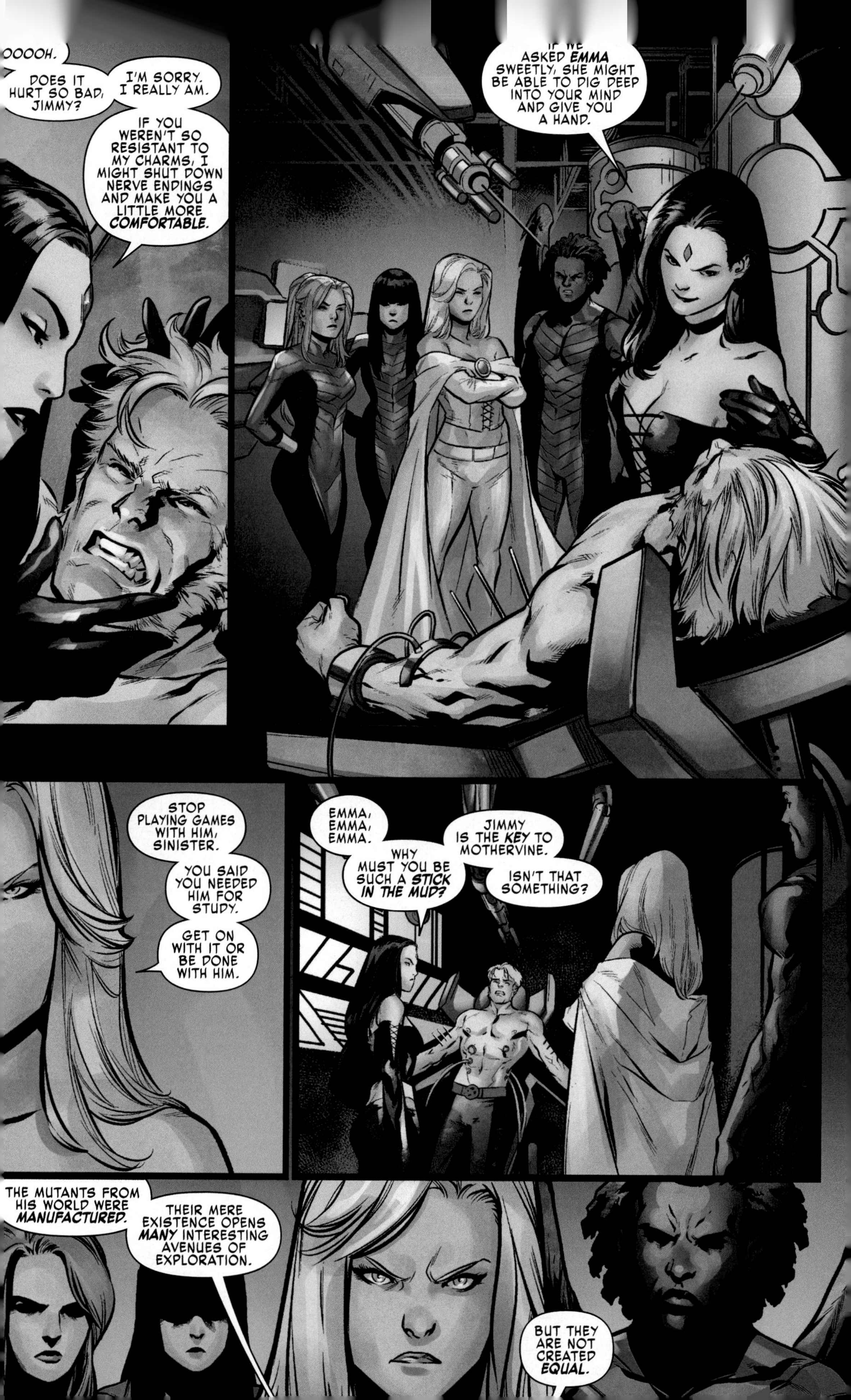
OOOOH.
DOES IT HURT SO BAD, JIMMY?
I'M SORRY. I REALLY AM.
IF YOU WEREN'T SO RESISTANT TO MY CHARMS, I MIGHT SHUT DOWN NERVE ENDINGS AND MAKE YOU A LITTLE MORE ***COMFORTABLE.***
IF WE ASKED ***EMMA*** SWEETLY, SHE MIGHT BE ABLE TO DIG DEEP INTO YOUR MIND AND GIVE YOU A HAND.
STOP PLAYING GAMES WITH HIM, SINISTER.
YOU SAID YOU NEEDED HIM FOR STUDY.
GET ON WITH IT OR BE DONE WITH HIM.
EMMA, EMMA, EMMA.
WHY MUST YOU BE SUCH A ***STICK IN THE MUD?***
JIMMY IS THE ***KEY*** TO MOTHERVINE.
ISN'T THAT SOMETHING?
THE MUTANTS FROM HIS WORLD WERE ***MANUFACTURED.***
THEIR MERE EXISTENCE OPENS ***MANY*** INTERESTING AVENUES OF EXPLORATION.
BUT THEY ARE NOT CREATED ***EQUAL.***

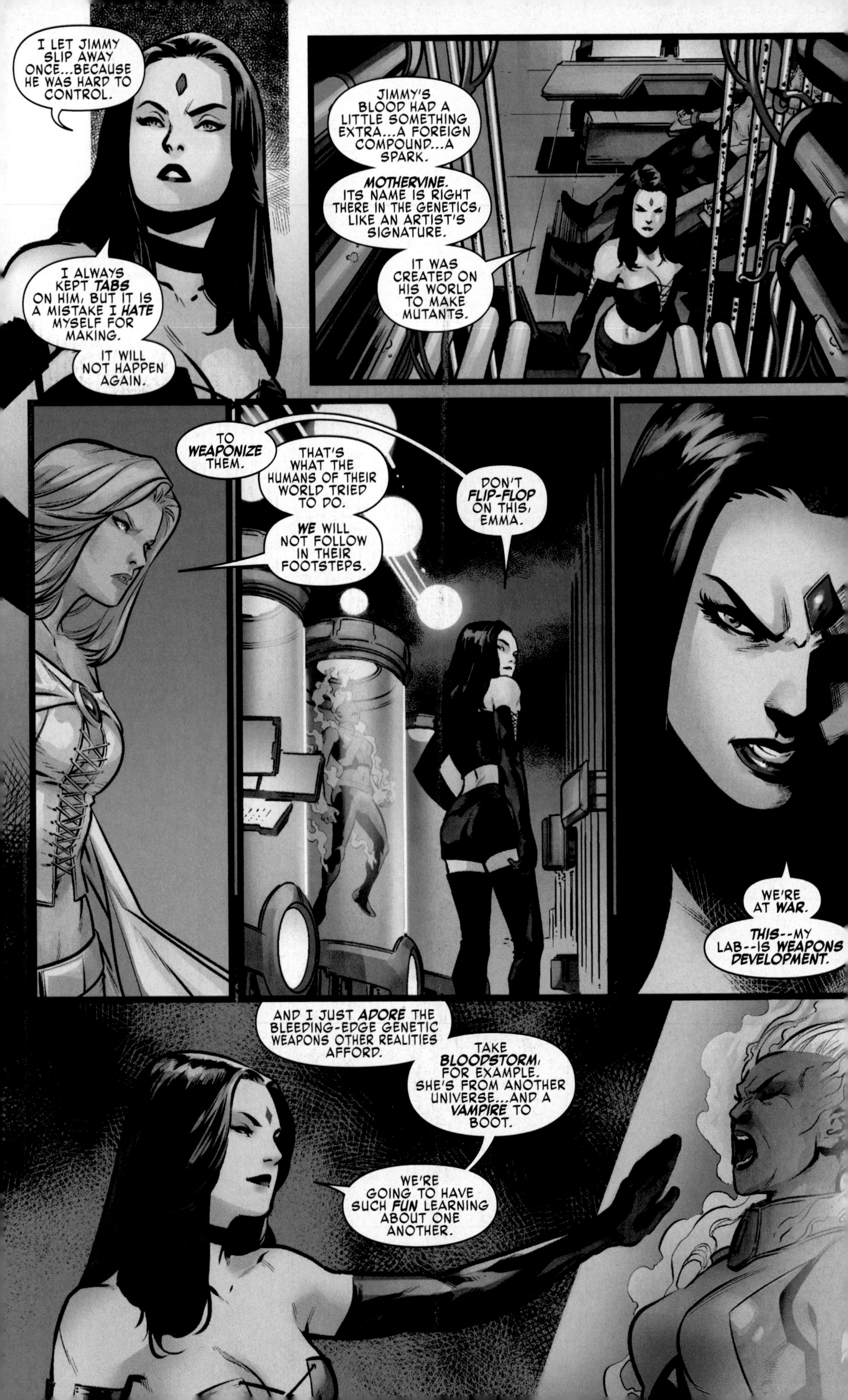
I LET JIMMY SLIP AWAY ONCE...BECAUSE HE WAS HARD TO CONTROL.
I ALWAYS KEPT TABS ON HIM, BUT IT IS A MISTAKE I HATE MYSELF FOR MAKING.
IT WILL NOT HAPPEN AGAIN.
JIMMY'S BLOOD HAD A LITTLE SOMETHING EXTRA...A FOREIGN COMPOUND...A SPARK.
MOTHERVINE. ITS NAME IS RIGHT THERE IN THE GENETICS, LIKE AN ARTIST'S SIGNATURE.
IT WAS CREATED ON HIS WORLD TO MAKE MUTANTS.
TO WEAPONIZE THEM.
THAT'S WHAT THE HUMANS OF THEIR WORLD TRIED TO DO.
WE WILL NOT FOLLOW IN THEIR FOOTSTEPS.
DON'T FLIP-FLOP ON THIS, EMMA.
WE'RE AT WAR.
THIS--MY LAB--IS WEAPONS DEVELOPMENT.
AND I JUST ADORE THE BLEEDING-EDGE GENETIC WEAPONS OTHER REALITIES AFFORD.
TAKE BLOODSTORM, FOR EXAMPLE. SHE'S FROM ANOTHER UNIVERSE...AND A VAMPIRE TO BOOT.
WE'RE GOING TO HAVE SUCH FUN LEARNING ABOUT ONE ANOTHER.

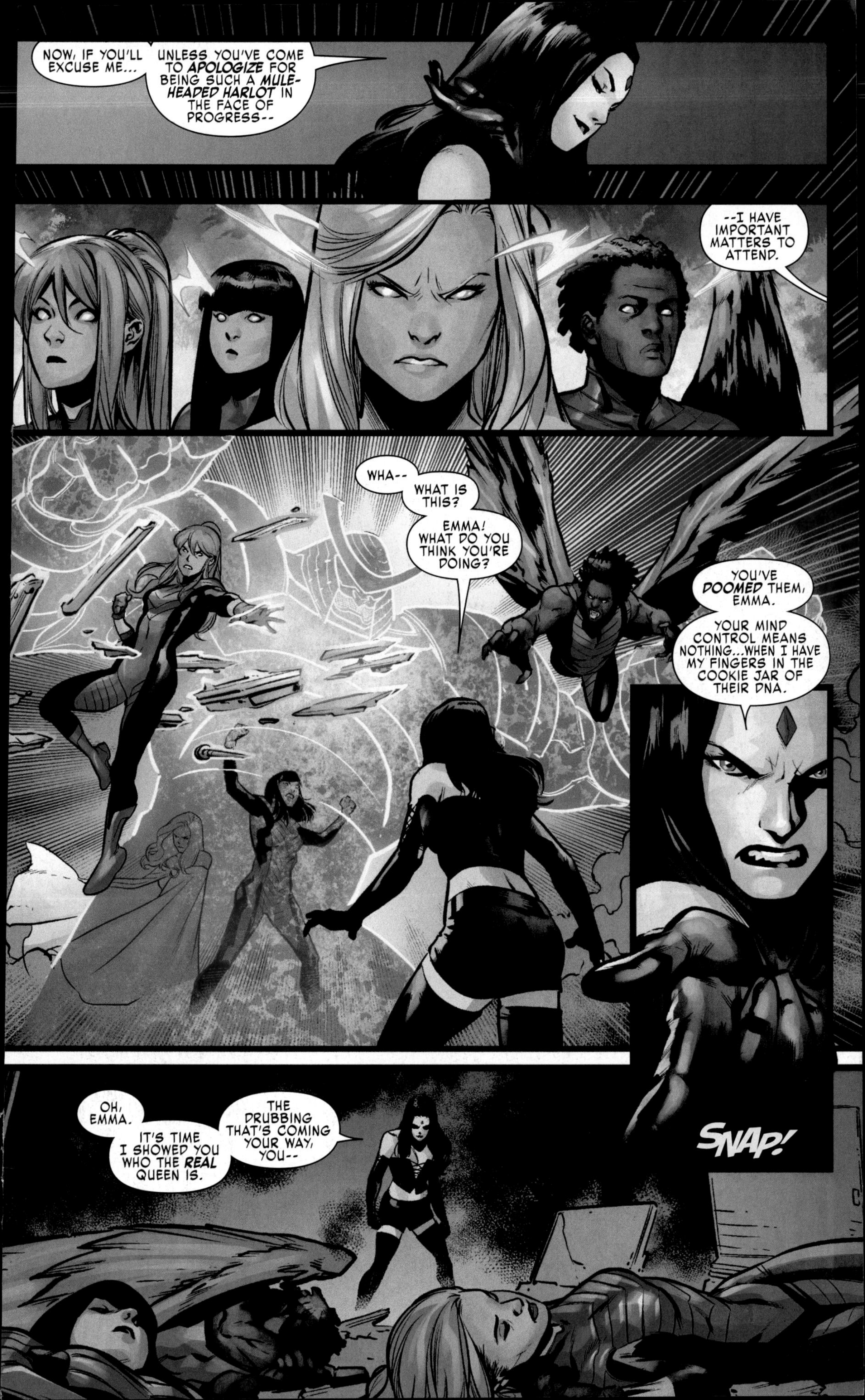

NOW, IF YOU'LL EXCUSE ME...
UNLESS YOU'VE COME TO *APOLOGIZE* FOR BEING SUCH A *MULE-HEADED HARLOT* IN THE FACE OF PROGRESS--
--I HAVE IMPORTANT MATTERS TO ATTEND.
WHA--
WHAT IS THIS?
EMMA! WHAT DO YOU THINK YOU'RE DOING?
YOU'VE *DOOMED* THEM, EMMA.
YOUR MIND CONTROL MEANS NOTHING...WHEN I HAVE MY FINGERS IN THE COOKIE JAR OF THEIR DNA.
SNAP!
OH, EMMA.
IT'S TIME I SHOWED YOU WHO THE *REAL* QUEEN IS.
THE DRUBBING THAT'S COMING YOUR WAY, YOU--

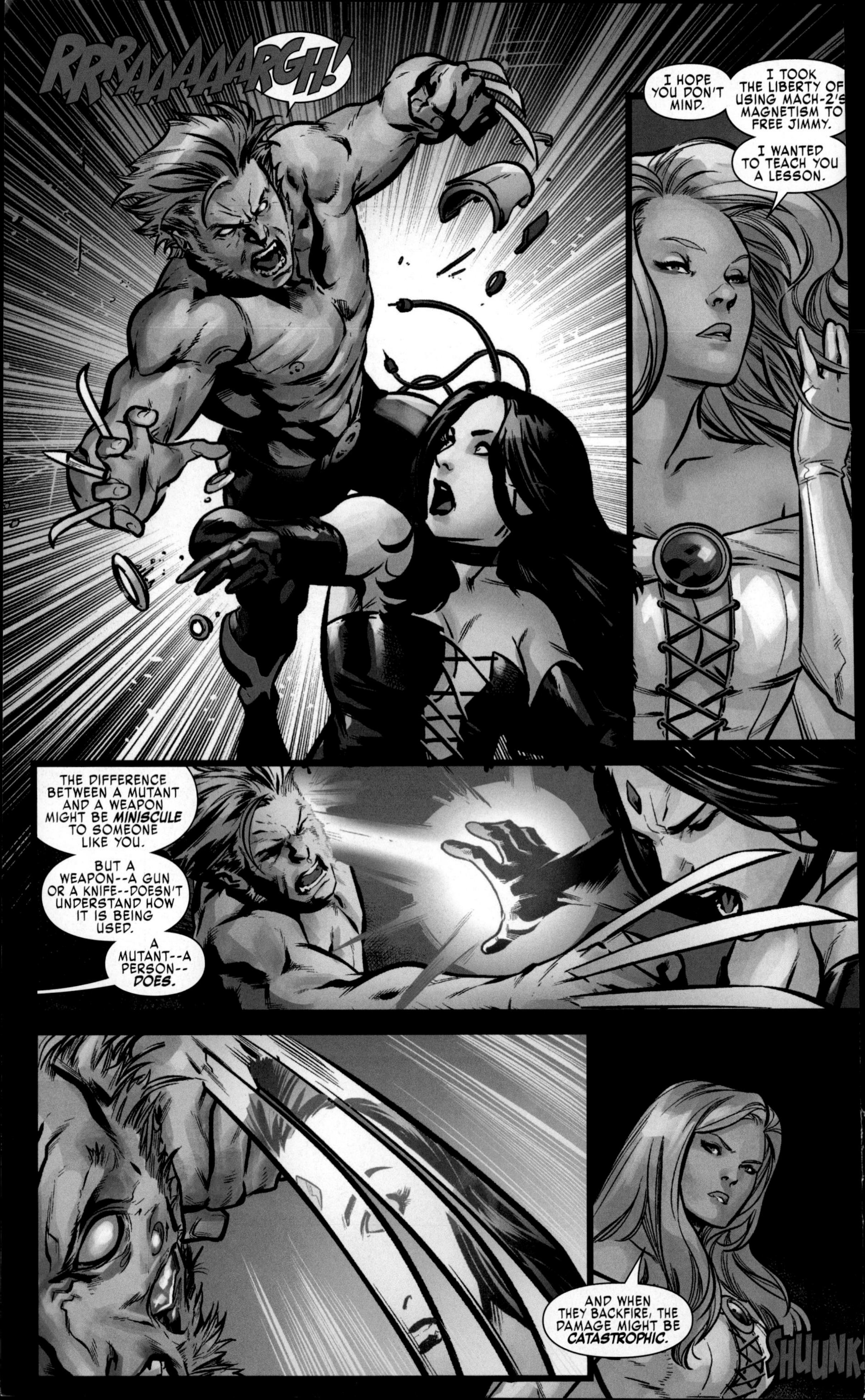
RRRAAAAAARGH!
I HOPE YOU DON'T MIND.
I TOOK THE LIBERTY OF USING MACH-2'S MAGNETISM TO FREE JIMMY.
I WANTED TO TEACH YOU A LESSON.
THE DIFFERENCE BETWEEN A MUTANT AND A WEAPON MIGHT BE *MINISCULE* TO SOMEONE LIKE YOU.
BUT A WEAPON--A GUN OR A KNIFE--DOESN'T UNDERSTAND HOW IT IS BEING USED.
A MUTANT--A PERSON--*DOES.*
AND WHEN THEY BACKFIRE, THE DAMAGE MIGHT BE *CATASTROPHIC.*
SHUUNK

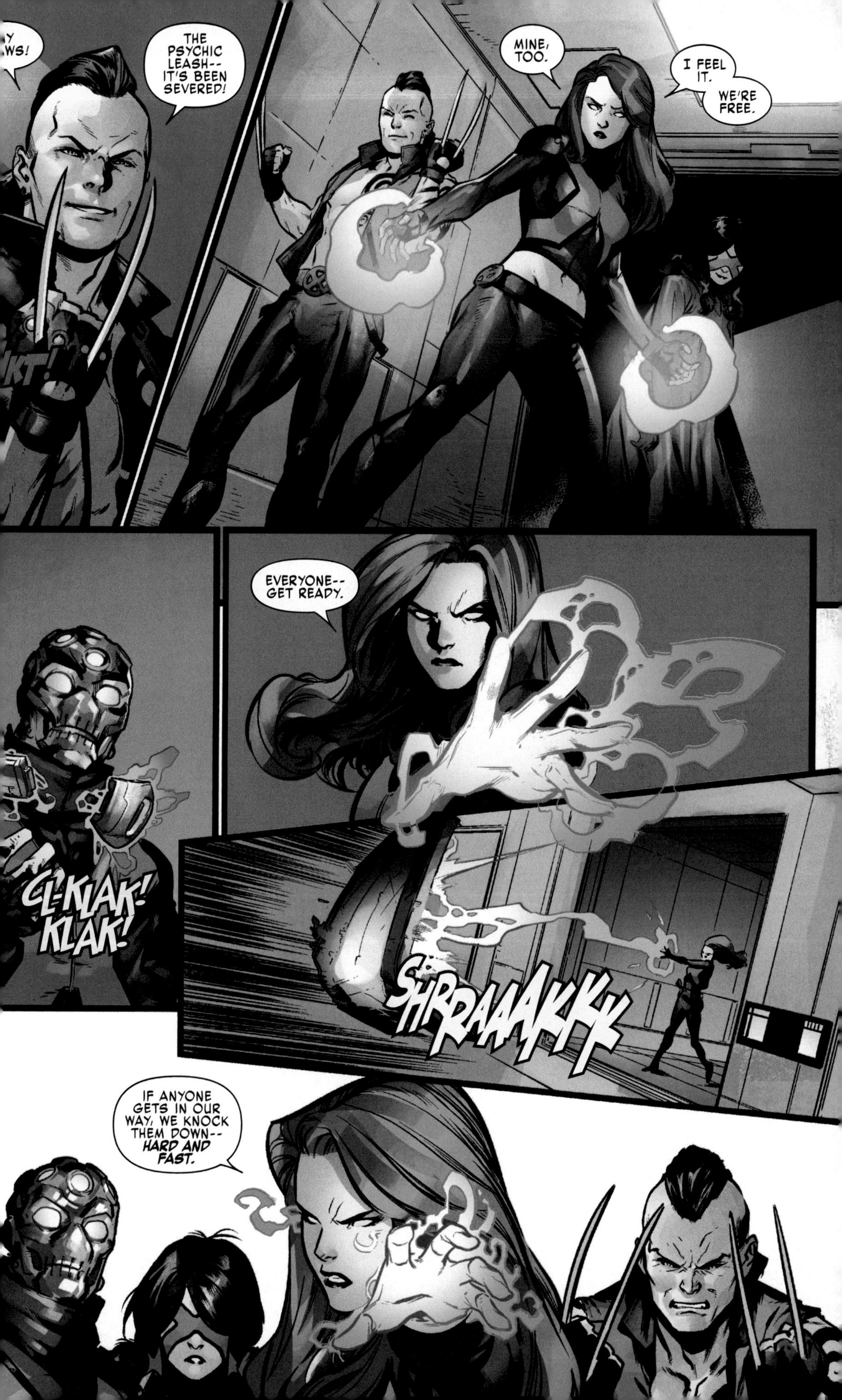
THE PSYCHIC LEASH-- IT'S BEEN SEVERED!
MINE, TOO.
I FEEL IT.
WE'RE FREE.
EVERYONE-- GET READY.
CL-KLAK! KLAK!
SHRRAAAKKK
IF ANYONE GETS IN OUR WAY, WE KNOCK THEM DOWN-- *HARD AND FAST.*

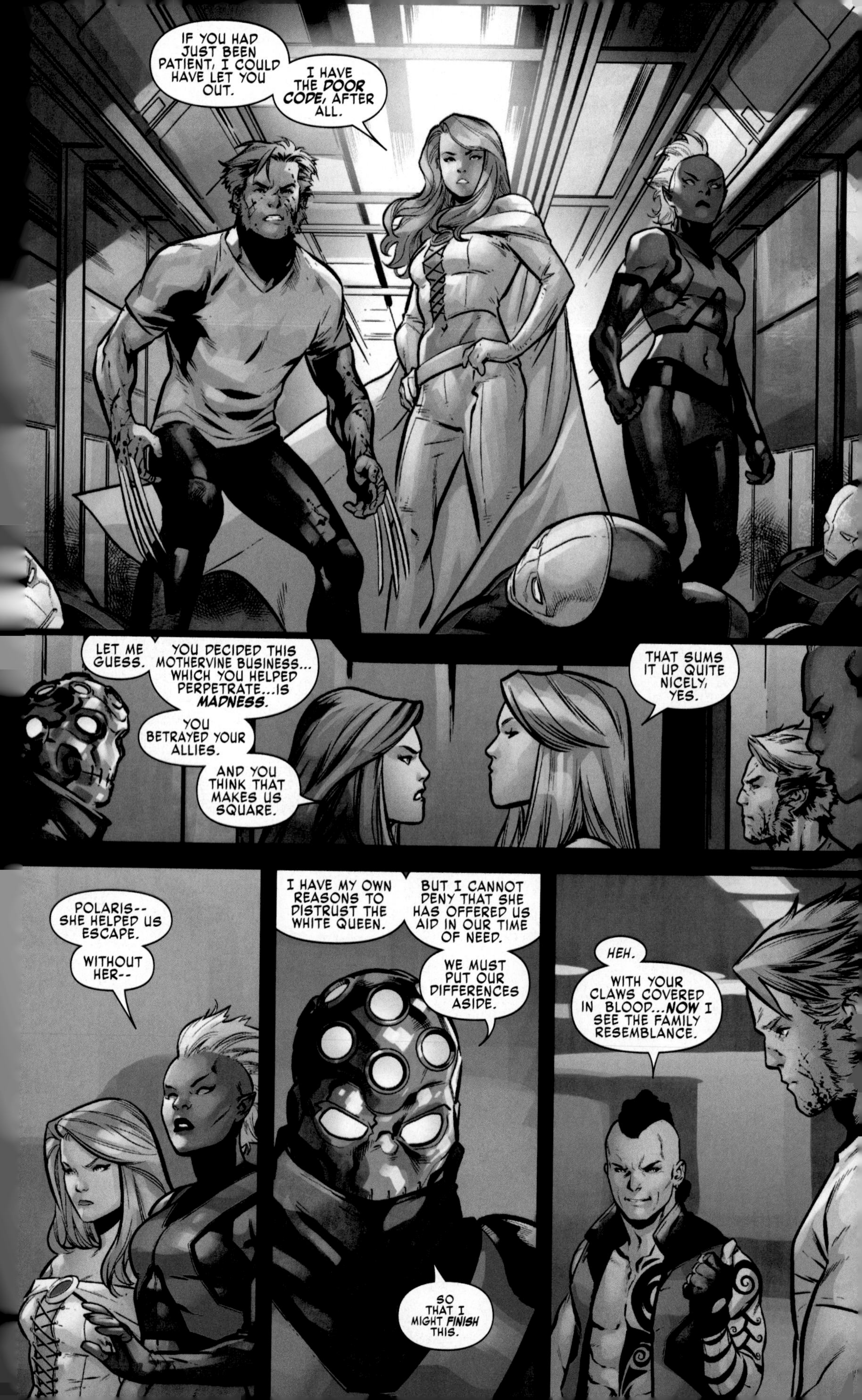
IF YOU HAD JUST BEEN PATIENT, I COULD HAVE LET YOU OUT.
I HAVE THE DOOR CODE, AFTER ALL.
LET ME GUESS.
YOU DECIDED THIS MOTHERVINE BUSINESS... WHICH YOU HELPED PERPETRATE...IS MADNESS.
YOU BETRAYED YOUR ALLIES.
AND YOU THINK THAT MAKES US SQUARE.
THAT SUMS IT UP QUITE NICELY, YES.
POLARIS-- SHE HELPED US ESCAPE.
WITHOUT HER--
I HAVE MY OWN REASONS TO DISTRUST THE WHITE QUEEN.
BUT I CANNOT DENY THAT SHE HAS OFFERED US AID IN OUR TIME OF NEED.
WE MUST PUT OUR DIFFERENCES ASIDE.
SO THAT I MIGHT FINISH THIS.
HEH.
WITH YOUR CLAWS COVERED IN BLOOD...NOW I SEE THE FAMILY RESEMBLANCE.

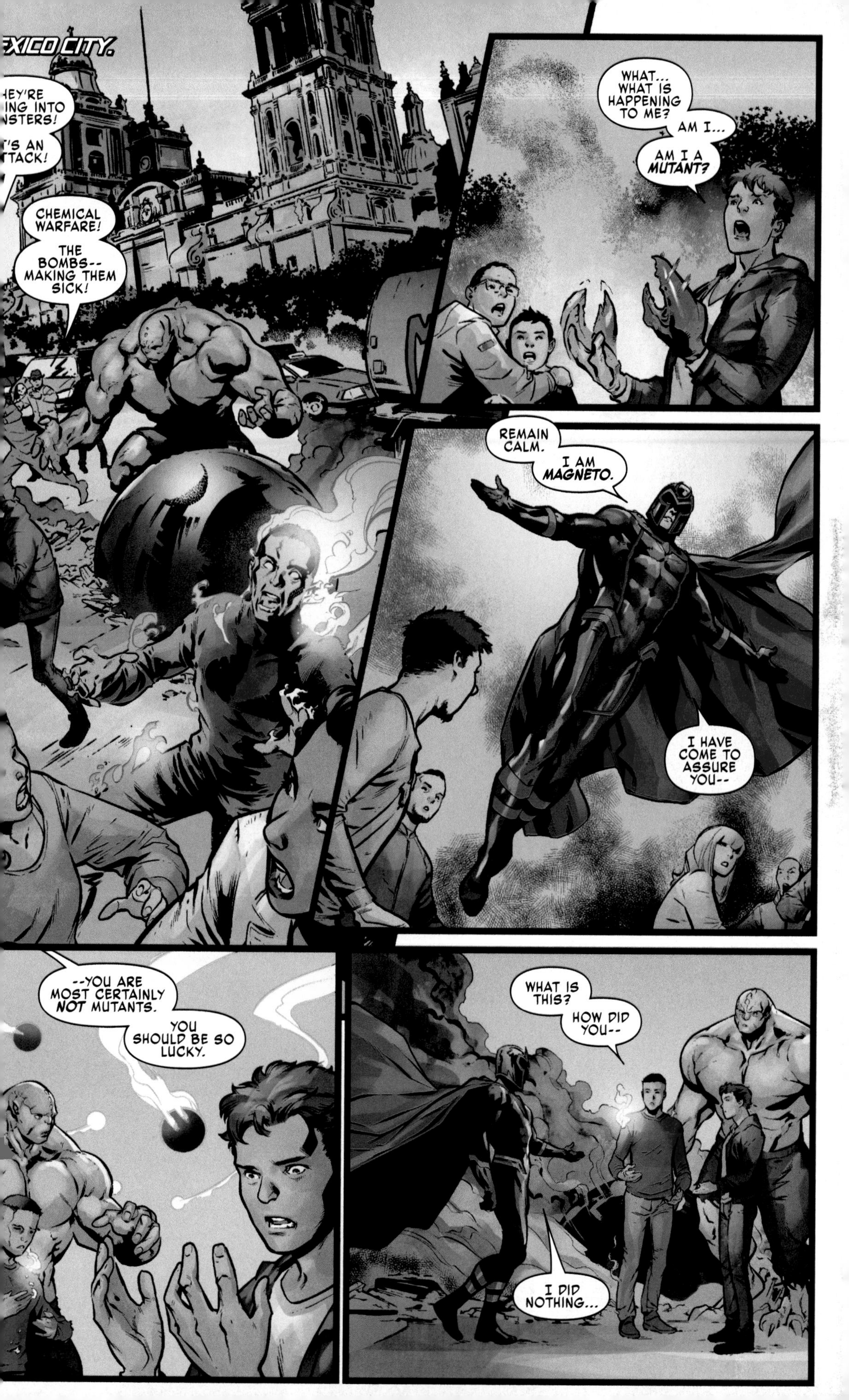

EXICO CITY.
HEY'RE ING INTO NSTERS!
T'S AN TTACK!
CHEMICAL WARFARE!
THE BOMBS-- MAKING THEM SICK!
WHAT... WHAT IS HAPPENING TO ME? AM I...
AM I A MUTANT?
REMAIN CALM.
I AM MAGNETO.
I HAVE COME TO ASSURE YOU--
--YOU ARE MOST CERTAINLY NOT MUTANTS.
YOU SHOULD BE SO LUCKY.
WHAT IS THIS?
HOW DID YOU--
I DID NOTHING...

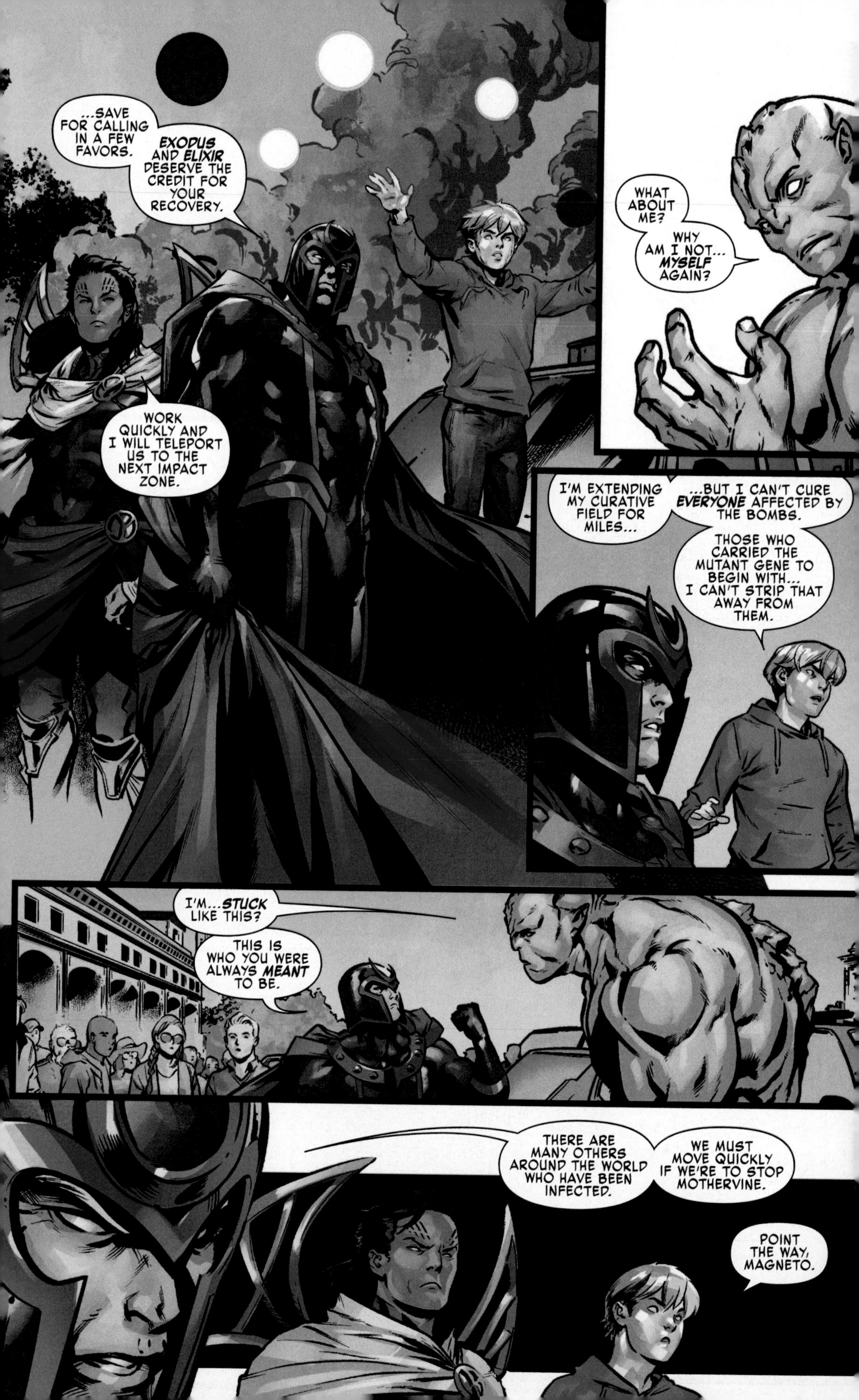
...SAVE FOR CALLING IN A FEW FAVORS.
EXODUS AND ELIXIR DESERVE THE CREDIT FOR YOUR RECOVERY.
WORK QUICKLY AND I WILL TELEPORT US TO THE NEXT IMPACT ZONE.
WHAT ABOUT ME?
WHY AM I NOT... MYSELF AGAIN?
I'M EXTENDING MY CURATIVE FIELD FOR MILES...
...BUT I CAN'T CURE EVERYONE AFFECTED BY THE BOMBS.
THOSE WHO CARRIED THE MUTANT GENE TO BEGIN WITH... I CAN'T STRIP THAT AWAY FROM THEM.
I'M...STUCK LIKE THIS?
THIS IS WHO YOU WERE ALWAYS MEANT TO BE.
THERE ARE MANY OTHERS AROUND THE WORLD WHO HAVE BEEN INFECTED.
WE MUST MOVE QUICKLY IF WE'RE TO STOP MOTHERVINE.
POINT THE WAY, MAGNETO.

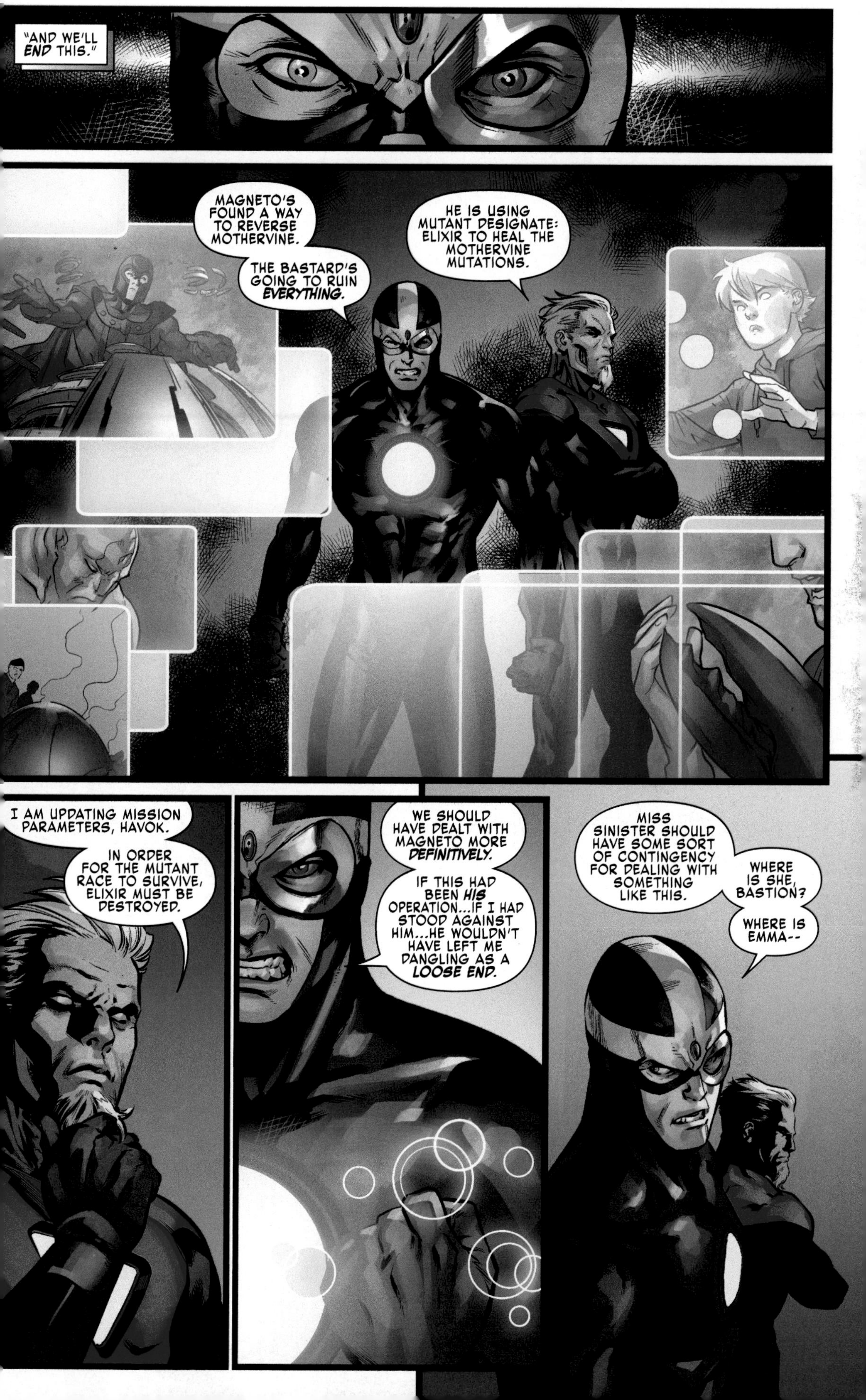
"AND WE'LL END THIS."
MAGNETO'S FOUND A WAY TO REVERSE MOTHERVINE.
THE BASTARD'S GOING TO RUIN EVERYTHING.
HE IS USING MUTANT DESIGNATE: ELIXIR TO HEAL THE MOTHERVINE MUTATIONS.
I AM UPDATING MISSION PARAMETERS, HAVOK.
IN ORDER FOR THE MUTANT RACE TO SURVIVE, ELIXIR MUST BE DESTROYED.
WE SHOULD HAVE DEALT WITH MAGNETO MORE DEFINITIVELY.
IF THIS HAD BEEN HIS OPERATION...IF I HAD STOOD AGAINST HIM...HE WOULDN'T HAVE LEFT ME DANGLING AS A LOOSE END.
MISS SINISTER SHOULD HAVE SOME SORT OF CONTINGENCY FOR DEALING WITH SOMETHING LIKE THIS.
WHERE IS SHE, BASTION?
WHERE IS EMMA--

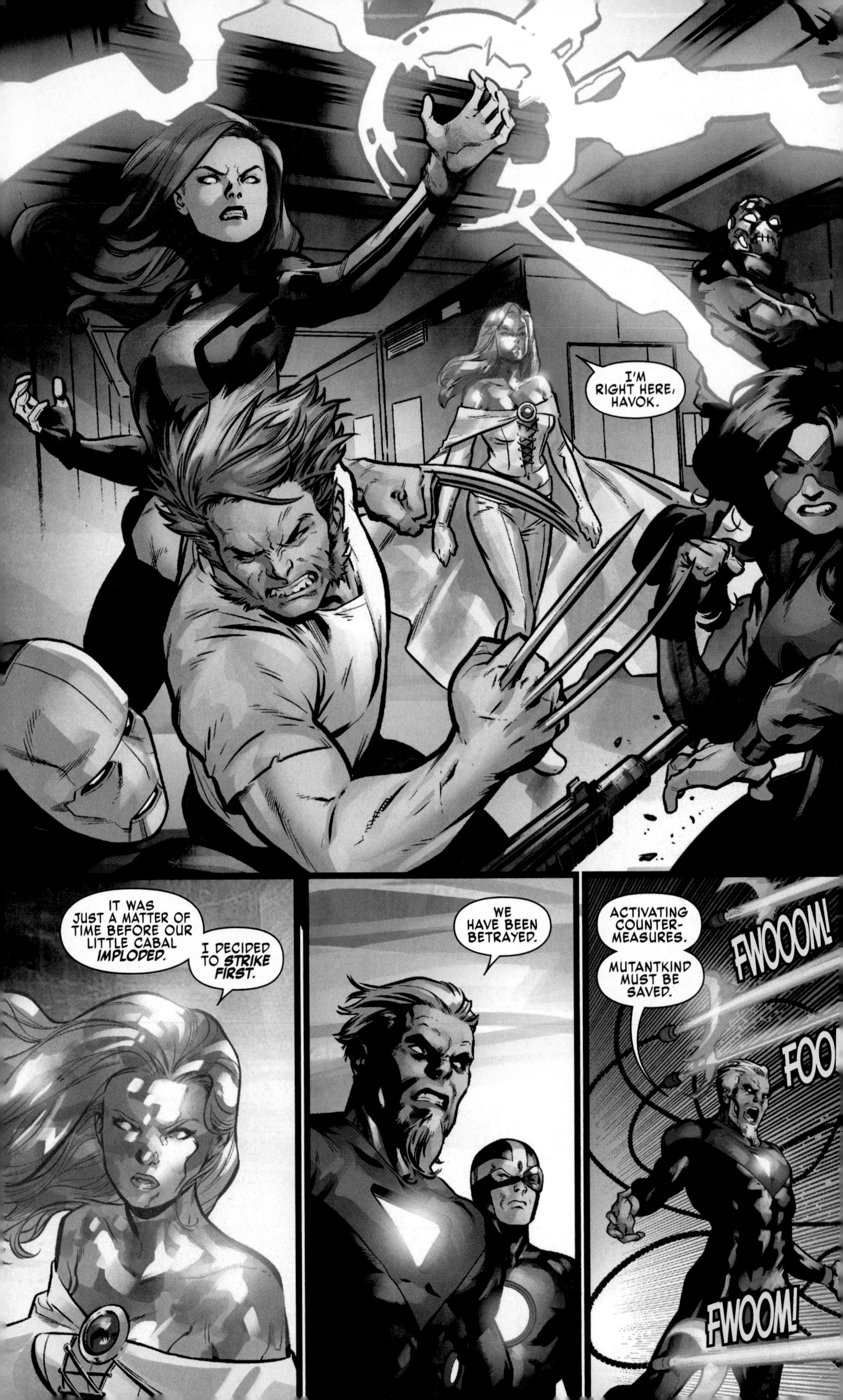
I'M RIGHT HERE, HAVOK.
IT WAS JUST A MATTER OF TIME BEFORE OUR LITTLE CABAL IMPLODED.
I DECIDED TO STRIKE FIRST.
WE HAVE BEEN BETRAYED.
ACTIVATING COUNTER-MEASURES.
MUTANTKIND MUST BE SAVED.
FWOOOM!
FWOOM!

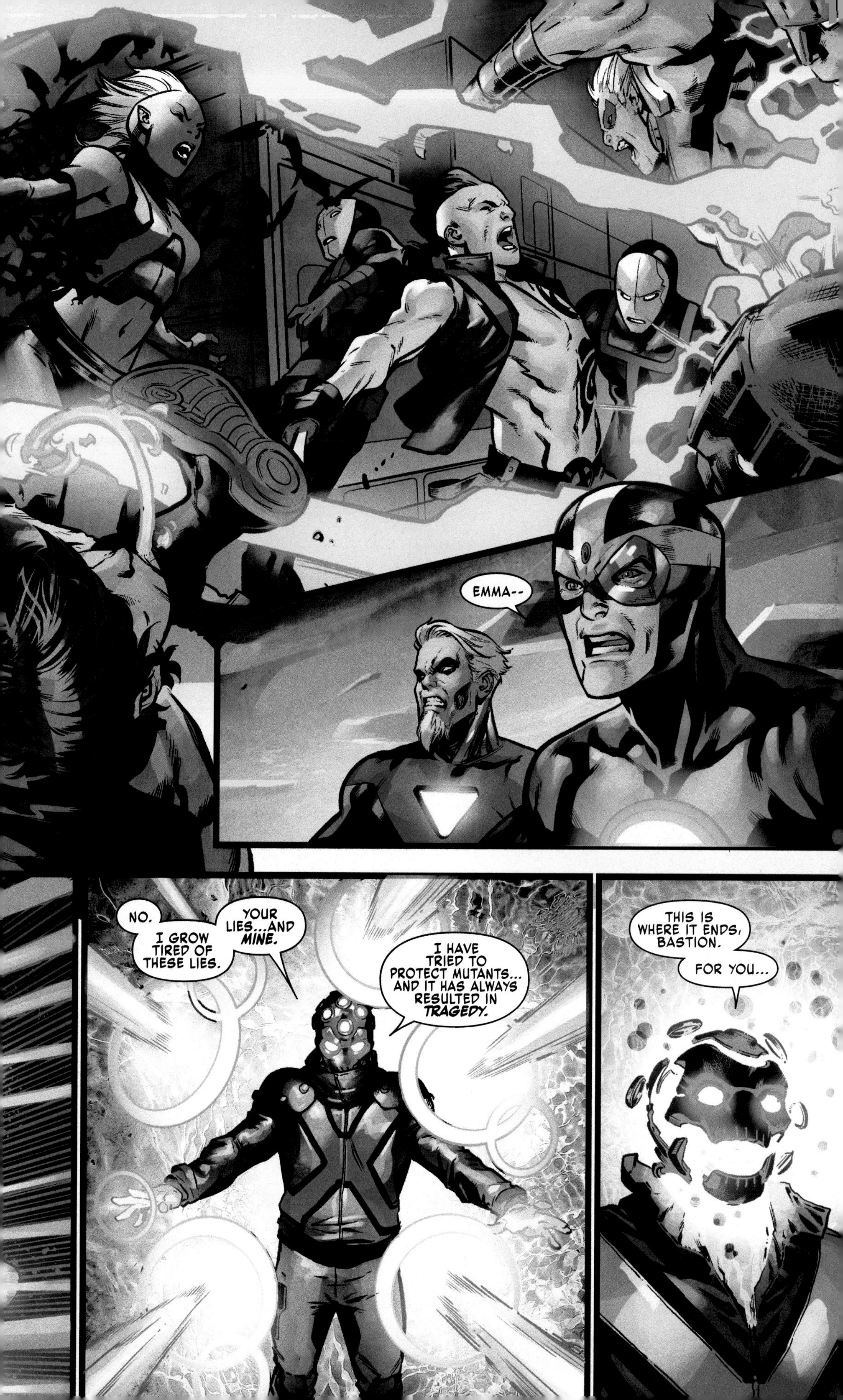
EMMA--
NO.
I GROW TIRED OF THESE LIES.
YOUR LIES...AND MINE.
I HAVE TRIED TO PROTECT MUTANTS... AND IT HAS ALWAYS RESULTED IN TRAGEDY.
THIS IS WHERE IT ENDS, BASTION.
FOR YOU...

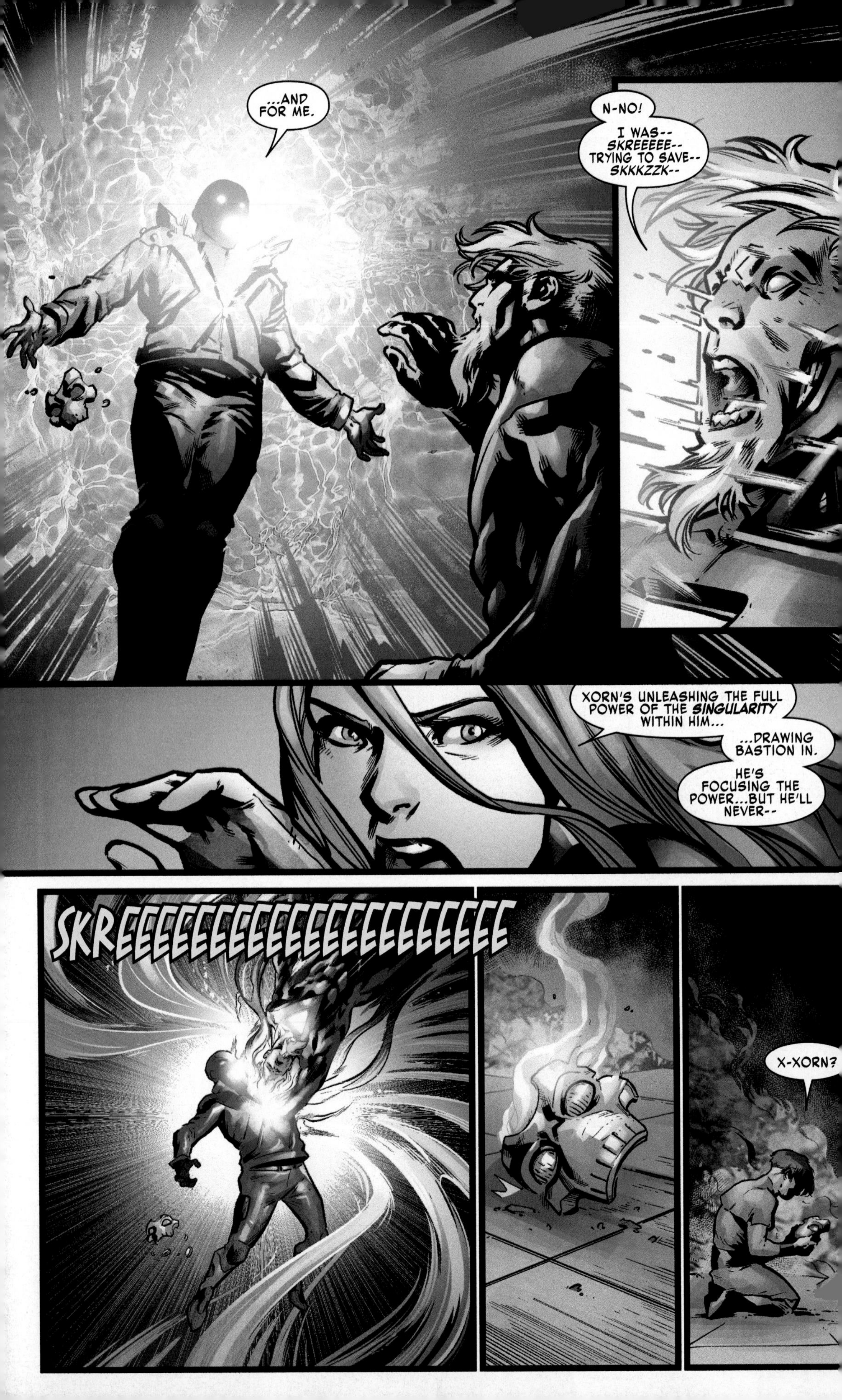
...AND FOR ME.
N-NO! I WAS-- SKREEEEE-- TRYING TO SAVE-- SKKKZZK--
XORN'S UNLEASHING THE FULL POWER OF THE SINGULARITY WITHIN HIM...
...DRAWING BASTION IN.
HE'S FOCUSING THE POWER...BUT HE'LL NEVER--
SKREEEEEEEEEEEEEEEEEEEEEEE
X-XORN?

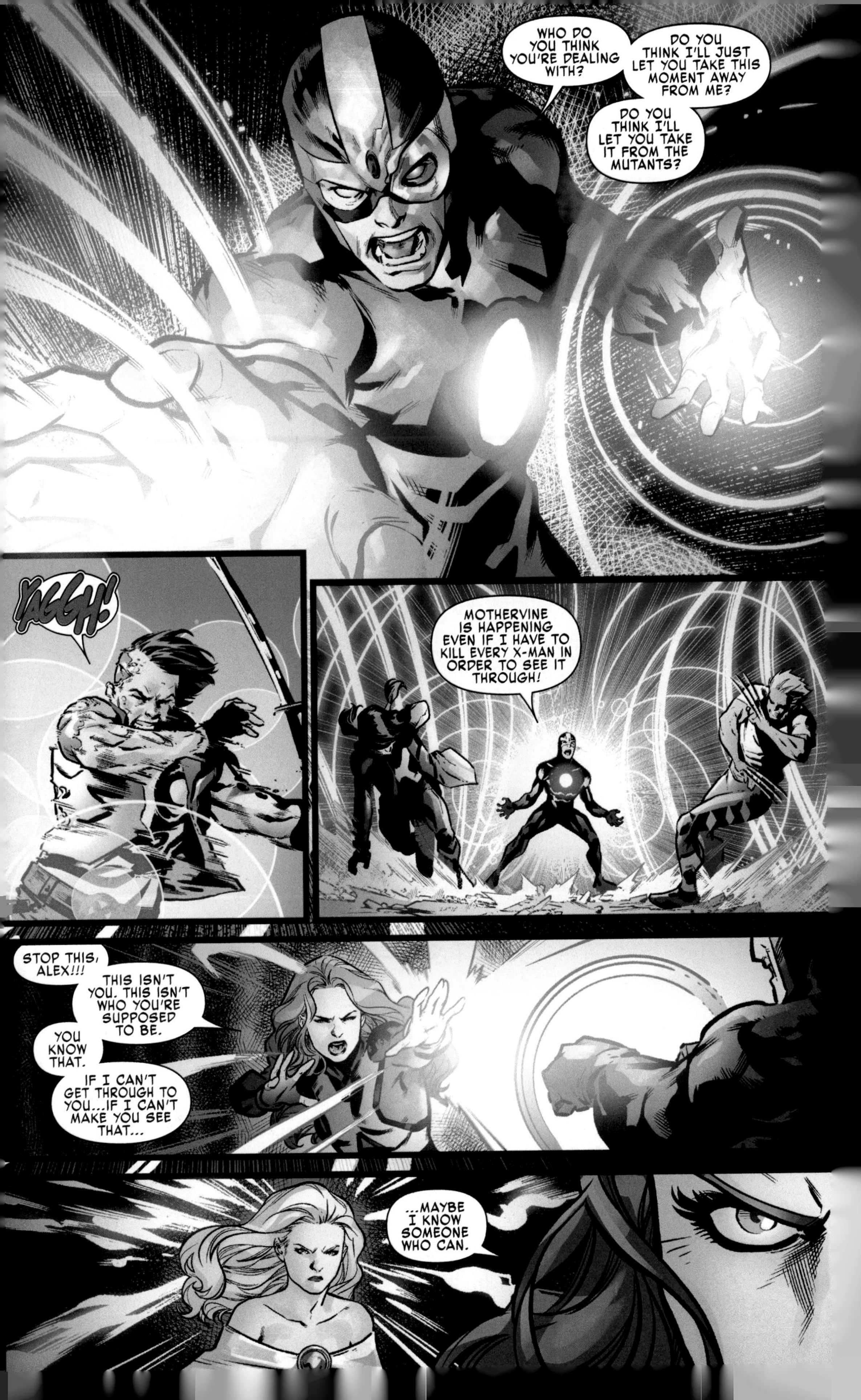
WHO DO YOU THINK YOU'RE DEALING WITH?
DO YOU THINK I'LL JUST LET YOU TAKE THIS MOMENT AWAY FROM ME?
DO YOU THINK I'LL LET YOU TAKE IT FROM THE MUTANTS?
YAGGH!
MOTHERVINE IS HAPPENING EVEN IF I HAVE TO KILL EVERY X-MAN IN ORDER TO SEE IT THROUGH!
STOP THIS, ALEX!!!
THIS ISN'T YOU. THIS ISN'T WHO YOU'RE SUPPOSED TO BE.
YOU KNOW THAT.
IF I CAN'T GET THROUGH TO YOU...IF I CAN'T MAKE YOU SEE THAT...
...MAYBE I KNOW SOMEONE WHO CAN.

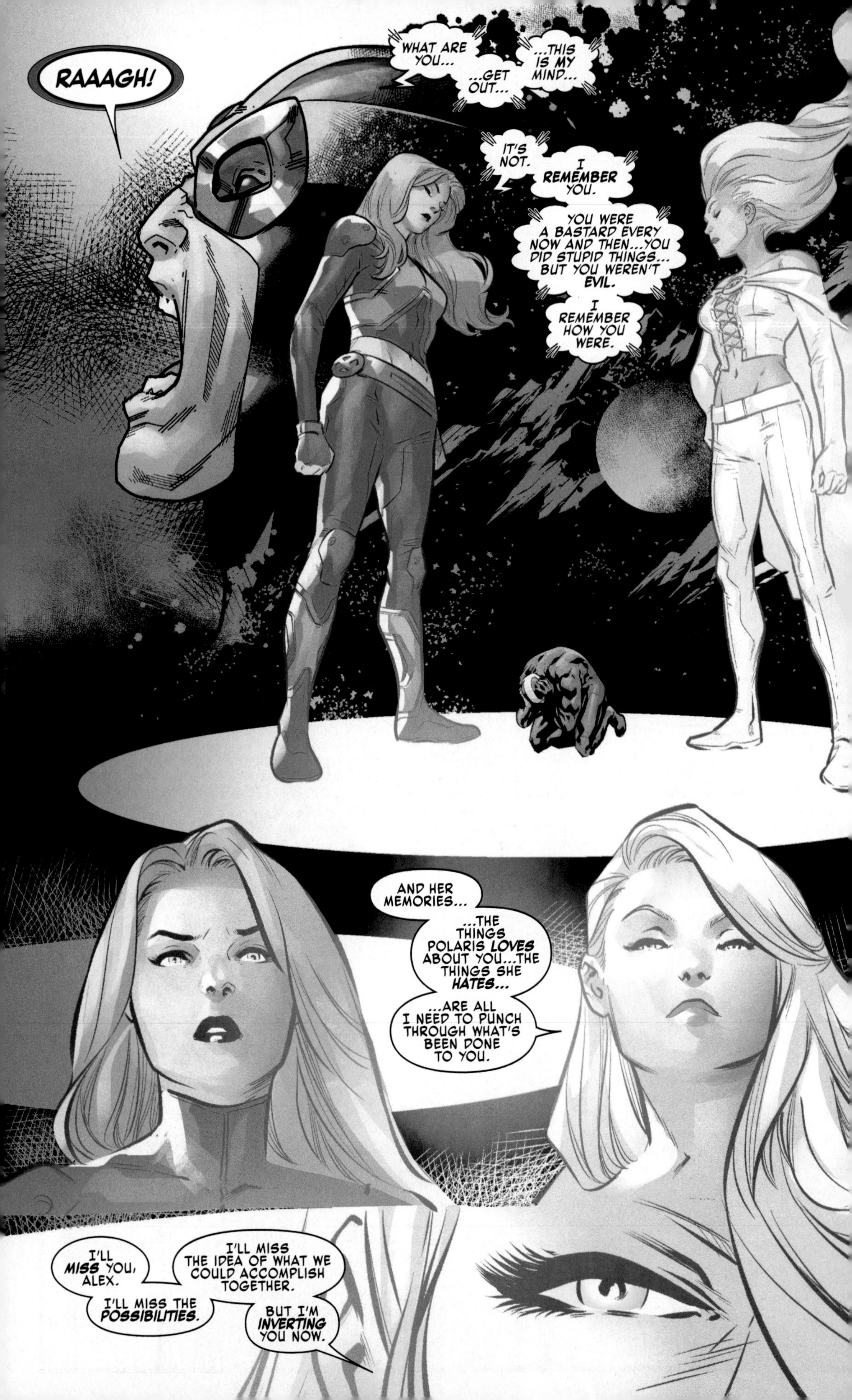
RAAAGH!
WHAT ARE YOU...
...GET OUT...
...THIS IS MY MIND...
IT'S NOT.
I REMEMBER YOU.
YOU WERE A BASTARD EVERY NOW AND THEN...YOU DID STUPID THINGS... BUT YOU WEREN'T EVIL.
I REMEMBER HOW YOU WERE.
AND HER MEMORIES...
...THE THINGS POLARIS LOVES ABOUT YOU...THE THINGS SHE HATES...
...ARE ALL I NEED TO PUNCH THROUGH WHAT'S BEEN DONE TO YOU.
I'LL MISS YOU, ALEX.
I'LL MISS THE IDEA OF WHAT WE COULD ACCOMPLISH TOGETHER.
I'LL MISS THE POSSIBILITIES.
BUT I'M INVERTING YOU NOW.

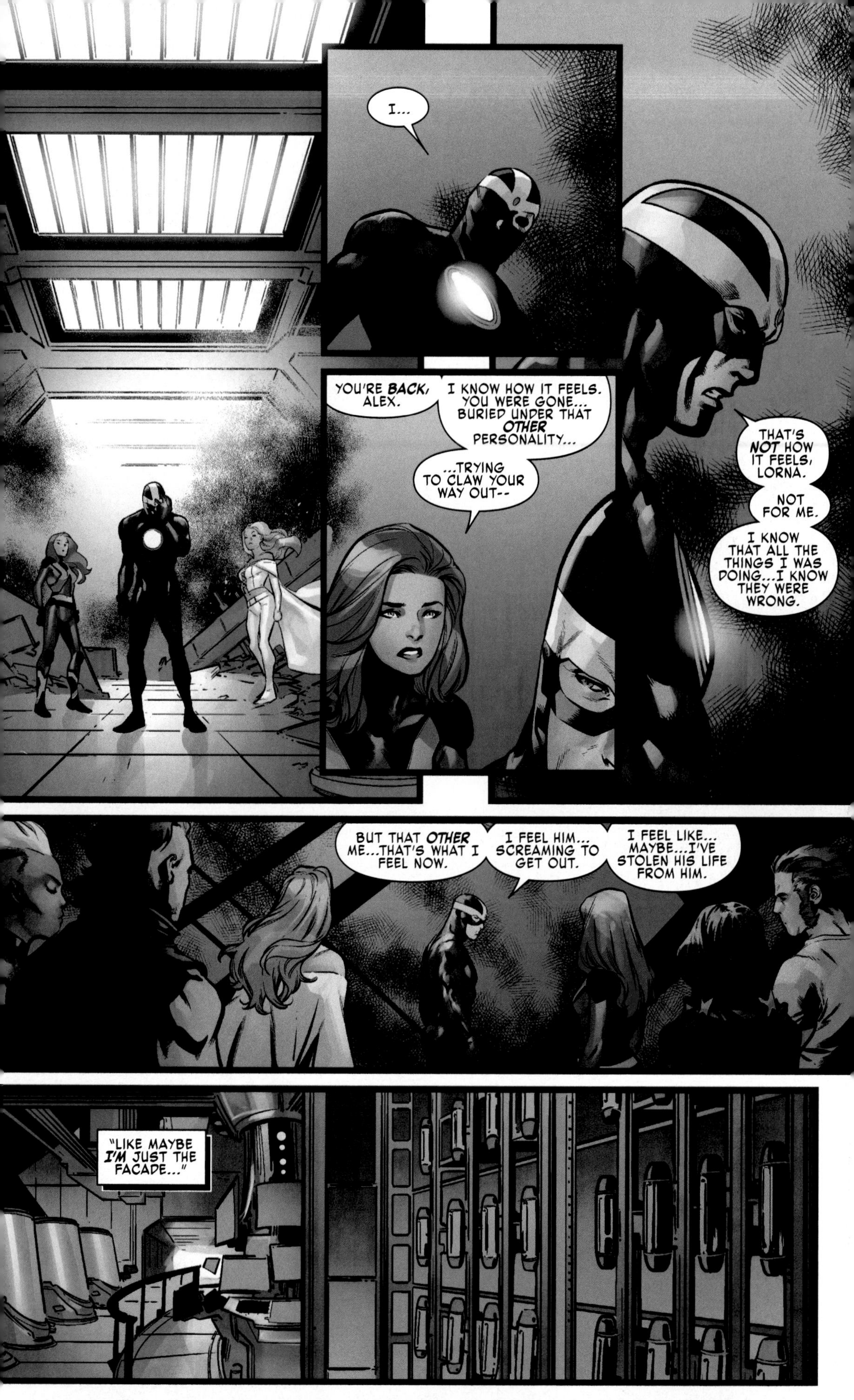
I...
YOU'RE **BACK**, ALEX.
I KNOW HOW IT FEELS. YOU WERE GONE... BURIED UNDER THAT **OTHER** PERSONALITY...
...TRYING TO CLAW YOUR WAY OUT--
THAT'S **NOT** HOW IT FEELS, LORNA.
NOT FOR ME.
I KNOW THAT ALL THE THINGS I WAS DOING...I KNOW THEY WERE WRONG.
BUT THAT **OTHER** ME...THAT'S WHAT I FEEL NOW.
I FEEL HIM... SCREAMING TO GET OUT.
I FEEL LIKE... MAYBE...I'VE STOLEN HIS LIFE FROM HIM.
"LIKE MAYBE **I'M** JUST THE FACADE..."

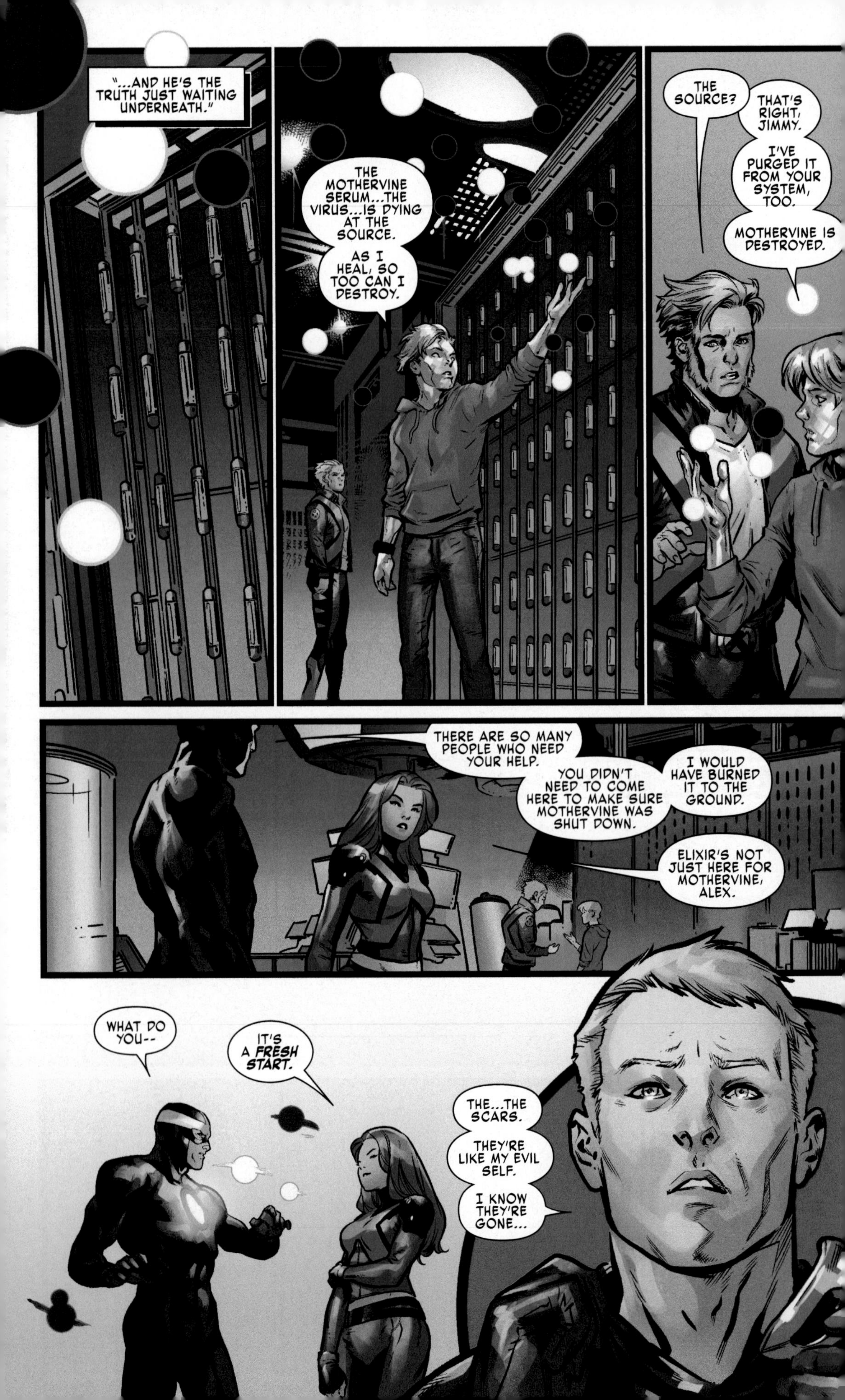
"...AND HE'S THE TRUTH JUST WAITING UNDERNEATH."
THE MOTHERVINE SERUM...THE VIRUS...IS DYING AT THE SOURCE.
AS I HEAL, SO TOO CAN I DESTROY.
THE SOURCE?
THAT'S RIGHT, JIMMY.
I'VE PURGED IT FROM YOUR SYSTEM, TOO.
MOTHERVINE IS DESTROYED.
THERE ARE SO MANY PEOPLE WHO NEED YOUR HELP.
YOU DIDN'T NEED TO COME HERE TO MAKE SURE MOTHERVINE WAS SHUT DOWN.
I WOULD HAVE BURNED IT TO THE GROUND.
ELIXIR'S NOT JUST HERE FOR MOTHERVINE, ALEX.
WHAT DO YOU--
IT'S A FRESH START.
THE...THE SCARS.
THEY'RE LIKE MY EVIL SELF.
I KNOW THEY'RE GONE...

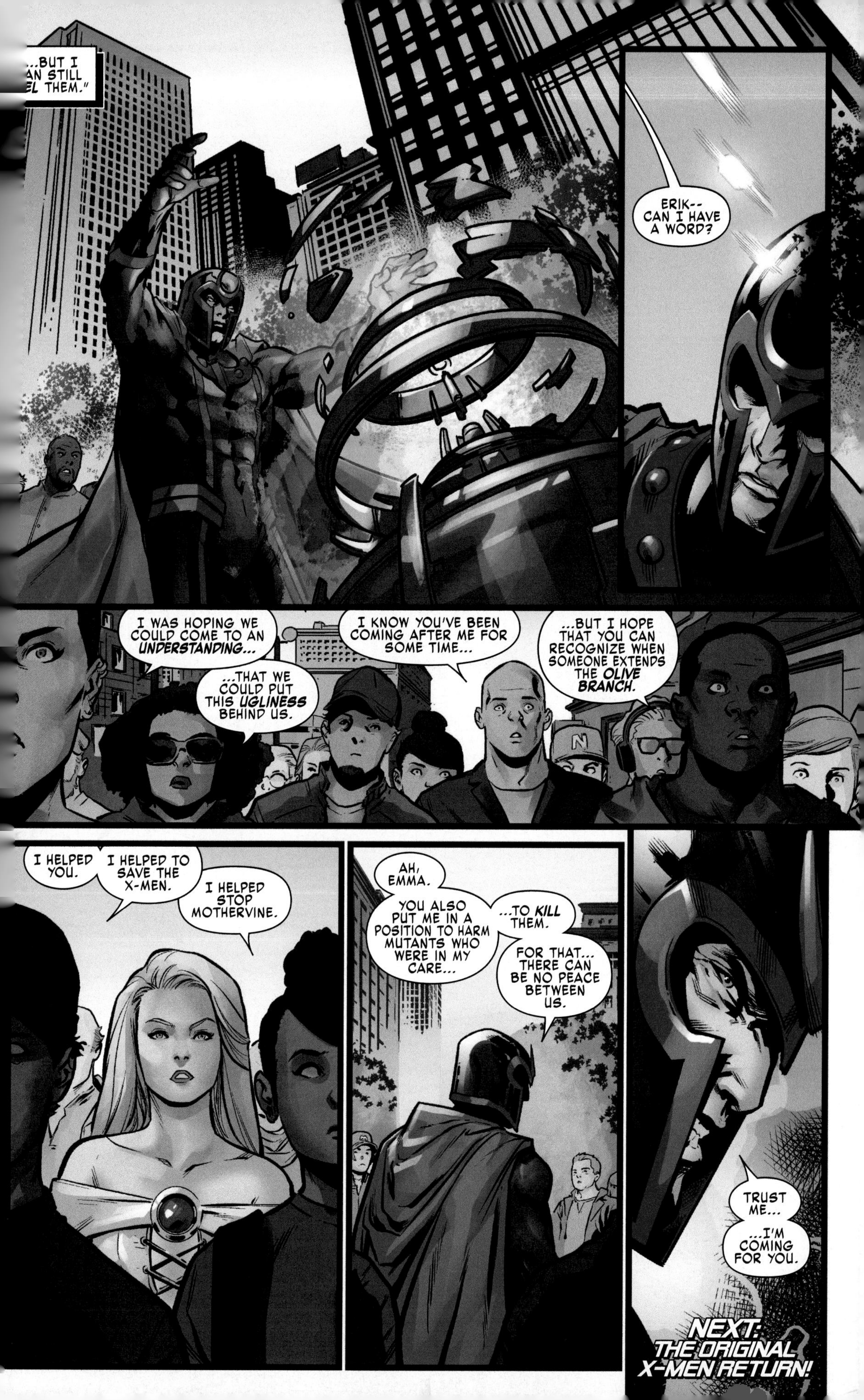

...BUT I AN STILL EL THEM."
ERIK-- CAN I HAVE A WORD?
I WAS HOPING WE COULD COME TO AN UNDERSTANDING...
...THAT WE COULD PUT THIS UGLINESS BEHIND US.
I KNOW YOU'VE BEEN COMING AFTER ME FOR SOME TIME...
...BUT I HOPE THAT YOU CAN RECOGNIZE WHEN SOMEONE EXTENDS THE OLIVE BRANCH.
I HELPED YOU.
I HELPED TO SAVE THE X-MEN.
I HELPED STOP MOTHERVINE.
AH, EMMA.
YOU ALSO PUT ME IN A POSITION TO HARM MUTANTS WHO WERE IN MY CARE...
...TO KILL THEM.
FOR THAT... THERE CAN BE NO PEACE BETWEEN US.
TRUST ME...
...I'M COMING FOR YOU.
NEXT: THE ORIGINAL X-MEN RETURN!

THINGS TO COME

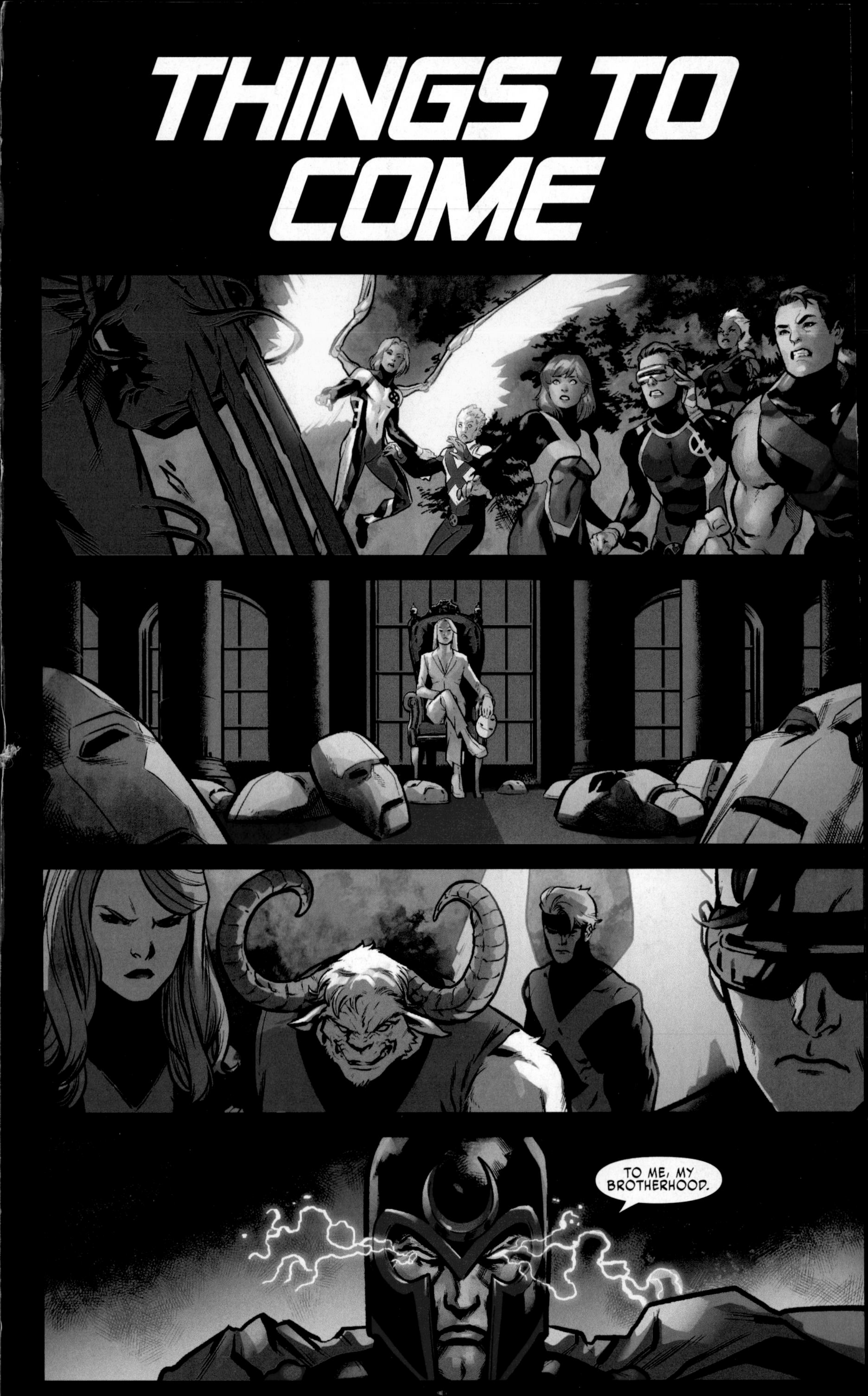
TO ME, MY BROTHERHOOD.